Cults, Converts and Charisma:
The Sociology of
New Religious Movements

Thomas Robbins

$ SAGE Publications
London · Newbury Park · Beverly Hills · New Delhi

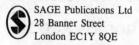

SAGE Publications Ltd
28 Banner Street
London EC1Y 8QE

SAGE Publications Inc
2111 West Hillcrest Street
Newbury Park, California 91320

SAGE Publications Inc
275 South Beverly Drive
Beverly Hills, California 90212

SAGE Publications India Pvt Ltd
C–236 Defence Colony
New Delhi 110 024

British Library Cataloguing in Publication data

Robbins, Thomas
 Cults, converts and charisma: the
 sociology of new religious movements.
 1. Religious movements. Sociological
 perspectives
 I. Title II. Current sociology
 306'.6

 ISBN 0–8039–8158–9
 ISBN 0–8039–8159–7 Pbk

Library of Congress catalog card number 88–060380

Typeset by System 4 Associates Limited, Farnham Common
Printed in Great Britain by J. W. Arrowsmith Ltd, Bristol, UK

Contents

Preface

I wish to acknowledge the indispensable assistance of Jean Peterson with regard to the technical preparation of the manuscript. The continual encouragement and editorial guidance and commentary of James Beckford, the former editor of *Current Sociology*, has also been vital to the completion of this report. Dr Beckford, co-author of the introductory chapter, would like to thank Roberto Cipriani and Enzo Pace for their help in bibliographical matters. For comments, bibliographical assistance and advice, I wish to thank David Bromley, James Richardson, Eileen Barker and Dick Anthony.

Thomas Robbins is an independent scholar. He received a doctoral degree in Sociology from the University of North Carolina and has taught or held research appointments at Yale University, Queens College of the City University of New York, Central Michigan University, the Graduate Theological Union and the New York School of Social Research. He is co-editor of *Cults, Culture and the Law* (Chico, CA: Scholars Press, 1985), *In Gods We Trust: New Patterns of Religious Pluralism in America* (New Brunswick, NJ: Transaction, 1981), and *Church–State Relations: Tensions and Transitions* (New Brunswick, NJ: Transaction, 1987). He has published numerous articles on religious movements in sociology and religious studies journals.

1

INTRODUCTION

The period from the late 1960s to the present has been one of religious ferment and tumult, especially in the USA, where in 1978 historian William McLoughlin labeled the period America's 'Fourth Great Awakening 1960–90 (?)' (McLoughlin, 1978: 178–216). This introductory chapter consists mainly of a short historical summary of some of the developments of the past decades which will provide a predominantly descriptive base and preface for the subsequent report on research, theory and analysis. A short discussion of methodological issues is also included.

The present report deals largely with new religious movements (NRMs) in North America and Western Europe, paying primary attention to the USA.[1] It does not deal at all with Latin American, Asian, African or Eastern European movements. Since the present writer is familiar mainly with Anglo-American sources, a special final section of this chapter, contributed by James Beckford, discusses bibliographical sources for continental Western Europe and Quebec. Nevertheless, the overall organization of this report is *topical* (e.g. chapters on conversion processes, organizational patterns, etc.), and it is assumed that much of the analytical material is applicable to Western European as well as to Anglo-American movements, although Beckford (1981b, 1985a, 1986a, see later discussion) covers continental variations and sources.

Initial Emergence of Exotic Groups from the 'Counterculture'

The period from the late or middle 1960s through the early or middle 1970s was the time of the 'counterculture' of flamboyant political and aesthetic protest among educated American youth. Sociologists such as Robert Bellah and Charles Glock have interpreted the cultural tumult as essentially a religious crisis or cultural crisis of meaning in which dominant value complexes such as utilitarian individualism were being challenged (Bellah, 1976a; Glock, 1976; see Ch. 2). The 'cults' which flourished in the 1970s have been said to be 'successor movements' to the broader countercultural excitation (Bellah, 1976a; Tipton, 1982a; see Ch. 2).

Certainly one dimension of countercultural ferment was an enhanced interest in oriental mystical ideas and varieties of Hinduism and Buddhism, particularly on college campuses. To some extent this phenomenon can be viewed as a popular extension of the interest in Zen Buddhism and other forms of mysticism on the part of the bohemian artists and writers of the 'Beat Generation' of the late 1950s and early 1960s (McLoughlin, 1978: 192–202). After the repeal of the Oriental Exclusion Act in 1965, an increasing number of gurus and swamis began to visit or settle in the United States (Melton, 1987). Various new modes of psychotherapy developing in this period were influenced by oriental mysticism which was accommodated to the American tradition of positive thinking and mind cure.

A second aspect of the 'counterculture' centered around the use and mystique of psychedelic drugs, which became associated with various utopian and mystical ideas. The best-known of the psychedelic popular-izers, psychologists Richard Alpert and Timothy Leary, linked psychedelic experiences to Hindu–Buddhist symbols; indeed, Dr Alpert was eventually apotheosized as the Guru, Baba Ram Das.

It is an interesting speculation as to what degree there was an intrinsic interface between the visual experience of hallucinogenic drugs and the mystical 'monistic' worldview in which phenomenal reality is an illusion concealing an immanent 'inner' reality of universal oneness. Early members of the Love Family, which regarded itself as the resurrected body of Christ, previously had experiences with LSD involving ego loss, a sense of oneness with God and an awareness of the unity of all creation which seemed to dovetail with the prophet Love's message (Balch and Cohig, 1985). Some early research has suggested that youthful converts to oriental groups such as Hare Krishna or Meher Baba in the late 1960s were frequently disillusioned 'psychedelic utopiates' seeking a 'purer' substitute for drug-induced ecstasies (Downton, 1979; Robbins and Anthony, 1972). Gregory Johnson wrote:

> Conversion to Krishna served to sustain the promise of 'psychedelic utopianism' within narrowly defined (and legally immune) limits. Perhaps the most significant aspect of hallucinogenic drug use was its redefinition of the possible pathways to knowledge. In a similar fashion, the ceremonies of the Krishna Temple offered direct unmediated communion with supernatural transcendent forces. The experience became regularized, controllable and predictable within the bhakti yoga discipline. Transcendence became a routine state of being (Johnson, 1976: 48).

Johnson's essay is contained in a well-known volume edited by Charles Glock and Robert Bellah (1976) which has special historical significance as it depicts the initial emergence of a complex of novel religiotherapeutic groups as a successor to the fading late 1960s 'hippie' scene in the San Francisco Bay area.

Much of the sociological literature on American new religions in the early to middle 1970s was oriented towards the identification of elements of symbolic continuity between mystical or apocalyptic religion and the 'drug subculture' or broader counterculture which facilitated the recruitment of deviant 'heads' and 'hippies' into exotic religious groups and promoted the social reintegration of the converts (see Ch. 2).

A third key element of the counterculture was the growth of political activism on college campuses and the rise of the 'New Left'. Nurtured by the escalation of the Vietnam War, student political radicalism seemed to decline abruptly in the early to mid 1970s. In the 1970s the sudden waning of youthful political activism, combined with a persistence of other countercultural values, created a favorable setting for the upsurge of esoteric countercultural religiosity which was also part of a broader American 'return to religion'. Bromley and Shupe write:

> During the 1970s visible political protest activity waned, although a substantial reservoir of discontent and disillusionment remained among youth. Beginning late in the 1960's a resurgence of religiosity began which became highly visible by the early 1970s. This religious revival was broadly based, cutting across age groups and social classes, and took a variety of different forms. The new religions, and particularly those of oriental origin, attracted many youthful devotees although, like the political movements of the previous decade, the visibility and notoriety of these new movements far outstripped their numerical size . . . the discrediting of secular solutions and the failure of the scientific revolution to provide a metaphoric system of meanings to replace those it had weakened produced a new interest in religious meaning systems. Among youth both Eastern religious groups, which critiqued many traditional values and new versions of Western Christian religion which sought to reaffirm traditional cultural values were enthusiastically received. (Bromley and Shupe, 1979a: 87)

'Burned-out' political activists were conspicuous among recruits to the new religions of the 1970s, particularly in the San Francisco Bay area (Bellah, 1976b; Kent 1988). Yet several studies report that only a minority (20 to 30 percent) of converts to NRMs in the early 1970s were former political activists (Downton, 1979; Richardson et al., 1979; Rochford, 1985).

Resurgence of the 'Old-Time Religion'

The 'resurgence of interest in religion in the 1970s was broadly based and entailed continual increases in indicators such as the percentage of adults reporting that they attended church in the last week or the proportion of polled adults who perceived the churches to be gaining social influence' (Bromley and Shupe, 1979a: 90–1). A number of American notables including former Black Panther Eldridge Cleaver, ex-Yippie Jerry Rubin, ex-radical Rennie Davis, Watergate defendant Charles Colson, pornographer Larry Flynt and folk-singer Paul Stookey became associated with exotic gurus, human potential groups, or fervent evangelical ('born-again') Christianity.

While broad-based, the surge of religion in the 1970s and in the preceding decade was not evenly distributed. Mainline 'liberal' denominations such as the Methodists or the Presbyterians continued to lose members or barely hold their own throughout the 1970s. But 'conservative' churches, including evangelical, Pentecostal and fundamentalist groups showed marked growth during the period of the 1960s and 1970s (Kelley, 1972) and are continuing to exhibit high growth rates.

The religious surge of the 1960s and 1970s was thus *disproportionately concentrated in evangelical–Pentecostal–fundamentalist groups*, as well as guru groups and quasi-religious therapeutic movements. 'By the mid-70s it was estimated that as many as fifty million Americans had had a born-again experience. The religious upsurge was strongly based in the middle classes, and church attendance increased most rapidly in young adult groups' (Bromley and Shupe, 1979a: 90). The surge of conservative churches also embraces the continuing substantial unorthodox 'heretical' Christian groups such as Jehovah's Witnesses (Beckford, 1975a) and the Mormon Church (Stark, 1984), both of which appear to exhibit high birth rates and high rates of adult recruitment.

An additional property of the growth of conservative churches has been an increase in the number of *independent churches* and Christian fellowships which are not affiliated with broader denominational structures. Some of these entities emerged out of the 'Jesus Movement' whose 'experiential fundamentalism' (Richardson and Davis, 1983) flourished, particularly on the West coast, around the turn of the seventh decade (Adams and Fox, 1972; Balswick, 1974; Ellwood, 1973; Enroth et al., 1972; Heinz, 1976; Petersen and Mauss, 1973). This movement was marked by the combination of countercultural styles evoking psychedelic and radical protest milieux with fundamentalist and Pentecostal religion. This crucial interface of the counterculture and 'Old-Time religion' was embodied in picturesque 'street Christians' and 'Jesus Freaks' who competed with gurus and esoteric therapy groups for the allegiance of youthful spiritual seekers. Nevertheless, as Enroth et al. (1972) argued, the movement was poorly institutionalized and possessed a kind of built-in tendency toward disintegration (see also Pilarzyk and Jacobsen, 1977). Many ex-Jesus People dropped out of bohemian groups and gravitated toward more conventional fundamentalist and Pentecostal churches, while others became enmeshed in a number of highly authoritarian and intolerant communal groups such as the Children of God or the Alamo Foundation which emerged on the fringe of the Jesus Movement (Enroth et al., 1972). These groups had firm doctrine, clear boundaries and stern authority and thus possessed a greater staying power than the various outreach programs, coffee houses, festivities and communes which constituted the vibrant but ephemeral Jesus Movement.

The Jesus Movement and 1970s evangelical revival thus may be said to constitute a basic 'cultic milieu' (Campbell, 1972) within which particular groups developed. The psychedelic subculture and West coast 'hippie' scene were other such milieux. Another generative milieu was the diffuse 'human potential movement' or burgeoning of therapeutic mystiques oriented toward 'growth' and 'self-actualization' (Wallis and Bruce, 1986: 157–90) which responded to the normalization of psycho-therapy as a routine experience for affluent persons who were reluctant to think of themselves as 'sick' (Anthony et al., 1978). A fourth generative milieu may have been the large *science fiction subculture* which emerged in the 1950s and 1960s and from which the Church of Scientology arose as did the 'UFO cults' (Bainbridge, 1987; Balch and Taylor, 1976; Morth, 1987; Wallis, 1977). Several other movements actually emerged from or were strongly influenced by Scientology (Bainbridge, 1978; Tipton, 1982a; Wallis and Bruce, 1986; see Ch. 4) which has really more or less created its own 'cultic milieu' (Stark and Bainbridge, 1985: 178–83).

By the middle 1970s 'new religions' had become a highly conspicuous feature of the religious scene. Wuthnow (1986) has reviewed various surveys, and estimates that by the mid 1970s the vast majority of the public in the United States and Canada had become aware of new religions and 'perhaps as many as 10 percent had been participants in at least one' (Wuthnow, 1986: 7). In seedbeds such as the San Francisco Bay area or Montreal more than 20 percent of the population may have participated in a movement (Wuthnow, 1986; Bird and Reimer, 1982).

Conflicts Over 'Cults'

The emergence of authoritarian and 'totalistic' movements, 'destructive cults' (Shapiro, 1977), or 'extreme cults' (Enroth, 1977) began to elicit considerable attention in the mid 1970s as parents of devotees alleged that ruthless gurus and self-proclaimed prophets were using potent 'brainwashing' techniques to enslave young persons and destroy their capacity to exercise volition. In the early and mid 1970s various ad hoc citizens' groups opposing cults formed and began to proclaim a crusade to 'free minds' and 'reunite families' (Sage, 1976). By the end of the decade a powerful 'anti-cult movement' had crystallized and had begun to elicit attention from sociologists (Shupe and Bromley, 1980a; Harper, 1982).

Initially 'anti-cult' groups tended to be associated with the controversial practice of 'deprogramming' or the intensive counterindoctrination of converts to controversial movements which was sometimes conducted in a context of physical imprisonment (Shupe et al., 1978; see Chs. 2 and 6). Lively debates about deprogramming have transpired in law journals and elsewhere (Robbins, 1985f), but the legal status of coercive deprogramming in the United States remains ambiguous (Bromley et al., 1983; Robbins, 1986c, 1987).

By the mid 1980s the anti-cult movement (ACM) appeared to be undergoing 'professionalization', a process in which research and the roles of psychiatrists, psychologists and social workers became more salient (Bromley and Shupe, 1987; Shupe, 1985). The consequences of professionalization may include increasing 'moderation' and a de-emphasis on coercive deprogramming. The trajectory of past 'countermovements' suggests that an intense 'scare' period will eventually pass, and the countermovement will 'linger on in relative obscurity' (Shupe and Bromley, 1985a: 67). But there are few signs of such degenerative languishing at present (Bromley and Shupe, 1987).

Initially the movements targeted by anti-cultists tended to be primarily communal groups emerging from the Jesus Movement such as the Children of God (Davis and Richardson, 1975), the Alamo Foundation and The Way International. Other 'totalistic' groups such as Hare Krishna (Judah, 1974; Rochford, 1985) or the International Society of Krishna Consciousness (ISKON) have also been widely excoriated, as has Scientology, a religio-therapeutic movement (Bainbridge and Stark, 1980; Wallis, 1977). To a lesser extent the Divine Light Mission (Downton, 1979), Erhard Seminars Training or est (Stone, 1981; Tipton, 1982a), the Love Family (Balch, 1985b) and the Bhagwan movement of Shree Rajneesh (Carter, 1987; Hummel and Hardin, 1983; Palmer, 1988; Wallis and Bruce, 1986) have been widely stigmatized as 'destructive cults'.

By the late 1970s the Unification Church of Reverend Sun Myung Moon (UC) was clearly emerging as the most controversial and stigmatized NRM. No other contemporary 'cult' has received as much scholarly and journalistic attention as have the 'Moonies', about whom have been assembled three sociological monographs (Barker, 1984; Bromley and Shupe, 1980; Lofland, 1977), one collection (Horowitz, 1978) and numerous scholarly and journalistic articles (e.g. Parsons, 1986) plus several hostile book length accounts by deprogrammed apostates (e.g. Edwards, 1979). Nevertheless, the movement is not really very large; its 'success' has been primarily in the realms of finance and political connections, although its intense 'white-hot mobilization' has been heavy-handed (Lofland, 1977, 1979, 1985). By the 1980s controversies over alleged Moonist brainwashing began to be overshadowed by attention to the movement's media and political linkages, financial practices and commercial diversification (Bromley, 1985; Grafstein, 1984; Robbins, 1985a).

Movements such as the UC, Scientology, ISKON and the Alamo Foundation are now highly diversified and arguably imperialist qua 'messianic capitalism' (Grafstein, 1984) and exploitative. The possibilities for conflicts with environmental forces have been maximized and the movements are consequently enmeshed in continual costly legal disputes (Beckford, 1985a; see Ch. 6). By the mid 1980s the toll of these conflicts had begun to tell on embattled NRMs. At this writing, the Reverend Moon has emerged from prison after serving time for tax fraud; ISKON is appealing a 9.5 million dollar civil judgement for falsely imprisoning a minor through mind control; some Hare Krishna leaders have been indicted for fraud and are being investigated for intragroup violence and sales of drugs; top Scientology officials have been jailed for stealing government documents; the Children of God have been more or less driven from the United States (Wallis, 1987a); Shree Bhagwan Rajneesh has pleaded guilty to immigration fraud and been deported, while his Oregon commune, which lost a long legal struggle to incorporate a city, has been disbanded (Carter, 1987); and finally, the Love Family has broken up (Balch and Cohig, 1985). The survival of some of the best-known groups now appears to be in doubt (Bromley and Hammond, 1987).

Jonestown. One of the strengths of the ACM has been its access to the media and the substantial degree to which dominant media images of cults have reflected ACM perspectives (Beckford and Cole, 1987; Shupe and Bromley, 1980a). Perhaps the significant turning point which consolidated the media hegemony of negative stereotypes of cults (Shupe and Bromley, 1980a: 219–31) was the horror of the People's Temple holocaust in Jonestown, Guyana, where over 900 American followers of Reverend Jim Jones, who had recently relocated from California, were either murdered or committed suicide in November 1978 (Hall, 1981, 1987). The 'lesson of Jonestown' has been eagerly extrapolated to urgent warnings against cults (e.g. Yanoff, 1984), although there are in fact many differences between the prominent groups mentioned above and the People's Temple movement (Melton, 1985; Richardson, 1980, 1982b). The Jonestown holocaust is not historically unprecedented (Chidester, 1983; Hall, 1987; Robbins, 1986a); yet, this catastrophe has appeared so historically absurd that it has not been quickly assimilated to research. Sociological analyses of Jonestown have not been plentiful (see Ch. 6).

Some journalists and 'cultwatchers' have been eager to discover 'the next Jonestown', hopefully before the fact. Attention has been drawn to certain groups which Levin and Alan (1984) have called the 'cults of the 80s', which recruit from disaffected urban minorities who do not feel part of the economic recovery and patriotic revitalization of the early and mid 1980s, and which are said to be supplanting the white, middle-class 'cults of the 1970s'. There have been a number of violent confrontations with police involving groups such as MOVE in Philadelphia. Violent proclivities have also been identified in the Aryan supremacist 'Christian Identity' movement and in polygamist fringe Mormons.

Normalization and Decline

The difficulties which certain highly controversial groups are now encountering is one sign that the surge of new movements and expansion of the 'new religious consciousness' have leveled off. New religions do not now appear as dynamic and creative as they appeared in the 1970s. On the other hand, many contemporary movements seem less wild and dissident than they did in earlier years. They are clearly wanting to be 'mainstreamed'. Yet it is questionable to what degree they have really changed the religious culture. Martin Marty writes:

> By the mid-1980's such extraordinary religion had established itself, although without essentially changing the map of American religion. Present in a number of thriving cults and persistent in holistic health movements, and small-group therapies, and most of all in private spiritual pursuits, most of this religion had begun to fit quietly into the larger landscape. What the public called cults no longer made news as a harbinger of the spirit that might alter consciousness and national life, bringing in a new age. Instead they were seen as only slightly less conventional denominations among the denominations, study accents among other Great Book interests, or, most of all, as merely self-preservative groups constantly fighting for legal rights and privilege — and

often thus winning support of both mainline and evangelical–moralist partisans. In other words, they made news on the familiar and ordinary church–state legal front, not on the horizon of extraordinary spiritual promise (Marty, 1985: 17).

These tendencies have been reflected in the changing focus of socio-logical inquiry relating to unconventional movements which has shifted such that a growing concern with 'cult controversies' and pertinent church–state issues (Beckford, 1985a; Harper, 1982; Kilbourne and Richardson, 1984a,b; Richardson, in press; Robbins et al., 1985; Shupe and Bromley, 1980a, 1985a) has partly supplanted an earlier scholarly fascination with the cultural meaning of new religions and what new movements portend for societal transformation and interpretation of the human condition (Glock and Bellah, 1976; Tipton, 1982a; Wuthnow, 1976b; see Ch. 7). Although a predominant concern with processes of conversion and commitment in religious movements has endured throughout the past two decades (see Snow and Machalek, 1984), there now appears to be an increasing focus on *processes of defection and deconversion* from religious movements (Beckford, 1987b, 1985a: 135–48; Bromley, 1988a; Jacobs, 1984, 1987; Lewis, 1986; Richardson et al., 1986; Skonovd, 1981; Wright, 1987) as well as on the ineffective-ness, break-up and 'failure' of some new religions (Balch and Cohig, 1985; Stark, 1987a; Wagner, 1983; Wilson, 1987).

A recent volume, *The Future of New Religions* (Bromley and Hammond, 1987) probes the survival prospects for a number of controversial groups including the Children of God (Wallis), Scientology (Bainbridge, Wallis), Hare Krishna (Rochford, Shinn, Gelberg), the Unification Church (Lofland, Mickler), Nichiren Shoshu (Snow) and the ACM (Shupe and Bromley). In his chapter, Benton Johnson (1987a) suggests that in the present climate different kinds of movements face different prospects. A continuing or even growing market for 'therapeutic business firms' is predicted, but the prospects for any particular movement are more questionable due to the fierce competition between firms and the volatility of therapeutic faddism (see Ch. 4): 'It is exceedingly unlikely that any movement will achieve a high impact on American society' (Johnson, 1987a: 256).

A modestly promising future is predicted for Hare Krishna (ISKON) and 'other commune-based Hindu imports' (but see Ch. 4 for recent developments). Some groups are receiving increasing support from the growing Indian immigrant community and can elaborate their communal settlements into tourist attractions (Johnson, 1987a; see also Rochford, 1985). But recent scandals and investigations involving allegations of violence and drug dealing (Huber and Gruson, 1987) may imperil ISKON. The prospects are not considered promising for 'world-transforming' or 'world-rejecting' movements such as the Unification Church which 'wants to dominate the world by direct action. As long as it persists in this ambition, it will face a barrage of challenges from which ISKON will be spared' (Johnson, 1987a: 258). The greater complexity of the mission of such groups enhances both the resistance they encounter and the risk of committing disastrous errors. Schism and conflict within the UC may ensue upon the demise of the Reverend Moon, whose following already contains four distinct 'ideological subgroupings' (Mickler, 1987).

Roy Wallis argues that with the waning of the counterculture the recruitment base for 'world-rejecting' movements such as the UC has been eroded (Wallis, 1978c, 1984, 1987a). This view has interesting implications: will the de-emphasis of grim pre-millennial tribulationist prophecy, which is arguably implicit in the activism and triumphalism of the New Christian Right (Hadden, 1987b), curtail fundamentalist apocalypticism? Or will a perceived failure of the goal of 'Re-Christianizing America' lead to intensified doomsaying prophecy and a new proliferation of world-rejecting movments? Or will the locus of apocalyptic world-rejection shift to the urban poor and minorities? How will the spectre of AIDS affect apocalyptic prophecy? (Palmer, forthcoming, see Ch. 2).

'World-affirming' movements which help persons to cope with stress through 'a modern version of. . .magic' (Wallis, 1984: 122) may continue to be viable, as Johnson suggests with respect to 'therapeutic businesses'. Impressionistically, the 'New Age' groups appear increasingly to appeal primarily to middle age adults. Exotic religions, particularly 'eastern' groups, appear to be far weaker on campuses compared to a decade ago. Evangelical and quasi-fundamentalists still show some strength on campuses. Well-known controversial groups such as the Unification Church, Hare Krishna, Scientology, or the Divine Light Mission 'have been experiencing a decline in membership' (Appel, 1983: 13; see also Rochford, 1985: 299). Were the sources of the growth of some new religions in the late 1960s and 1970s largely generational? (see Ch. 2). There are some survey data indicative of a strong and continuing spiritual hunger among young people (Appel, 1983: 10–16). There are many small movements throughout the United States which exist below the level of national media awareness; 'it is possible that the largest proportion of people involved in cults belong to groups so small as to go unnoticed by the general public' (Appel, 1983: 15). Nevertheless, certain American trends such as the decline of central urban commons and market areas and their replacement by privately owned enclosed malls (whose managers are empowered in some states to curtail solicitation) bode ill for the missionary efforts of both religious and political movements.

Clearly the major media seem to have withdrawn some of their earlier attention from the topic of 'cults' (Shupe, 1985) partly in favor of the roiling controversies over politicized Christianity. It is, of course, difficult to distinguish between media reality and 'real' reality. Beckford (1985d) has criticized the narrow focus of sociologists on a handful of controversial 'cults' which may now be in decline, while other 'holistic' movements are flourishing. At least one expert argues that 'alternative religions', though still too small to mount a meaningful challenge to either mainline or evangelical Christianity, have nevertheless, 'grown to the point that they can, if allowed to continue without significant legal obstacle, provide an alternative that can and will gain the increasing allegiance of middle America' (Melton, 1987: 56). But Bibby and Weaver (1985) use survey data to demonstrate that the earlier claims by Robbins et al. (1978) that new religions have grown at the expense of mainline denominations have not been borne out in Canada. Wuthnow (1986) cites data from Melton (1978) indicating that the emergence of new cultic and sectarian groups slowed down in the middle 1970s compared to the late 1960s and very early 1970s; 'the general picture appears to be one of growth until 1975 or 1976, followed by stability and decline' (Wuthnow, 1986: 16). On the other hand there is currently media as well as evangelical concern over an alleged growth of Satanic ritual. There have also been prominent media stories reporting the continuing cultural dissemination of occult and 'New Age' beliefs, as well as the proliferation of authoritarian fundamentalist fringe groups (Babbie, 1987; Lindsey, 1986). Neo-Paganism, sometimes associated with feminism or homosexual affirmation (Neitz, 1988; Spencer, 1987), may be on the increase. Currently 'New Age' practices and thought are gaining entry into educational, business and even military institutions (Garvey, 1985), and their spread is regularly denounced by TV evangelists. Concern has also been voiced regarding the recruitment and putative exploitation of elderly persons by cults (Brooks, 1986; Rudin, 1984). So there is some ambiguity in both present trends and future prognoses regarding NRMs.

Conclusion: Phases of Ferment

To summarize this descriptive introduction, we suggest that the spiritual ferment of the past two decades in America can be tentatively divided into three overlapping periods or stages.

The initial period, which lasts from the middle 1960s through the early 1970s is the period of diffuse countercultural protest: student protest, psychedelic utopianism, hippies, etc.

As radical political activism waned, while other countercultural values were assimilated into the dominant culture, particular religiotherapeutic movements or 'cults' emerged as 'successor movements' to the broader countercultural protest (Bellah, 1976a). The second period thus began at the end of the 1960s and is now waning. The latter half of this period was marked by increasing controversy over 'destructive cults.' A shrill 'anti-cult movement' (ACM) emerged and 'deprogramming' entered the English language. Surviving movements became increasingly financially and commercially diversified as they shifted away from dependence on street solicitation and sought to retrench and consolidate. Recruitment appeared to drop off among some of the better known groups, and consolidation strategies were imperiled by legal challenges to diversified messianic 'empires' (see Ch. 6).

The growth of 'conservative' and evangelical churches and denominations in the USA has been a basic religious trend for over two decades. The evangelical revival has become conspicuously politicized. The resurgence and politicization of 'the Old-Time religion' has increasingly overshadowed 'cults' as a journalistic and scholarly preoccupation. The third period, which continues through to the present, appears so far to be a period of charismatic–fundamentalist renewal (Hunter, 1983, 1987), televangelical right-wing politics (Hadden and Shupe 1987; Liebman and Wuthnow, 1983; Shupe and Bromley, 1984; Wallis and Bruce, 1986), patriotic revitalization and moral agitation. Wuthnow (1986) reports that survey data indicate that the proportion (19 percent) of those Americans acknowledging being evangelicals did not change from 1976 to 1982, although particular evangelical organizations have grown and have expanded their activities in several directions.

The present volume deals mainly with what we have called the 'second phase' of the persisting ferment and with its continuing consequences, i.e. extant sociological analyses of 'new' movements, converts and conversion–commitment–disengagement processes. We deal only tangentially with evangelical politics or televangelical economics, or with hippies or political protest. We are aware that the surge of cults and gurus may have 'passed its peak', and that many exotic groups may prove ephemeral. Compared to the phenomenally growing Mormons, most new groups, comments Rodney Stark, are 'attempting to spread the wrong message in the wrong time and place' (Stark 1984: 25). Somewhat similar thoughts have been articulated by Eileen Barker:

Sociologists of religion should expend as much energy in checking the failures of the movements during the next ten years as they did in charting successes over the past decade. We may then get a clearer idea of whether the new religions portend yet another great awakening or whether, as I have come to suspect, they represent simply a highly publicized collection of options selected from the enormous variety already available in modern societies, which celebrate neither belief nor ideology under any single canopy (Barker, 1985: 47).

There are those who fear that 'now that the boom in new religions appears to be fading...we may have missed our best [research] opportunities' (Balch, 1985a: 38). This anxiety may be well grounded; yet, may not the sociologist of religion fly with Minerva's owl which, as Hegel noted, *takes wing at twilight*!

Below we briefly discuss some methodological issues arising in the study of contemporary NRMs. The reader may wish initially to leave this section until the substantive bulk of the report has been scrutinized. Following the note on methods there is a short essay prepared by James Beckford on bibliographical sources and emergent patterns pertaining to continental Western Europe and Quebec. Some readers may also care to defer attention to this section until the Anglo-American substantive material has been assimilated. Dr Beckford's essay concludes Chapter 1.

Subsequent chapters review what the author considers to be the most pertinent substantive subtopics. We begin in Chapter 2 by examining the 'big theories' about sociocultural transformations and dislocations, which have been advanced to 'explain' recent spiritual flux and ferment. Chapter 3 reviews the recent literature on processes of conversion, commitment and disengagement in religiotherapeutic movements. In Chapter 4 we look at analyses of the institutionalization and organizational patterns of contemporary NRMs. Chapter 5 surveys typologies of NRMs which have been formulated in recent decades, as well as attempts to assimilate recent movements to the tradition of church–sect theory. Chapter 6 probes sociological analyses of the conflicts and controversies revolving around 'cults.' Finally, Chapter 7 tries to evaluate the impact of the dynamic explosion of NRM research on the sociology of religion. This chapter also deals with the questions of objectivity, sympathy and responsibility, which are touched upon in Chapters 1 and 6. The emerging interfaces between the sociology of religion and other areas such as social movements and the sociology of medicine, articulated through the study of NRMs, are also scrutinized in this final chapter. Chapter 7 is followed by a large bibliography which covers all the preceding chapters.

A Note on Methods

From a methodological standpoint the sociological research on cults has been somewhat slipshod. As Robert Balch complains in his cogent paper, 'What's Wrong with the Study of Cults and What We Can Do About It' (Balch, 1985a), sociologists have not standardized their methods of data collection to provide a basis for comparative analysis. Researchers have generally 'approached cults and sects in. . .a biased and unsystematic manner. . .any secondary analysis of the current research is apt to get bogged down by ambiguous terms, in incomplete data, and idiosyncratic research methods' (Balch, 1985a: 24). Balch identifies serious problems of bias, terminological confusion (e.g. 'conversion' equated with recruitment), overgeneralization, unwarranted causal inferences and inadequate methods of collecting data.

The problem of bias has been widely discussed (Barker, 1983b; Bromley et al., 1987; Kilbourne and Richardson, 1984b; Richardson, 1985d; Robbins, 1985b; Stone 1978a; Wallis, 1984: 132–44) and will be discussed in the final chapter of this report. Donald Stone observes that 'the new religions often serve as spiritual inkblots: reports of movements may tell us more about the observers than about the observed' (Stone, 1978a: 143). As the present writer has noted, different analyses of 'cults', particularly involving the issue of 'mind control', tend to be somewhat incommensurate in the sense that they may employ either an internal–empathic interpretive framework or an external–critical framework. The 'findings' of a study are partly predetermined when one interpretive framework is used to evaluate the practices of cults while the opposite framework is applied to deprogramming and countercult processes (Robbins, 1984, 1985b). Results are also predetermined by 'epistemological exclusionary rules' whereby a class of respondents such as committed converts or recriminating apostates are treated a priori as incapable of valid insights while another class is assumed to have a monopoly of truth. Underlying these peccadillos is the reality that many controversial 'issues' are essentially *interpretive* and evaluative rather than factual (Shupe and Bromley, 1980a: 152–3; see Ch. 7).

The problem of relying on the retrospective accounts of converts or ex-converts has been extensively discussed (Balch, 1985a; Beckford, 1978a; Jules-Rosette, 1981; Snow and Machalek, 1984; Taylor, 1976; Wallis and Bruce, 1986). Such accounts are fundamentally interpretive and are influenced by the respondents' present situations, particularly with respect to involvement in an ideological group in which members learn a new interpretive framework and 'vocabulary of motive' which patterns their accounts (Balch, 1985a; Beckford, 1978a; Snow and Machalek, 1984).

Retrospective accounts are often associated with sampling problems. Recriminating defectors with ties to an anti-cult social network are organized and thus more visible and easier to locate than other ex-converts (Balch, 1985a; Robbins, 1985b). Probabilistic samples of the members of a particular movement, or of ex-members either of a particular group or of 'cults' in general, are nearly impossible to draw. Yet, without probabilistic sampling, significance tests are technically not susceptible to interpretation. What Robbins (1985b) calls 'network samples', whereby the 'anti-cult network' essentially studies itself, have produced some analytical distortions (e.g. Conway and Siegelman, 1982) and have conveyed the misleading impression that most ex-converts have required deprogramming to leave cults. Alternative sampling strategies have recently been suggested (Balch, 1985a; Robbins, 1985b). Nevertheless, any given 'sample' drawn exclusively from a particular group is likely to be highly specialized and therefore skewed in some way. Area samples such as produced by the Bay Area Study (Wuthnow, 1976a,b, 1978) and the Montreal Area Study (Bird and Reimer, 1982) are not likely to produce substantial subsamples from particular small groups, although they may be quite informative with respect to respondents' attitudes, beliefs and behavior.

Direct observation is used frequently by sociologists to study new movements, and the prevalence of this approach represents one way in which the growth of new religions has 'anthropologized' the sociology of religion. 'Ideally, researchers should observe members in a wide variety of formal and informal settings and/or who are known to members or leaders to be engaged in research are vulnerable to the criticism that they have been either deliberately or inadvertently duped by manipulative groups (Beckford, 1983b; Schwartz, 1985).

Direct observation tends to sensitize the careful observer to changes in a movement as well as to internal conflicts, factions, geographical variations, etc. Reliance on defectors' accounts or other data sources may produce overly static and monolithic images of movements. 'Immersion in the day to day flow of group activities tends to give researchers greater insight into the way members perceive reality' (Balch, 1985a: 32; see also Bromley et al., 1987). 'Researchers who study groups from a distance tend to view cult members as passive victims of forces beyond their control, and they are more likely to use clinical terminology . . . which fails to capture the members' point of view' (Balch, 1985a: 33). Sociologists incline more toward a 'humanistic perspective' which emphasizes the active agency of 'seekers' in conversion processes (Straus, 1976, 1979b; Richardson, 1985a). Yet, 'empathy can be just as trouble-some as antagonism' (Balch, 1985a: 33) as the empathist may end up adapting the 'official' or organizational definition of reality and become desensitized to coercive, manipulative and other ironic nuances in social processes within a movement. *Any observational process will necessarily be selective.*

For Balch good observational practices are essential to research on religious movements, as are the basic descriptive data or ethnographies which careful observation produces. Unfortunately, sociological journals do not like to publish 'mere' descriptive accounts, and thus sociologists' descriptions become abbreviated and distorted in order to be accom-modated to the 'theoretical' embellishment necessary for publication. Theoretical and comparative inferences from such descriptive data as exist are impeded by the non-standardization of data collection techniques and foci. Balch (1985a) and Robbins (1985b) have suggested the construc-tion of something akin to anthropologists' Human Relations Area Files, in which comparable information on hundreds of groups has been collected and catalogued. The basic categories of such classifiable data, according to Balch, should be: (1) demographic characteristics of membership; (2) historical development; (3) structure and content of belief system; (4) leadership; social organization; (5) relationship of members to outsiders; (6) economic practices; (7) material culture; (8) patterns of everyday life; (9) talk patterns; (10) sexual patterns; (11) child rearing; (12) deviance and social control; (13) recruitment strategies; (14) commitments and sacrifices required of members; (15) socialization techniques; (16) con-version patterns; and (17) defection patterns (Balch, 1985a).

It is conceivable, however, that the very volatility and effervescence of NRMs, which quickly shift their patterns in response to the inspirations of gurus as well as environmental pressures (Balch, 1985a; Balch and Cohig, 1985; Carter, 1987) will undercut any program of cataloguing groups on the model of the anthropological files.

At this point some note should be taken of the ingenious and imaginative use of a range of 'unobtrusive' data sources by Stark and Bainbridge (1985). A treasure trove has been found in the *Encyclopedia of American Religions* compiled by J. Gordon Melton (1978) which lists and describes 'more than 1200 different religious groups active in the United States' (Stark and Bainbridge, 1985: 41) and also pinpoints the location of spiritual centers. The Melton volume is supplemented by Stark and Bainbridge with census data, including neglected past national census studies of religious bodies. A third key data source is the local classified yellow pages, which can be used as a guide to the location and distribution of spiritual bookstores, foodstores, etc. An additional data source is provided by various esoteric and occult publications including 'client cult directories' such as the *Spiritual Community Guide* and the *International Psychic Register*, plus *Fate* magazine, whose tabulated subscription lists were made available to the authors. Further sources include a Transcendental Meditation training manual, printed in 1972 and listing 1977 trained initiators working in 135 centers (Stark and Bainbridge, 1985: 226), plus secondary analyses of various polls and surveys.

Stark and Bainbridge have given some thought to the defects and biases of each source, yet they have generally been able to utilize *multiple indices* to survey the geographical and cross-national distribution of cults and the correlations between the strength of cults and other variables such as the strength of churches. Certain difficulties arise here such as the problematic strategy of counting the number of esoteric spiritual centers in a locality as a measure of 'cult strength', which the authors (Stark and Bainbridge, 1985: 179) and their critics (Wallis, 1984: 59–69, 1986a; Wallis and Bruce, 1986) debate (see Beckford below, p. 22). This issue is pertinent to the claim of greater receptivity to NRMs in Europe compared to the USA (Stark, 1985b). Nevertheless Stark and Bainbridge have clearly pioneered in the use of computers and non-obtrusive measures to study NRMs.

In general, sociological research on NRMs has fallen far short of Dr Balch's standards. Sweeping theories have been presented either without supportive empirical data or with merely illustrative data from a single group. The conspicuous lack of *control groups* in many studies has drawn pointed comment (Barker, 1986, see Ch. 2).

In this report the terms 'new religious movement' (NRM) and 'cult' are used interchangeably, although the latter term generally denotes the controversial or stigmatized aspect of NRMs. While this report deals primarily with sociological research on NRMs, there are some appropriate citations to pertinent works by psychologists (e.g. Singer, 1979) and psychiatrists (e.g. Galanter, 1985), but no exhaustive review is attempted in this area (Halperin, 1983).

The Literature on Western NRMs
Outside the USA and the UK (James Beckford)

Sociological studies of NRMs in the West have been dominated by American and British scholars in two senses. First, their ways of posing questions and theoretical problems have been extensively followed and replicated by scholars writing in European languages other than English. Second, the sheer number of English-language reports on NRMs easily outweighs those in other languages. This is partly why the only European contributions to the analysis of NRMs which are reviewed at length here come from Britain. This is also why it is possible to base this report primarily on British and American material, for it follows that many of the arguments are also applicable to NRMs in continental Europe. But there is an urgent need to place the British and American works in a broader context and to examine the issues on which continental European, Scandinavian and Quebecois sociologists (some of whom write in English, of course) have established independent approaches to the topic of NRMs. The contributions of British scholars will be included only if they deal with NRMs in continental Europe (Wilson and Dobbelaere, 1987).

Although no cross-national comparative research has been conducted on NRMs in Western Europe a few selective guides to the literature in more than one language have appeared. Among the earliest are Romarheim's (1977, 1979) accounts in Norwegian of new religious developments in Scandinavia. In addition, Berger and Hexel's (1981) discussion of competing explanations of NRM membership and growth is the most thorough overview in German. Beckford and Richardson's (1983) bibliography in English covers a much wider range of material than that of Berger and Hexel and in fact the issue of the Belgian journal *Social Compass* (30.1.1983) in which this bibliography was published was devoted to the topic of NRMs with special reference to their presumed association with dissension among young people. Beckford's (1983c) introductory essay sketches the outline of the major works on NRMs in Western Europe at that time. More recent synoptic works include Filoramo (1986), Beckford and Levasseur (1986) and Barker (1987a). The most analytical discussion of the sociological literature in French is Hervieu-Léger (1986, Ch. 4), although, significantly, much of the literature that she reviews is either American or British. A number of contributions to Rouleau and Zylberberg (1984) pursue the analysis in equally interesting, but different directions from a French Canadian point of view, and a bibliography drawn up in Quebec (Foucart, 1982) covers many other French-language publications.

Collections of articles which deal in the main with Western Europe include *Conscience et Liberté* (1982), *Concilium* (1983) and most issues of the Danish journal *Update* (which has recently been absorbed by *Areopagus*, a journal of broader theological interest published in Hong Kong). The general tenor of *Update* was ideologically critical of NRMs, but relatively dispassionate discussions of a sociological character were published from time to time (see, for example, Volume 8, No. 2, 1984 on NRMs in several European countries). The same is true of the Italian journal *IDOC–Internazionale* which favors a Catholic-oriented critique of NRMs. By contrast, the London-based journal which specializes in the study of NRMs, *Religion Today*, probably leans towards the interests of the movements. It is also a more academically oriented publication.

Before examining the non-English-language literature in detail, it is useful to mention some general points of similarity with the British and American material. First, European and Quebecois sociologists were just as unprepared as their British and American counterparts for the sudden and rapid proliferation of controversial NRMs which began in the late 1960s. Second, the movements' controversial aspects, such as alleged brainwashing, tax evasion and political ambitions, have attracted more sociological interest than have, for example, their teachings, history, or forms of organization. There is, third, a widespread but questionable assumption that NRMs are relatively rare and unusual phenomena which call for special explanation — often in terms of psychological or social pathology.

Two themes, which are relatively weak in the American literature, emerge clearly from the predominantly non-English-language publications on NRMs in Western Europe and Quebec. They will now be examined by means of a selective literature review.

First, there is considerable diversity in the meaning of non-English terms designating the kind of phenomena that are conventionally labelled 'NRMs' by British and American sociologists (for example, 'sects', 'new sects', 'youth sects', and 'youth religions', etc.). It is not surprising, then, that the choice of NRMs deserving sociological explanation also varies with the religious history of the countries in which sociologists are working. Thus, some French, Belgian and Quebecois authors tend to minimize distinctions between the 'classical' Protestant sects of the nineteenth century (Jehovah's Witnesses, Christian Scientists, Mormons, etc.), movements of 'renewal' within Catholicism (Hervieu-Léger, 1986; Mat-Hasquin, 1982; Rouleau and Zylberberg, 1984), presumably in order to emphasize the contrast with Roman Catholicism. In a variant on this tendency, some Italian publications concentrate on movements of renewal within the Roman Catholic Church, sometimes categorizing them as NRMs (Nesti, 1973; Guizzardi, 1974; Pace, 1983), and on the long history of religious movements prior to the twentieth century (Filoramo, 1979, 1986; Macioti, 1987; Ambrosio, 1984). Work in Germany is characterized less by historical depth (but see Geldbach, 1987) and tends to be focused on the NRMs which have been formally identified by the Federal Ministry of Youth, Family and Health (Bundesministerium, 1980) as worthy of special scrutiny. The list includes the Ananda Marga movement which has virtually escaped British and American attention but which became highly controversial in Germany following the self-immolation of some members there. For an equally adventitious reason, the Three Holy Hearts movement (Lecerf, 1975; Woodrow, 1977) has colored French and Belgian conceptions of NRMs. Dutch researchers have considered including evangelical movements such as Youth for Christ, Navigators and Campus Crusade, Teen Challenge, Youth with a Mission and Operation Mobilization in their lists of NRMs (Köllen, 1980; but see also Witteveen's 1984, reasons for excluding them). And some Scandinavian scholars have shown greater interest in studying revival movements within the Lutheran tradition and/or in American sectarian organizations than in the cults that are controversial elsewhere (Sihvo, 1973; Biézais, 1975; Sundbacq, 1980, Holm, 1981; Heino, 1984. Wikstrom, 1984; Aargaard and Duddy, 1984). Finally, there has been very little research on NRMs in Spain (where freedom of religion has been granted to non-Catholic groups only in the recent past), but interest in yoga-related activities appears to be growing fast (Belil, 1984; García, 1986; Rodriguez, 1985).

In view of the fact that Stark and Bainbridge (1985) have written probably the best-known American commentary on Europe's receptivity to sects and cults (Stark, 1985b) it is interesting to note in passing that the practice of virtually all European sociologists is either to make no distinction between 'sect' and 'cult' or to distinguish between them on grounds entirely different from those used by Stark and Bainbridge (see in particular Campiche, 1987, for a cogent rejection of the distinction). Ironically, Stark and Bainbridge acknowledged that 'What is cult and what is sect is not decided by scholars, but by societies . . . [A] group may be a cult in one [society] and a sect in another' (Stark and Bainbridge 1985: 489) but they nevertheless persisted in imposing *their* distinction on the European data. If they had familiarized themselves with European literature on NRMs (in both English and other languages) they might have been persuaded to see the question of Europe's receptivity to cults and sects differently. We return to this point later.

The second distinctive theme of European and Quebecois sociological commentaries on NRMs has to do with the variable response to the movements in different countries. Most of today's NRMs have made their way to Western Europe and Quebec via the USA and have retained the status of outposts or dependencies of American-based leaders (Hummel and Hardin, 1983; Chagnon, 1985; Pelletier, 1986). These foreign 'branches' therefore tend to be organized along the same lines as in the USA. But the (mainly hostile) public response to them varies from country to country (Beckford, 1983), reflecting not only religious history but also the recent history of social problems and criticism in each place. This is most clearly illustrated in Hardin's (1983) and Hardin and Kehrer's (1982) analysis of the grounds for misgivings about NRMs in various sectors of West German society where the anti-cult movement is a highly articulate and powerful network. More than 500,000 copies of the anti-cult books and booklets written by a single Lutheran pastor with special responsibilities for 'youth religions' have been sold, for example, (Duddy, 1984). Baffoy (1978), van der Lans and Derks (1983), Filoramo (1986, Ch. 6), Morelli (1981), Aargaard and Duddy (1984), Valentin (1984) and Mayer (1985a,b) perform comparable analyses for, respectively, France, The Netherlands, Italy, Belgium, Denmark, Austria and Switzerland.

Although no *comparative* studies of public responses to NRMs, other than Beckford's (1981, 1983, 1985a), have been conducted in Europe or Quebec, an important collection of papers dealing in part with the problems facing NRMs in several countries has been published in German (Neumann and Fischer, 1987). The legal problems associated with NRMs in West Germany have also been intensively examined in Neumann and Fischer (1987). Finally, some of the complications arising from official investigations of NRMs in France (Vivien, 1985) and the European Parliament are discussed in Beckford (1986a).

What emerges clearly from this European and French-Canadian material is a picture which may be confusing in its country-by-country detail but important in so far as it indicates that the grounds for constituting NRMs as problematic and controversial vary from place to place (and perhaps across time as well — see van Driel and Belsen's [1987] analysis of the changing tenor of print media items about NRMs in The Netherlands and West Germany). This, in itself, represents a break away from a tendency in English-language treatments of NRMs to assume that the relatively standardized *modus operandi* of the movements in different countries is accompanied by a standard response modelled on the American or British patterns. Beckford (1983c) has tried to capture the broad variations in a three-fold typology of societal responses to NRMs: the voluntarist, the organicist and the reticulate. Further details of the third type of response, displayed principally in West Germany but also echoed in Scandinavia, have been supplied by Shupe et al. (1983). There is also some confirmation of this response in Dobbelaere et al.'s (1987) analysis of the dominant themes in Belgian press accounts of the

Unification Church. But it should not be overlooked that NRMs may not actually be considered especially problematic in some countries. Nordquist (1982) argues that the Swedish public, for example, is 'uninterested' in the topic, and Derks (1983) claims that the Dutch public has nothing to fear from NRMs or from their ex-members' state of mental health.

In view of the evidence about the differential responses to NRMs in Western European countries, a further note of caution must be sounded about the usefulness of disaggregated statistics of rates of receptivity to cults or sects in Europe. In particular, Stark and Bainbridge's argument that 'secularization produces religious revival and innovation' (1985: 477) and that the decline of formal churches in Western Europe has been matched by faster growth rates of cults and sects than in the USA (Stark, 1985b) must be seriously challenged. Not only is the statistical basis for the claim that the rate of cults per million of population is 2.3 for the USA and 3.2 for England and Wales questionable but it also totally begs the question of the relative *strength* of the movements in terms of their resources, property, standing and power in the two places. It seems perverse to make assessments of Europe's receptivity to NRMs without taking these things into account, and it is difficult to accept the claim that 'religious movements usually will build temples and station staff in places where they are strong and spurn places where they are weaker' (Stark and Bainbridge, 1985: 485). The latter part of the assumption appears to preclude virtually all missionary activity, for example, and runs directly contrary to findings from Scandinavia (Nordquist, 1982). Moreover, the data cannot support Stark and Bainbridge's belief that recruits to sects are ex-members of churches and recruits to cults were formerly unchurched. Indeed, in the predominantly Roman Catholic countries of Europe, there is a problem about the extent to which the term 'unchurched' is meaningful. A broader question is whether the basically voluntarist and pluralist connotations of 'membership', as the term is used in American sociology of religion, have the same resonance in the context of many European societies. This may be why European sociologists of religion have so far failed to evince much interest in Stark and Bainbridge's speculations (see, for example, the brief critical remarks by Campiche, 1987; Wallis, 1987c; and Hervieu-Léger, 1986, 218). It may also be why there is relatively strong interest in Europe in such phenomena as 'diffused religion', 'folk religion' and 'implicit religion'. They are possibly regarded as stronger candidates than sects or cults for the role of successor to the declining churches.

In sum, the European and French-Canadian contributions to socio-logical debates about NRMs in the West are relatively distinctive for their emphasis on, first, the social and cultural processes whereby the movements are constituted as 'new' religious phenomena of various kinds, and second, the factors affecting the societal response that the movements elicit in different countries.

In addition, a number of less significant points of distinctiveness can be listed: in comparison with American (and to a smaller extent British) scholars, continental European and French Canadian sociologists tend to display less enthusiasm for empirical research, maintain greater personal distance from the movements, are less preoccupied with legal conflicts (with the exception of West Germany) and are more divided over the question of whether NRMs are evidence of advanced secularization or nascent resacralization.

The conclusion of this brief survey of literature on Western NRMs outside the USA and the UK is that the predominantly Americanized form of the movements is refracted in different ways in different countries. As a result, there are limits to the extent to which one should speak of *an* agreed problematic of NRMs in the West: there are numerous problematics. The comparative sociology of the sociology of NRMs urgently requires study.

Note

1. With regard to Anglo-American NRMs, there are a number of existing review essays and bibliographies by sociologists (Anthony and Robbins, 1987; Barker, 1986; Beckford, 1987a; Beckford and Richardson, 1983; Choquette, 1985; Kilbourne and Richardson, 1984a; Robbins, 1981, 1983b, 1985f; Robbins and Anthony, 1979b, 1982b, 1987; Robbins et al., 1978; Snow and Machalek, 1984). A larger number of readers and collections deal largely with contemporary NRMs (*American Studies*, 1985; Anthony et al., 1987; Barker, 1982a, 1983b; Bromley and Hammond, 1987; Bromley and Richardson, 1983; Coleman and Baum, 1983; Douglas and Tipton, 1982; Fichter, 1983; Glock and Bellah, 1976; Hadden and Long, 1983; Heenan, 1973; Kaslow and Sussman, 1982; Kilbourne, 1985; Long and Hadden, 1983; Needleman and Baker, 1978; Richardson, 1978a, in press; Robbins and Anthony, 1981; Robbins et al., 1985; Stark, 1985a; *Thought*, 1986; Wallis, 1975a, 1982a; Wallis and Bruce, 1986; Wilson, 1981; Zaretsky and Leone, 1974a. Numerous monographs cover particular movements; however, there are only a few synthesizing monographs which attempt an overview of the general topic (Appel, 1983; Beckford, 1985a; Bromley and Shupe, 1981; Wallis, 1984). Reference works by Melton (1978, 1982, 1984, 1985) may prove useful.

2

NEW RELIGIOUS MOVEMENTS AND SOCIETY: THEORIES AND EXPLANATIONS

This chapter deals with theories which have been developed to explain the apparent proliferation and growth of NRMs in the period of the late 1960s through the 1970s. Some of the analyses are *ideas* which have not been adequately tested or may not even be testable. After the fact it is often too easy to identify 'problems' or a 'crisis' which can 'explain' the development of social movements. Theories of the socio-historical causation of social movements are not easily susceptible to direct empirical investigation.

The Issue of Historical Specificity

We are dealing, in this chapter, with *explanations* for enhanced spiritual ferment and turmoil in recent decades. But this explanatory enterprise pre-supposes the specificity and uniqueness of that which is to be 'explained'. Does the recent flux described in our introductory chapter really constitute a discrete and bounded social phenomenon which distinctly stands out against the broader flow of American or European religious history? A historian has recently commented:

> It is possible to locate a period in American history when so-called small sects were not growing at a faster clip than denominations then viewed as large and stable. This fact is crucial and central to any discussion of American religious pluralism. Yet dozens of recent books and an almost endless amount of journalistic commentary, much of it based on the work of very able sociologists, have assumed that sects and cults...began to affect religious life in this country only around 1960. Our failures in Vietnam have properly had to answer for many things, but the disruption of "normal" religious behavior is not one of them (Moore, 1985: X).

In *Religious Outsiders and the Making of Americans*, H. Lawrence Moore (1985) argues that religious 'outsiders' have continually played a key role in American religious history but that the importance of their contribution has been obscured by a tradition of 'consensus' history. This distortion is said to survive in treatments which assume that some kind of Protestant ethic/civil religious unity has heretofore dominated American culture and has only recently become an 'empty and broken shell' (Bellah, 1975) such that new spiritual movements have now appeared to define new cultural motifs (e.g. Anthony and Robbins, 1982b; Bellah, 1975, 1976a).

In Moore's view, religious movements have continually used the 'language of dissent' to define themselves dualistically against a posited established culture (e.g. the culture of secularism and materialism against which today's television evangelists thunder). This is a constant pattern, not a set of intermittent disruptions of 'normal' denominational pluralism. 'The notion that sectarianism as a factor in American religious life rises and falls in response to dramatic social upheaval does not seem to fit facts' (Moore, 1985: 124). Christian Science, Mormonism and Watchtower have grown as 'ordinary manifestations of tensions that were always present in American society'. 'Striking parallels' can thus be seen in the development of groups such as Scientology, Hare Krishna and the Unification Church and the earlier history of Christian Science (Moore, 1985: 124–7). Several writers have recently pointed to the similarities of recent NRMs, consciousness and alternate lifestyle movements and the various sects, utopian communities and pseudosciences which arose during the 'Second Great Awakening' in the nineteenth century (FitzGerald, 1986; Oden, 1982). For other historical comparisons, see Bromley and Shupe (1981), FitzGerald (1986), Hampshire and Beckford (1983), Kent (1987), Pritchard (1976) and Robbins and Anthony (1979a).

Some support for elements of Moore's perspective can be found in recent work by Rodney Stark and William Bainbridge (1985), particularly some fascinating census data research into 'cult membership in the twenties' (Stark and Bainbridge, 1985: 234–62; Stark et al., 1979, 1981), indicative of 'amazing stability in cult activity over the 40 years between the 1920s and 1970s. This suggests the need for more basic theories of cult formation than those suggested by scholars who regard the rise of new religions as a *new* phenomenon' (Stark et al., 1981: 137). The unearthing of familiar patterns of cult receptivity in data over 50 years old seems to indicate that 'cults are not merely ephemeral residues of the radical 1960s. They are a vital aspect of American religion, and their distribution offers a sensitive indicator of the sacred in a supposedly secular age' (Stark and Bainbridge, 1985: 262).

On the other hand, the broader pattern of endemic religious innovation and dissidence in American culture does not negate the existence of historically particular sources of particular 'awakenings' or specific themes and symbols arising in different periods of cult formation, e.g. the Vietnam war may still be an important factor underlying the recent (1965–85) ferment. Wuthnow (1986) has analyzed survey data indicative of discontinuities entailing an expansion of new movements in the 1960s and early 1970s and a subsequent levelling off of the growth of esoteric spirituality (see Ch. 1).

How 'new' is the 'New Religous Consciousness' (Melton, 1987)? Fundamentalism, Pentecostalism and pre-millennial prophecy are hardly new, and there is clear continuity between contemporary 'monistic' mysticism (Anthony and Robbins, 1982a) and the 'harmonial' and occult themes manifested earlier in Christian Science and Theosophy (Melton, 1987; Moore, 1985: 105–27). The latter also display continuity with the symbolic universe of 'New Age' and human potential groups, although the impact of the post-Second World War science fiction subculture, as reflected particularly in Scientology and its offshoots (Bainbridge, 1987; Morth, 1987), may be novel. Hindu–Buddhist–Sufi mysticism has been present in the United States and Europe for some time (Melton, 1987) and the larger present audience for such ideas may reflect primarily the spread of higher education and the growth of the intelligentsia (Wuthnow, 1986). 'The blossoming of the alternative religions of the 1970s is not so much a new event in Western culture as a continuation of the flowering of the occult mysticism and Eastern thought that began in the nineteenth century' (Melton, 1987: 47–8).

Affirmations of continuity by Moore and Stark–Bainbridge arise in part as reactions to the analyses and theories we will describe below. A plethora of theories have related the recent growth of NRMs to *linear* changes in culture and social structure: secularization; mass higher education; breakdown of the family; basic value shifts; national crisis of meaning; disruptions of civil religions; emergence of a 'culture of narcissism'; lack of sustained economic growth; waning of 1960s political radicalism; and the 'counterculture', etc.

Theories of Sociocultural Transformation

A number of theories appear to regard the spiritual ferment of the past decades as a distinctively modern phenomenon which reflects funda-mental social and cultural change. The change processes which are identified as underlying the proliferation of NRMs sometimes entail states of disorganization or breakdowns, e.g. of normative patterns regulating interpersonal and communal relations (Aidala, 1985; Hunter, 1981; Westley, 1978a,b); or a posited crisis of moral meanings or cultural values (Anthony and Robbins, 1982b, 1983; Bellah, 1976a, Glock, 1976; Wuthnow, 1976a,b). The gradual advance of secularization is credited with laying a foundation for enhanced religious diversity and innovation; (Turner, 1983; Wallis, 1984; Wilson, 1976, 1982). What most (though not all) of these theories have in common is the positing of a relationship between the rise of a contemporary NRM and occurrence of a fundamental, linear transformation in American (or modern Western) society and culture.

Revolution and the Occult

We begin with a brief consideration of theories which identify cultic effervescence as a *pre-revolutionary condition* (which is not necessarily uniquely modern). This seems to have been the viewpoint of Charles Dickens who depicted an exotic occultism flourishing among the degenerate and demoralized upper class of the Ancien Régime in *A Tale of Two Cities*:

> The leprosy of unreality disfigured every human creature in attendance upon Monseigneur. In the outermost room were half a dozen exceptional people who had had, for a few years, some vague misgiving in them that things in general were going wrong. As a promising way of setting them right, half of the half-dozen had become members of a fanatic sect of convulsionists and were even then considering within themselves whether they should foam, rage, roar and turn cataleptic on the spot — thereby setting up a highly intelligible fingerpost to the future. . . .

A less vivid though more theoretically elegant formulation to the effect that an explosion of exotic new religious movements foreshadows a major revolution has more recently been set forth by Edward Tiryakian (1967), who maintains that the appearance of deviant and 'non-institutionalized' religions represents a vital 'lead indicator' of imminent revolutionary upheaval. Tiryakian focuses attention on 'the covert, non-institutional sphere of society' in which 'new basic cultural definitions of the situation are generated as responses to societal strains' (Tiryakian, 1967: 83). Employing a Parsonian schema, Tiryakian identifies the crucial 'covert' realm as the Latency subsector of the Latency (Pattern Maintenance and Tension Management) sector of the Social System. Non-institutionalized religious phenomena constitute the typical content of this key subsector, thus, 'significant increases in the outbreak of non-institutionalized religious phenomena' are indicative of a normative breakdown and foreshadow a coming revolution (Tiryakian, 1967: 91–5; see also Groves, 1986). Yet from the standpoint of the 1980s, many of the currently surging 'Old Time Religion' groups might appear to be 'restorationist' rather than innovative or proto-revolutionary.

A later formulation by Tiryakian (1974), which stresses the potentially creative and transformative role of the 'esoteric culture', has been more specific in identifying groups preoccupied with a hidden and exclusive gnosis and oriented toward 'occult practices' manipulating concealed natural forces as his true focus. Modern occult practices do not represent a mere 'atavistic throwback' indicative of a 'breakdown in moderniza-tion', but rather potentially inspire 'new systems of social action' and can play a creative role in emergent processes of social change (Tiryakian, 1973, 1974; see also Campbell and McIver, 1987; Jorgensen, 1982). From Tiryakian's standpoint the most significant contemporary groups would be magical–occult groups perhaps including techno-scientistic movements such as the 'modern magic' of Scientology (Bainbridge and Stark, 1980). But Stark and Bainbridge consider such groups to be regressive and headed toward increasing marginality. 'They reject the whole scientific culture as well as Christian–Judaic traditions...They will not thrive unless the modern world collapses' (Stark and Bainbridge, 1985: 455–6). Truzzi, by contrast (1971, 1974, 1975), looks at occultism as popular culture.

For Stark and Bainbridge, groups such as TM and Scientology, which are said to conceal a magical core behind a pseudo-scientific facade, 'are very vulnerable to scientific evaluation and most likely will be revealed as magic if and when such evaluations are made' (Stark and Bainbridge, 1985: 456). Yet such groups may persist for some time, as has unscien-tific psychoanalysis. Nevertheless, 'faiths of the future will contain no magic, only religion' (Stark and Bainbridge, 1985: 450). Ben-Yehuda (1985) develops a neo-Durkheimian analysis of contemporary occultism in terms of deviance theory and the shifting boundaries of 'science'. However, the 'deviant' quality of 'occult knowledge' may be ambiguous (Campbell and McIver, 1987).

The above formulations lead into the topic of the relationship of NRMs to *secularization*, discussion of which is deferred until the end of this chapter. We now turn to some of the analytical frameworks, generally developed in the 1970s, which relate the growth of NRMs to the emergence in the 1960s of an 'alienated' youth culture or 'counterculture'.

Functionalism and the Integrative Thesis

Considering the attention given in the late 1970s and early 1980s to agitation over the depredations of 'destructive cults' (Appel, 1983; Clark et al., 1981; Conway and Siegelman, 1978), it is ironic that much of the sociological commentary on NRMs in the early 1970s tended to highlight the 'adaptive' and 'integrative' consequences of participation in NRMs in terms of rehabilitating drug users and reassimilating alienated nomadic youth into conventional educational and occupational roles (Adams and Fox, 1972; Anthony and Robbins, 1974; Johnson, 1976; Petersen and Mauss, 1974; Robbins, 1969; Robbins and Anthony, 1972). The early literature on 'the integrative hypothesis' has been reviewed by Robbins et al. (1975). More critical evaluations have since been offered by Beckford (1978c, 1981a) and Wallis (1984: 73–84).

Wallis (1984) notes that only certain types of movements were featured in analyses affirming the integrative impact of NRMs. These movements tended to proscribe drug use and to discourage promiscuity and were sometimes politically conservative, as with a number of 'Jesus groups' (Gregg, 1973; Petersen and Mauss, 1974). They often possessed an orientation suggestive of a work ethic, as with the 'selfless service' ethos of followers of Meher Baba (Anthony and Robbins, 1974; Robbins, 1969; Robbins and Anthony, 1972). Such groups did 'not insist on such a sharp break between members and their families and former friends as is often the case with world-rejecting sects. The institutions of the wider society are not so uniformly condemned' (Wallis, 1984: 73). Such groups also offered novel and deviant means of salvation which drew upon themes related to bohemian youth culture. Devotees of the Happy–Healthy–Holy (3HO) Sikh movement of Yogi Bhajan (Tobey, 1976) assumed Punjabi names, wore turbans, became vegetarians and sometimes resided in communal centers. Nevertheless, as Tobey (1976) and subsequently Wallis (1984) noted, 3HO did not enjoin a retreat from worldly involvements, rather, 'marriage, responsible employment, and social service are normative for all its members' (Wallis, 1984: 73). Such movements appeared to provide a kind of haven or asylum from *both* the system *and* the counterculture in which individuals could temporarily sustain the deviant *style* of the counterculture while changing their practical values and behavior in the direction of the conventional expectations (Adams and Fox, 1972; Petersen and Mauss, 1974; Robbins et al., 1975; Wallis, 1984: 74–5).

The 'Integrative Hypothesis' was formalized by Robbins et al. (1975), who posited 'that new youth culture religious movements have consequences of reconciling and adapting alienated young persons to dominant institutions, and in so doing, they perform latent pattern maintenance for the social system' (Robbins et al., 1975: 49). Robbins (1969) suggested continuity with well-known earlier tendencies of American 'sects' to recruit from anomic first generation urbanites who were 'socialized in dominant values' through sectarian involvement (Johnson, 1961).

Robbins et al. identify four processes through which 'these movements facilitate the social reintegration of converts' (Robbins et al., 1975: 49).

(1) *Adaptive socialization* refers to the overt inculcation of norms, values and skills which are conducive to successful coping and adaptation to conventional institutional milieux. The norms are often negative, e.g. do not take drugs, drink, be promiscuous, etc. (2) *Combination* denotes the capacity of movement symbol systems to 'combine or synthesize counter-cultural values with traditional or mainstream orientations...' (Robbins et al., 1975: 51). Significant here are the 'identity synthesis' (Gordon, 1974) and 'returning fundamentalist' (Richardson and Stewart, 1978) formulations which depict 'Jesus people' as persons from conserva-tive Christian backgrounds who rebelled and became immersed in deviant countercultural expressivity, but subsequently emerged and synthesized their spiritual hunger, alienation and residual feeling for conservative Christianity by involvement in a movement combining the latter with stylistic deviance (see also Adams and Fox, 1972; Balswick, 1974; Petersen and Mauss, 1973; Tipton, 1982a).

(3) *Compensation* and (4) *redirection* were identified as processes which did not involve 'explicit norms either proscribing deviant involvements... or legitimating non-deviant commitments...' (Robbins et al. 1975: 52). *Compensation* highlights the diminished alienation from conventional (e.g. bureaucratic) roles on the part of the devotee who has spiritual 'compensations'. *Redirection* entails the diminished appeal of deviant routines and roles from which the devotee has now been 'redirected' toward spiritual 'substitutes', e.g. spiritual 'highs' replacing chemical 'highs' (Robbins et al., 1975; see also Downton, 1979; Johnson, 1976).

Robbins et al. distinguish between *adaptive* and *marginal* movements. The former 'facilitate the reassimilation of converts into conventional vocational routines'. In contrast *marginal* movements 'actually *remove* members from conventional pursuits and lock them into social marginality' (Robbins et al. 1975: 56). Examples of the latter include ISKON, the Unification Church and the Children of God (COG). Rather speculatively, Robbins et al. argue that marginal movements nevertheless have latent integrative consequences in terms of redirecting converts from drug use and political radicalism. Wallis (1984: 76) does not find this claim very convincing. Studies indicate that members of totalistic movements such as Hare Krishna, the UC and the COG became disenchanted with drugs *prior* to conversion (Beckford, 1978c; Judah, 1974; Wallis, 1984: 76) and that the devotees were not politically radical or seriously alienated before recruitment (Beckford, 1978b,c; Judah, 1974). Converts to adaptive groups were often 'well on their way back from the margins of society before they had any contact with the religious movement' (Wallis, 1984: 76; see also Beckford, 1978c and McGee, 1974: 56–69).

In Wallis' view, there is a tendency (e.g. Robbins and Anthony, 1972) to 'overstress the active role of the movements and its beliefs and practices in producing the outcome of a more behaviorally and morally conforming member of society' (Wallis, 1984: 76). Nevertheless, there are a number of studies by social scientists pointing to socially and psychologically adaptive–integrative consequences associated with involvement in NRMs. These studies have been cited in several theoretical articles (Anthony, 1982b; Kilbourne and Richardson, 1984a; Robbins and Anthony, 1982a; Robbins et al., 1975). Some of these studies may, however, be subject to methodological criticisms (Beckford, 1978c, 1981a; Wallis, 1984: 136–8).

Early sociological analyses reductively imply that the integrative 'function' of these groups was their be-all and end-all. Seeking to mitigate earlier reductionism Robbins et al. (1975: 59–61) tried to distinguish theoretically between the adaptive sociological *consequences* of NRMs and (1) the *motivations* of recruits to convert, (2) the *origin* and development of these groups, (3) the *truth* or falsity of group beliefs, and (4) the vital *symbolic mediation* of integrative effects through beliefs and rituals which must be subjectively understood. Subsequently Robbins and Anthony (1979b) published a follow-up piece which sought to evaluate the possibility of long-run *disintegrative* as well as *transformative* consequences for society arising from contemporary NRMs, in contrast to merely *integrative* and pattern-maintenance effects 'functions'.

Beckford (1978c, 1981a) has mounted a solidly theoretical and normative critique of the functionalist–integrative genre which spotlights problems involving reductionism, the logical requirements of functionalist explanation and, in particular, 'the relationship between "ought" and "function"'. Functionalist analyses of the integrative impact of NRMs are said to manifest a spurious ethical neutrality which actually obscures clear moral evaluation of religious movements and the consequences of involvement. Such groups may indeed provide 'meaning' to anomic youth, but what particular meanings? 'Once religion is identified with "meaningfulness-in-general", all possibility of distinguishing its humane from its non humane forms dies' (Schuler, 1983–4: 233). Beckford (1981a) notes that, paradoxically, both detractors and defenders of stigmatized cults tend to frame their arguments in similar quasi-functionalist terms: 'The functionalist perspective commonly switches to the psychological level of the individual in order to show either integrative or destructive effects of cultism on its practitioners. Psychological well-being then replaces social solidarity as the allegedly normal state of the system' (Beckford, 1981a: 120).

Another aspect of the functionalist perspective on the individual's psychological well-being is that diametrically opposed evaluations of cults can be produced from a consideration of the same observations. It is agreed, for example, among both supporters and opponents of cults, that they have the effect of generating in their members individually and collectively impressive outputs of emergy and enthusiasm. Yet, whereas one side in the debate interprets this observation as evidence of the healthy functioning of individuals, the other side considers that it substantiates the suspicion that 'unnatural' energies are being canalized into antisocial activities (Beckford: 1981a: 120; see also Shupe and Bromley, 1980a: 152–53).

Beckford notes that although the 'integrative' analysis may covertly *legitimate* religious movements, it does so in a reductive and condescending manner: 'The implication is that cults are valued for precisely the kind of reasons which their own members might wish to reject (Beckford, 1981a: 125). See Batiuk (1987) and Campbell (1982) for additional critiques of the functionalist treatment of NRMs. ·

The 'Postmovement' Dynamic. As Wallis (1984) and others have noted, a key element of the 1970s functionalist–integrative genre was the highlighting of a strategic relationship between the surge of NRMs in the 1970s and the 'counterculture', particularly its waning and an emergent disillusionment with the promises of psychedelic utopianism and political radicalism. This relationship has also been explored by social scientists who do not belong in the functionalist tradition, such as Foss and Larkin's formulations regarding 'postmovement groups' (Foss and Larkin, 1976, 1978, 1986). 'Postmovement groups' refer to the religious, political and therapeutic groups which came to prominence in the middle and late 1970s. Such groups tended to be highly authoritarian, charismatically led, puritanical and intolerant. Examples include the Hare Krishnas, the Progressive Labor Party, the Children of God, 'Trotskyite sects' and the LaRouchites (in their early Marxist incarnation). According to the authors, each group appropriated 'a fragment of the vision articulated in the youth culture of the 1960s (peace, love, revolution, ego transcendence and so on)' but maintained 'a fierce exclusivity based on doctrines claiming a monopoly of truth' (Foss and Larkin, 1976: 269), which was extrapolated into an authoritarian regimentation. 'The servility of the members was used as evidence of spirituality, ego transcendence, or manifestations of peace and love' (Foss and Larkin, 1979: 270).

'During the 1970s, such cultural themes of the youth movement of the 1960s, as consciousness exploration, voluntary poverty, ''community'', and generational revolt were inverted in some of the patriarchal or mock-bureaucratic 'new religions' and some of the more authoritarian of the new psychotherapies such as Synanon, Scientology and — to some extent — est, whereas New Leftism was inverted into neo-Leninism' (Foss and Larkin, 1986: 86). Conventional authority relations were reproduced in unconventional form (see also Straus, 1986, on Scientology's authoritarian social control processes).

From the standpoint of social movement theory Foss and Larkin's later formulation (1986) is significant in terms of viewing the development of particular groups and movements as reflecting a phase of a broader 'Movement' or 'revolution' qua period of unrest. Comparisons are made to the French Revolution, Russian Revolution and English Civil War in which different phases generated different kinds of groups. Religious cults qua postmovement groups emerged in the context of the waning of 'The Movement' and the resulting disillusionment. Thus, devotees of The Divine Light Mission in the early 1970s were characterized by Foss and Larkin (1978) as expressing their disillusioned conviction of the absurdity of the world through half-mockingly 'worshipping the absurd' as embodied in a plump teenage guru and his opulent lifestyle.

Foss and Larkin's analysis cuts across the distinctions between political, religious and therapeutic movements, although it is arguably reductive in the sense that it treats the significance of religious movements as derivative from more fundamental sociopolitical dissidence.

The Tipton Thesis. A better-known formulation is embodied in Steven Tipton's analysis of the role of 1970s movements in responding to value conflicts arising from the interface of the persisting influence of the expressive counterculture and the resurgence of the more traditional American value-orientations of conformist utilitarian individualism and absolutist biblical literalism. Tipton's study of est, Zen devotees and charismatic Christians manifests substantially more continuity with the functionalist–integrative genre than does the analysis of Foss and Larkin. It is in part the grand culmination of the themes of 'combination' and 'identity synthesis' in the earlier functionalist analyses of the integrative consequences of NRMs.

Tipton's analysis was spelled out in his widely reviewed *Getting Saved from the Sixties* (Tipton, 1982a) and in several provocative articles dealing with est (Tipton, 1982, 1983) and American Zen (Tipton, 1979). Tipton sees the 1970s as a period witnessing a conflict and confusion of moral ideologies:

> The conflict of values between mainstream American culture and counter-culture during the 1960s framed problems that alternative religious movements of the 1970s have

resolved by mediating both sides of the conflicts and transforming their divergent moral meanings. Contrasting styles of ethical evaluation have shaped this conflict and its mediation. These styles distinctively characterize the romantic tradition of the counter-culture and the two traditions that underpin mainstream culture, biblical religion, and utilitarian individualism (Tipton, 1979: 286).

American society 'continues to revolve around technological produc-tion, bureaucratic organization, and a massed urban population. Outright rejections of the instrumental behavior rationalized by utilitarian culture are likely to flourish only within small subcultures or for short periods in the life-cycle of their adherents' (Tipton, 1979: 302). Thus most Americans who have been influenced by discordant value-orientations such as the countercultural ethos of expressive spontaneity or fervent born-again Christianity must 'respond to the practical demands exerted on adults by the different traditions with which they live'. Thus, the 'situational–expressive' moral ideology of the 1960s counterculture which enjoined making life anew day-by-day becomes problematic in terms of 'the human condition that calls for order and regularity':

> . . . these movements have carried on situational–expressive ideals by recombining them with moralities of authority, rules, or utility. Neo-oriental groups, like Zen Buddhism, recombine the situational–expressive ethic with the regular ethic of rationalized religion. Neo-Christian groups recombine the situational expressive ethic of the hip counter-culture with the authoritative ethic of revealed biblical religion. The human potential movement combines the situational–expressive ethic with the consequential ethic of utilitarian individualism . . . These movements draw from the old targets of biblical religion, rationalism and utilitarian culture itself, as well as from non-western traditions, in order to synthesize their ethics. In this, they are 'religious' in the literal sense that they 'bind together' heretofore disparate cultural elements, revitalizing tradition as they change it' (Tipton, 1979: 310).

Particularly important is Tipton's analysis (1982a,b) of cultural mediation in est and the movement's orientation toward what Tipton terms 'rule egoism'. The moral ethos of est embodies the countercultural or 'situational– expressive' premise that the purpose of life is to feel good, to 'experience aliveness'. But feeling good is said to be related to attaining *goals*, and this in turn requires following *rules*. Est puts forward a countercultural 'expressive theory of good' which is subtly extrapolated in a manner which legitimates conformity and thematizes the capitalist moral linchpin of sanctity of contracts; 'est justifies following rules and keeping agreements, because these produce good consequences: Follow the rules if you want to experience aliveness . . . compliance with rules is justified on egoistic grounds' (Tipton, 1982b: 89).

Tipton's monograph *Getting Saved from the Sixties* (1982a) is one of the few sociological works on NRMs which has received widespread attention outside of the disciplinary community. However, some scholars influenced by Marxian and critical perspectives have received Tipton's volume with hostility and have perceived Tipton's account of NRMs in the 1970s as too celebratory:

> Does mysticism signify emancipation or a more successful adaptation to actual power-lessness? Is the postulate of individual perfection any more than a defense against despair? How do the movements of anti-modernism shore up the given social order with more resilient psyches? (Schuler, 1982–3: 234–5).

In Schuler's view Tipton does not clearly answer these vital questions, because he is a prisoner of a 'sociological tradition' which theorizes in terms of 'such abstractions' as 'religion', 'integrative function', and 'bureaucracy'...[which] assume an ahistorical status that wipes out differences and submerges conflict' (Schuler, 1982–3: 235). The Zen, human potential and charismatic groups Tipton describes are seen to 'collaborate in a common moral project' such that each ideology is allegedly not really being scrutinized by Tipton for its specific pathological qualities of passivity and false consciousness:

> Despite negative attitudes towards consumerism, the non-dualistic ontology of Zen, its beliefs in the illusion of suffering and individuality, the elimination of desires and conflict, and pursuit of perfection lead us away from recognizing the specific irrationality that governs our lives...*est* perfects defensiveness by eliminating guilt, failure, disappointment and leaving you totally responsible for your existence...the revival church teaches that you are nothing until you submit to its authority and draw your life from God. At both extremes, the world is accepted, neither challenged nor understood. Criticism becomes a spiritual disorder, while shell-shocked psyches are patched up for further service (Schuler, 1983–4 235).

Ironically, Schuler seems really to accept much of the integrative thesis, i.e. (to put it simplistically) NRMs encourage their potentially alienated devotees to *accommodate to the status quo by allowing them to feel inwardly liberated*. What is objected to is Tipton's alleged complacency and his failure to forcefully condemn NRMs for false consciousness and ultimate passivity. 'In essence, mysticism may be the moral buttress of the totally administered society, a Zen ethic to replace the Protestant one...An exotic path to pacification gives the illusion of change, but the end will probably gratify Wall Street' (Schuler, 1983–4: 232).

In Tipton's defense it might be argued that the critical standpoint from which he is denounced is grounded in the dogmatic assumption that all tensions are to be properly resolved only on the level of comprehensive social change. Attributions of 'false consciousness' can be seen as projections of political agendas. Apropos of Christian Science, historian R. L. Moore asks, 'On what grounds. . .can we say that she misperceived her plight other than our own political priorities?. . .Mary Baker Eddy solved a number of her personal problems by founding a church. Other women solved their problems by joining it' (Moore, 1985: 120). For Tipton's critical analysis of 'therapy as a way of life' see Bellah et al. (1985).

One implication of Tipton's analysis may be that contemporary 'alternative religions' are a generational phenomenon which will become increasingly marginal as the influence of the 1960s counterculture wanes (Downton, 1979; Wallis, 1984). Or have some of the expressive values of the countercultural period been institutionalized such that the kinds of conflicts which NRMs are seen by Tipton as mediating will continually arise? Tipton's analysis (1982a) of charismatic Christians coping with the tension between biblical absolutism and utilitarian individualism may be particularly relevant to the Christian revivalism of the 1980s (see also Hunter, 1983, 1987).

Cults and Cultural Confusion

In retrospect Tipton's analysis can be seen as the coordination of two interrelated perspectives: the integrative thesis, and the pervasive notion that the growth of NRMs of the 1960s and 1970s responded to a broad cultural transformation and crisis of meaning (Bellah, 1976a; Glock, 1976; Wuthnow, 1976b) arising in part from disruptions to American civil religion (Anthony and Robbins, 1982b; Bellah, 1975; Eister, 1972, 1974; Johnson, 1981).

Robert Bellah and others have identified American civil religion and/or 'public theology' as a constellation of religio-political meanings and rituals which articulate a sense of national purpose (Bellah, 1981). Bellah has noted, however, that, 'Today the American civil religion is an empty and broken shell' (Bellah, 1975: 145). In *The Broken Covenant* Bellah identified the spiritual effervescence of the period as groping toward a 'birth of new myths' as a response to the erosion of civil religion. Elsewhere (1976a) Bellah argued that the new spiritual groups which flourished in the 1970s represented 'successor movements' to the late 1960s 'crisis of meaning' and to the countercultural revolt against 'technical reason' and materialist utilitarian individualism, although evolving NRMs will likely make accommodations to resurgent utilitarian individualism. This latter acknowledgement is the take-off point for Tipton's analysis (see above) of the value mediating role of NRMs in the 1970s. But the Bellah–Tipton view has not gone unchallenged: 'Millennial religion has clearly rubbed off on sociology...A legitimacy crisis is proclaimed, so Tipton, Bellah and others anticipate a new awakening. They slip from description to sweeping explanations set against the panorama of American history' (Schuler, 1983–4: 234).

Bellah's cultural explanation has also been challenged by anthropologist Marvin Harris, who has scoffed at the notion that the devotees of gurus and cults of the 1970s were rebelling against materialism and technology (Harris, 1981: 141–65). While Bellah sees the success of American society in economic and material terms producing a spiritual rejection of materialism, Harris argues that the American vision of economic success was proving, in the 1970s, to be illusory such that the NRMs of this period were not so much 'revolting against success' as hedging against failure and regressing to magical means of grasping material goals through chanting mantras, trusting in Jesus and 'psychological training'.

Moral Ideologies. A number of other writers besides Tipton have focused on pervasive moral ambiguity in modern American culture and the troubling conflicts over moral responsibility which increasingly arise. Frederick Bird focuses on 'the extent to which and ways in which new religious movements encourage among adherents a reduced sense of moral accountability' (Bird, 1979: 335). This sense is produced in a different manner and with different consequences in *devotee, discipleship* and *apprenticeship* groups (see Ch. 5). Somewhat similarly, Anthony and Robbins identify the source of recent spiritual ferment as a deepening climate of moral ambiguity which reflects the decline of a cultural tradition of dualistic moral absolutism which incorporates a premise of personal responsibility and autonomy (Anthony and Robbins, 1982a,b; Robbins et al., 1978). The pervasive moral confusion is said to have produced two comprehensive resolutions on a spiritual level. *Monistic* worldviews extrapolate relativistic and subjectivistic tendencies in cultural modernism and affirm metaphysical unity or 'oneness' and the illusory quality of the phenomenal world (and the derivative primacy of inner consciousness). In contrast *dualistic* worldviews stridently reaffirm motifs of ethical dualism and millennarianism derived ultimately from the American evangelical and puritan traditions (Anthony and Ecker, 1987; see Ch. 5). Both perspectives provide a basis for constructing meaning in the face of apparent moral chaos (Anthony and Robbins, 1982a,b). Resurgent dualistic moral absolutism confers moral meaning on disorienting chaos by prophesying the imminent wrathful destruction of the corrupt, relativistic culture and by identifying Antichrist as the demiurge underlying unsettling contemporary trends such as the growth of communism, pornography, homosexuality, bizarre cults, crime, etc. (Anthony and Robbins, 1982a,b; McGuire, 1982;).

Charles Glock (1976) also interprets the surge of NRMs in the 1970s in terms of a response to a disorienting shift of cultural values. Glock identifies the undermining of traditional conceptions of *personal autonomy* and responsibility as the essential cultural transformation of the 1960s and 1970s which engendered a quest for new structures of meaning. Glock's view of recent value shifts has been reinforced by some survey data from the 1970s on popular notions of causation of individual and social experience (Glock and Piazza, 1981; and Wuthnow, 1976a,b), which suggest a shift away from traditional individualistic–voluntaristic perspectives on the locus of causation toward both 'mystical' and 'scientific' orientations (traditional 'theistic' views remain salient). These shifts, which may amount to a fundamental 'Consciousness Reformation' (Wuthnow, 1976b), were found to be correlated with the 1970s' growing experimentation in alternate lifestyles (e.g. liberal sexual practices, political radicalism, drug use and new religiotherapeutic mystiques) in the San Francisco Bay area (Glock and Bellah, 1976; Wuthnow, 1976a,b).

Bainbridge and Stark have mounted a sharp critique — 'The "Consciousness Reformation" Reconsidered' (Bainbridge and Stark, 1981; Stark and Bainbridge, 1985: 366–93). On the basis of a re-analysis of Wuthnow's original Bay Area Study data plus data from an additional social network study, Bainbridge and Stark find little evidence for the existence of 'secular' meaning systems of individualism, social science determinism and mysticism. The authors argue 'that the concept of *meaning system* is itself meaningless as long as it is a purely cultural construct. Meaning systems must have *social* meaning...it must be possible to locate them within social networks and organizations' (Stark and Bainbridge, 1985: 393). Bainbridge and Stark criticize the assumptions underlying some of the recent formulations affirming transformations of cultural values and meanings in recent American experience. Human beings are not generally theologians possessing coherent, overarching 'worldviews'. 'Purely cultural explanations' are misleading (Bainbridge and Stark, 1981: 1).

Wuthnow (1981a) responded with a theoretical treatise which sought to relate ambiguities allegedly permeating the Bainbridge–Stark essay to the conflict of Cartesian–dualist and holistic epistemological traditions in modern social science (see also Wuthnow, 1987). Bainbridge and Stark's view is said to reflect dualistic epistemology by imputing a purely subjective and cognitive quality to religious beliefs which are then 'reduced' to the 'objective' substratum of interpersonal bonds. Wuthnow decries 'sociometric reductionism'. The debate between Wuthnow and Bainbridge–Stark illustrates the significance of the flourishing study of NRMs as a catalyst for theoretical ferment in the sociology of religion (Robbins, 1988; see Ch. 7). See Aidala (1984) for a replication of Wuthnow's 'Consciousness Reformation' findings (using a study of youth communes) as well as an extrapolation and an additional critique.

Cultural Continuity. A number of social scientists identify various elements of substantial continuity between the values embodied in esoteric religio-therapeutic movements and prominent American cultural motifs. Wuthnow (1985) argues that seemingly unconventional and dissident movements such as Hare Krishna can nevertheless be seen to be congruent with mainstream tendencies in American culture. The new religions 'bear the distinctive imprint of the prevailing technological worldview' (Wuthnow, 1985: 46), even though they may present themselves as stalwart opponents of this worldview. Hare Krishna condemns materialism and technologism, yet spirituality for ISKON is resolved into standardized, repetitive *techniques* producing immediate empirical–experiential consequences. Like Hare Krishna, Transcendental Meditation and various other yoga, guru and therapy groups are marketing *spiritual technologies* (see also Anthony and Ecker, 1987). The 'experiential' emphasis of various mystical occult, human potential and charismatic groups which has frequently been contrasted to American materialism and utilitarianism is really convergent with a dominant American empiricist–materialist epistemology in which the primary criterion of truth is grounded in the tangible empirical consequences which a 'true' entity produces (Anthony and Ecker, 1987; Wuthnow, 1985; see Ch. 5).

> The groups did not legitimate themselves in terms of universal principles of absolute values, but in terms of the short-run consequences of their activities. In this important respect, they echoed suppositions characteristic of the culture at large...The groups that prospered most made their peace with the technical worldview...the emergence of religious protest itself presupposed conventional understandings of the social world. The new religions exploited techniques having immediate consequences and adopted consequentialist reasoning in support of their practices (Wuthnow, 1985: 53; see also Anthony and Ecker, 1987; Tipton, 1982a,b).

Similarly, Harris (1981) argues that the operations of many esoteric and putatively anti-materialistic and experientialist cults are conspicuously *instrumentalist* and treat religious awakening as a means for acquiring 'worldly wealth, power and physical well-being as manifestations of the search for spiritual salvation' (Harris, 1981: 150). Roger Straus, presenting a detailed analysis of the 'Ethics' or social control practices of the Church of Scientology, finds that 'the Scientology world in fact not only shares but glorifies the essential values, motives and rationality of American capitalist society' (Straus, 1986: 68). The 'Ethics' of Scientology resemble the operative ethic of American corporate capitalism in the sense that 'a great value is placed on the individual', yet theoretical individualism is 'bounded and implicitly defined by a functionalist, system-centered rationality' (Straus, 1986: 77). Conventional authority relations are reproduced in esoteric contexts (Foss and Larkin, 1986). Modern 'cultures' are complex. While no movement is likely to grow unless it has a 'cultural base', i.e. is congruent with some cultural expectations, it is hardly surprising that given movements might reflect some cultural norms while simultaneously repudiating others. Notwithstanding Wuthnow's (1985) analysis of Americanized guru groups as representing spiritual technicalism, Hare Krishna strikingly repudiates dominant American cultural values in several areas including child socialization, education and attitudes towards mind–body (Bromley and Shinn, 1988). The Unification Church is bizarre, collectivist and 'oriental', yet it also speaks to messianic American anti-communism (Anthony and Robbins, 1978; Robbins et al., 1976).

Civil Religion and its 'Narcissistic' Rejection. A key aspect of the analysis of the spiritual ferment of the past two decades in normative terms is the posited breakdown in the 1960s and 1970s of consensual motifs of civil religion and 'messianic anti-communism, which has operated as a unifying religio-political ideology in mid-twentieth-century America' (Robbins and Anthony, 1982b: 63). But, 'The war against communism ceased to be holy in Vietnam...The cult phenomenon substituted a myriad of fragmented visions for the central messianism we once called Americanism' (Appel, 1980: A19).

The surge of right-wing evangelicism can be seen in part as a reaction against the undermining of consensual 'Americanism' in the 1960s and 1970s (McGuire, 1982; Moore, 1985; Wuthnow, 1983). Anti-communist pre-millennialism comments on the decline of patriotism, i.e. 'Those who wore American flags in their lapels recognized the Antichrist in those who did not. So disloyal had most Americans become that pre-millennialists could identify the 'remnant' with those who cried when they heard the strains of ''America the Beautiful''' (Moore, 1985: 148).

Anthony and Robbins (1978, 1980–1) and Robbins et al. (1978) see the vision of the Moon movement as a sectarian version of eroding messianic civil religion which seeks to revitalize both the American tradition of 'dualistic moral absolutism' and its post-Second World War form, anti-communist 'cold war ideology'.

Various aspects of the linkage of the upsurge of NRMs in the 1960s and 1970s and discontinuities of American civil religion have been explicitly stressed by a number of writers (Anthony and Robbins, 1978; 1982b; Bellah, 1975, 1976a; Hammond and Gordon-McCutcheon, 1981; Heenan, 1973; Robbins et al., 1978). While Appel (1980) and Anthony and Robbins (1978) stress the decline and reactive reconstruction of the theme of America as a 'chosen people', other writers have emphasized the consequences of the undermining of civil religion for the weakening of the linkage between private and public value systems. Johnson (1981) argues that the radical differentiation of private and public realms in modern society creates a disjunction between personal identity and broader civic concerns, thus generating a proliferation of 'narcissistic' religiotherapy groups promoting a privatized inner awakening (see also Hunter, 1981 and Marx and Holzner, 1975). Extrapolating Johnson's argument, Anthony and Robbins (1982b) contrast two dissimilar responses to the posited erosion of civil religion and the enhanced disjunction of public and private spheres. Authoritarian 'civil religion sects' such as the Unification Church elaborate meaning systems which respond to cultural fragmentation by synthesizing political and spiritual themes. 'Narcissistic' mystical and therapeutic movements such as Arica or est reject the infusion of explicit civic–political values into spiritual expressivity and emphasize personal apotheosis.

The self-oriented retreat from broader social concerns has been a central theme of the critique of the cultural 'narcisssism' which was seen as pervading America by the social critics of the 1970s, who were hostile to proliferating religiotherapeutic movements and personal growth mystiques (Lasch, 1979; Marin, 1973; Schur, 1976). The overused 'narcissism' label, originally a depth-psychological concept, has tended to denote various meanings (Anthony et al., 1983) including: *social apathy and passivity* encouraged by self-awareness mystiques (Schur, 1976); latent or implicit *sociopolitical conservatism* related to the alleged complacency of 'harmonial' perspectives (Marin, 1973); and a psycho-pathological condition entailing *obsessive self-fixation* and an inability to sustain long-term commitments and relationships.

Johnson (1981) sees the erosion of civil religion as reinforcing or intensifying the traditional 'Protestant' disjuncture between the 'cure of souls' and the concern for bettering society. But Johnson argues that the label of narcissism is more properly applicable to *therapies* such as est or Scientology than to *religions* such as Hare Krishna, the Unification Church or Meher Baba, which may mitigate the consequences of narcissism by encouraging moral constraints, self-discipline and social altruism (Johnson, 1981; see also Snelling and Whitely, 1974). Yet these religions really have little potential for decisively resolving the widening cultural disjuncture between self-oriented and socially oriented values (Johnson, 1981).

What little research has been done on these issues appears to undercut the posited 'narcissist' quality of religiotherapeutic movements. Nordquist (1978) found a high level of 'social compassion' among members of the Ananda Yoga Community in California, but Nordquist's methods have been criticized by Wallis (1984: 136). Robert Wuthnow (1978: 77–98, 1981b) has challenged some of the basic assumptions underlying the widely assumed negative relationship between mystical 'passivity' and political activism. Contra Schuler (1983–4), Wuthnow sees the relativist and subjectivist epistemology of mysticism leading to a critical and reformist antinomianism.

Perhaps the most controversial of the 'human potential' movements which grew in the 1970s is Erhard Seminars Training or est. Scholarly and journalistic comment about it has been highly critical and has tended to interpret its meaning as a reconstruction of competitive and utilitarian individualism that is free of the moral constraints imposed by traditional civil religion (Marin, 1973). This view is consistent with a pessimistic interpretation of Tipton's study (Schuler, 1983–4; see above). However, an investigation by Donald Stone (1981; see also 1976, 1978b) casts some doubt on this analysis. Est has been criticized for its injunction that 'you are responsible for all your experience, you create it'. However, the concept of responsibility is detached by Erhard and est from the connotations of blame; devotees do not blame the disadvantaged for their plight.

Superficially, the 'narcissism' critique of NRMs which indicts them for emancipating adherents from the subordination of private egoism to collective purposes is not compatible with the critique of cultist 'brainwashing', which complains about the effects of too rigid constraint of devotees by group pressures and collective purposes and the consequent erosion of personal autonomy. But Anthony et al. (1983) note that the popular volume *Snapping* (Conway and Siegelman, 1978) seems to have implicitly 'synthesized elements of the brainwashing and narcissism themes' (Anthony et al., 1983: 6). Cultists are seen as surrendering their critical intellect in exchange for a sensate 'high', although cultist indoctrination ultimately locks them into mindless subjection through alterations of brain functioning qua 'information disease' (Conway and Siegelman, 1978). The brainwashing argument (see Ch. 3) is thus generalized to *non-totalistic* groups, while something similar to the narcissism argument is applied to rigidly collectivistic groups. The latter puritanical sects, which appear on the surface to have repudiated hedonism, are said to create homogeneous enclaves in which uncritical subordination to authoritarian leadership is exchanged for immediate emotional gratification (see also Parsons, 1986, 1987b, forthcoming).

Religious Movements in the Material World

The critique of narcissism in contemporary religiotherapies partly converges with the emphasis of some writers on the economic dimension of NRMs and the prevalence of mundane material incentives for devotees (Bird and Reimer, 1982; Grafstein, 1984; Harris, 1981; Johnston, 1980; Khalsa, 1986). Harris (1981) writes from a 'materialist' perspective as well as from the standpoint of the expectation in the late 1970s that an economic 'era of limits' had arrived. Harris (1981) as well as Bird and Reimar (1982) see the proliferation of esoteric religiotherapeutic groups in the 1970s representing a pervasive *revival of magic in the face of declining economic expectations*. The spread of cults signifies 'a misunderstood attempt to save America's dream of worldly progress by magical and supernatural means' (Harris, 1981: 41). The pursuit of wealth and power is emphasized in numerous movements such as Scientology or est (Harris, 1981; see also Grafstein, 1984). In the former groups, Jesus is often said to actively assist the followers' upward socioeconomic mobility and also heal illness when the believer has faith. In movements such as est or Silva Mind Control the devotee is enjoined to 'take responsibility' for his thoughts and thereby impose his thought on events to gain material and social rewards.

Harris also notes that the daily life and routines within many NRMs are dominated by the need to finance the expansion of the movement and its influence (Harris, 1981). The expansion of the economic operations of NRMs often reflects the deliberate decisions of charismatic leaders rather than being simply a by-product of institutionalization (Khalsa, 1986; see Ch. 4). Groups such as the Unification Church or the Bhagwan Movement have been said to represent 'capitalist success stories' because they have diversified profitable investments and commercial operations which generate substantial funds (Bromley, 1985; Grafstein, 1984; Khalsa, 1986; Robbins, 1988b).

'The heavily regulated and bureaucratic nature of American society, particularly its social services processes, encourages the functional diversification of religion as a means of evading regulatory constraints' (Robbins, 1987a: 136, see also 1985a). Thus, the religious claims advanced by Scientology, Synanon and other movements may possibly be viewed as 'end-runs around the constraints of accreditation and professional standards for psychotherapists' (Robbins, 1987: 136, see also Ofshe, 1980a; Robbins, 1985a). Religion, according to two anthropologists, is 'the only place where social experimentation is possible [in the U.S.A. today]' (Zaretsky and Leone, 1974a: xxxvi).

NRMs and the Social Structure. One of the theories which has *not* figured prominently in the social science literature is the notion of 'religions of the oppressed'. 'It would be a mistake to believe that it is the materially oppressed who flock to the current wave of new religions' (Barker, 1986: 336). By and large the NRMs which emerged in the 1960s and 1970s are *middle-class phenomena* (Kilbourne and Richardson, 1984a; Latkin et al., 1987; Stark, 1987a; Wallis and Bruce, 1986; Wuthnow, 1976a,b, 1986) and in this such groups are similar to the new left feminist and ecology groups of the period (Hannigan, 1987). Some religiotherapeutic groups recruit heavily from structurally 'autonomous' professionals (Wallis and Bruce, 1986). There are exceptions to the middle-class norm, e.g. the ill-fated People's Temple community is said to have resembled a lower-class (and heavily black) *cult* in terms of its rank and file, while resembling a countercultural middle-class *new religion* in terms of its leadership elite (Weightman, 1983; see also Richardson, 1980, 1982b) Nevertheless, 'If the middle-class members of the majority of movements complain about deprivation, it is likely to be spiritual, community or "real-relationship" deprivation to which they are referring' (Barker, 1986: 337–37).

Regarding the spiritual ferment of the late 1960s and 1970s Wuthnow notes:

> Those who actively participated in movements such as TM, Zen, and Yoga, and those who expressed attraction to them, were significantly better educated than average (Wuthnow, 1978). More generally, it was the better educated young people, particularly those whose campus experiences had exposed them to the counter-culture, who defected from conventional religious beliefs and practices and who adopted worldviews conducive to joining the new religions (Wuthnow, 1986: 14).

Possible exceptions were 'The Jesus people groups and more authoritarian movements such as the Unification Church, but even these movements often recruited indirectly from the educational system by picking up its dropouts — young people not making the grade, young people who were victims of campus isolation, cut off from families, and in many cases victims of alcohol or bad drug experiences' (Wuthnow, 1986: 23). Although still largely middle-class, Jesus groups, eccentric fundamentalist sects and new born-again groups tend to have a less elitist upper middle-class coloration compared to the oriental and human potential groups of the 1970s (Tipton, 1982a; Wuthnow, 1976a,b).

Wuthnow (1986) highlights the *tremendous expansion of higher education in the 1950s and 1970s* and the emergence of a vast educated intelligentsia or 'new class' as a fundamental demographic trend underlying the proliferation of NRMs. The mysticism which has always been 'the secret of religion of the educated classes' has now expanded (Campbell, 1978). The relativism implicit in higher humanistic education is related to the value shifts embodied in the 'Consciousness Reformation' (Wuthnow, 1976b). Other salient demographic trends include the increase in the 1960s of the proportion of young people in the population (this trend has since declined) and the movement of population to the west coast where traditional religious loyalties and institutions are weakest (Stark, 1987a; Stark et al., 1979; Wuthnow, 1986). Conceivably, the demographics of NRMs are now in transition. For example, 'New Age' groups are said to appeal largely to middle-aged people, while 'cults' are now increasingly targeting women and the elderly (Brooks, 1986; Rudin, 1984; Salvatori, 1987).

Religious Movements and Communal Dislocations

A major perspective on the recent proliferation of NRMs highlights the problems of community arising in an urbanized and mobile society dominated by bureaucratic megastructures. As traditional 'mediating structures' between individuals and families and the broader society (e.g. homogeneous 'folksy' neighborhoods, extended families, churches, personalistic work settings) which once provided supports and services for nuclear families are undermined by various trends, the family becomes increasingly isolated from other social institutions and therefore more precarious (Keniston, 1977). The structural isolation of the family may involve a radical discontinuity between the diffuse affectivity or 'loving' quality of familial roles and the impersonal quality of 'adult' roles in educational and vocational milieux (Anthony and Robbins, 1974; Robbins and Anthony, 1972). This discontinuity provides the context for a tendency for many young persons to seek surrogate families in extrafamilial relationships (Gordon, 1980). Various movements and guru groups appear to promise adult or adolescent (or even sometimes elderly) devotees alternative kinship systems featuring unconditional acceptance ('Jesus loves you'), warmth, normative structure and firm authority. The language of kinship ('brothers and sisters', 'father') is employed by new movements more seriously than in institutionalized churches (Doress and Porter, 1981). Surrogate families qua religiotherapeutic movements or born-again groups 'are generally less demanding families than the ones developed by Jim Jones and Reverend Moon, but they provide structure, meaning, and a full schedule of family activities' (Gordon, 1980: 10).

Religious movements can provide services and supports for families, including jobs, child day care, medical assistance, welfare and shared value commitments. The supports may be viable, however, only if a family becomes part of the movement. If such assimilation is resisted by one or more members, the effect on the family may be disintegrative, especially if the movement is close-knit, militant and authoritarian (Beckford, 1982b; Bromley et al., 1983; Kaslow and Sussman, 1982; Marciano, 1982; Schwartz and Kaslow, 1982; see later discussion on 'Cults and Families').

In general 'mediating structures' provide the opportunity for close, face-to-face contact with other persons with whom one shares common sentiments and solidarity. They also provide a moral foundation in the sense of sustaining communal values which are internalized by participants (Kerrine and Neuhaus, 1979). Cults, communes, encounter groups and the various idealistic social movements which proliferated in the late 1960s and early 1970s have been viewed as 'social inventions' which meet needs arising from the undermining of traditional mediating structures (Coleman, 1970). Settings are produced for extended communal relations which transcend kinship ties. A strong critic of the Unification Church of Sun Myung Moon has conceded, 'The Unification Church as surrogate family . . . does provide an effective therapeutic setting that offers linkage to the large society without its turmoils' (Horowitz, 1981: 165).

Social movements are often effective mediating structures because they emphasize universal values and often integrate these meanings into 'familial' or diffusely affective and expressive patterns of interpersonal relationships. Thus, the Unification community (of 'Moonies') becomes a surrogate family; 'but it is more than just a family', it is 'legitimated in terms of universal values. Thus, despite the childlike quality of some aspects of interaction within the community, the role of the Unification family member has an "adult" quality which inheres in its orientation toward broader civic and spiritual values' (Anthony and Robbins, 1982b: 224; see also Parsons, 1986, 1987a,b). The theme of 'sacrifice' is crucial here. 'Young converts see themselves as fighting selflessly for universal ideals of love and harmony and world unity in a world permeated by relativism, cynicism, and selfish egoism' (Anthony and Robbins, 1981a: 224). 'The Unification Church constantly emphasizes the breakdown of the American family, corruption and immorality in American life (divorce, pornography, suicide, drugs and scandal) and, by contrast, the work of the church toward the ''perfect family'' in a perfect world' (Doress and Porter, 1981: 297; see also Bromley et al., 1982).

The importance of religious movements as mediating collectivities for young persons arises from their capacity to create universalistic values and symbols which legitimate new patterns of interpersonal relationships and communal interaction. Converts to contemporary religious movements often believe that they enjoy a special communal fellowship in which 'loving' relations among spiritual brethren are perceived as derivative from each devotee's inner relationship to Jesus, the Holy Spirit, a spiritual master or an immanent mystical force (Anthony and Robbins, 1974, 1982b; Barker, 1979; Bradfield, 1976; Parsons, 1986). Satisfying relationships among devotees in a group thus constitute a legitimating 'plausibility structure' for the meaning system of the movement, which then provides a symbolic mystique which heightens the perceived satisfaction derived from the 'loving' quality of the spiritual fellowship.

Holistic Self-Conceptions. A related theme stresses structural differentiation and the concomitant fragmentation of individual life-space into diverse functionally specific social roles which has created a diffusion of personal identity (Hunter, 1981; Westley, 1978a,b, 1983). This condition enhances the appeal of symbolic mystiques and movements which are capable of holistic conceptions of self (Beckford, 1984). Various new collectivities emphasizing some mode of 'consciousness raising' employ intensive group dynamics processes to transform the identities of devotees through reinterpretation of personal experience and biography (Greil and Rudy, 1984b; Marx and Holzner, 1975; Marx and Seldin, 1975; Parsons, 1987a,b). Personal identity can appear problematic in a highly differentiated society where individuals have multiple limited involvements and interests, some of which must be performed in a 'detached' or non-emotionally involved manner. Proliferating new therapeutic movements and mystiques offer to participants a holistic sense of 'who am I' which transcends the diverse roles and limited instrumental commitments of participants (Anthony et al., 1978; Beckford, 1984;

Westley, 1978a,b, 1983). A pattern appeared to be emerging in the USA in the 1970s entailing 'discovered' personal identities which are treated as more fundamental than institutional role-identities (Parsons, 1986, 1987a, Turner, 1976). A 'Durkheimian' analysis of NRMs by Westley (1978, 1983) argues that their holistic themes reflect the 'cult of man' or sacralization of humanity which Durkheim envisioned as the integrative collective conscience of an adanced society with a highly developed division of labor. This provocative argument confers a new significance on the 'narcissism' of contemporary religiotherapeutic mystiques (discussed above). However, it encounters two difficulties: (1) religiotherapeutic groups which stress the sacred human potential tend to evolve over time toward an overtly supernaturalist or theist symbol system (Ofshe, 1980b; Stark and Bainbridge, 1985; Wallis, 1984; Wallis and Bruce, 1986; see Ch. 4); (2) there is the anomalous development whereby some controversial groups develop totalistic communal patterns such that their devotees actually cease to be involved in diversified roles and groups and thus appear to some observers to lack authentic 'selves' (Beckford, 1979). But authoritarian collectivism may indeed be quite compatible over the short run with 'narcissistic personalism' (Parson, 1986, 1987a); indeed charismatically led groups combining personalism and authoritarianism, although unstable, may be presently proliferating because they are compatible with the functional diversity, specialization and mobility of contemporary society (Parsons, 1986, forthcoming).

NRMs and 'De-Institutionalization'. A seminal essay, 'The New Religions and the Protest Against Modernity', by James Hunter (1981) interprets NRMs as responding to heightened problems of social existence in modern society, which is increasingly characterized by 'a split between public and private spheres of life' (Hunter, 1981: 3; see also Johnson, 1981). The gap is widening between (1) a highly institutionalized public realm dominated by large-scale formally organized bureaucratic structures in which thought, behavior and relationships are expected to be impersonal and controlled by a principle of functional rationality and (2) an increasingly fragmented and 'de-institutionalized' private realm in which the norms patterning child-rearing, courtship, marriage, sexuality and leisure are in flux. The 'under-institutionalized' private realm is now structurally incapacitated 'to provide reliable social parameters for the more mundane activity of everyday life and a plausible, well-integrated system of meaning which gives location and purpose to the individual's total life experience' (Hunter, 1981: 5).

The sharp polarity of the 'oppressively formidable public sphere' and the fragmented and de-institutionalized private realm sets up the basic 'dilemma of modernity' which provides the context for the growth of new spiritual movements. Although 'secular' (e.g. political, environmentalist, or feminist) social movements may also respond to this dilemma (Hannigan, 1987), religious groups possess an advantage in terms of their traditional symbolization of sacred kinship and holy communities of brotherhood, fatherhood, motherhood and fellowship (Anthony and Robbins, 1974; Barker, 1979; Bradfield, 1976). Throughout history religious movements have often been notable for their capacity to evolve universalistic legitimations for new patterns of extended communal and affiliative relations transcending biological kinship ties.

The relatively authoritarian and totalistic communal world of certain groups represents, according to Hunter, the option of 'total institutionalization' which entails 'a microcosmic totalitarianism as a means of tangibly reestablishing a home-world for its members. Synanon, the Unification Church, and the Children of God are especially notable in this regard' (Hunter, 1981: 10). However, many of the groups which are not *organizationally* totalistic, nevertheless manifest totalism or absolutism on the *cognitive* or ideological level, which operates in terms of orientations toward 'pure consciousness', 'external bliss', the achievement of 'God consciousness', etc. Thus most NRMs 'in one form or another profess to offer a superlative, providing its possessor with an ultimate system of relevance which transcends the bland ordinariness and meaninglessness of everyday life in the modern world' (Hunter, 1981: 9–10).

But if NRMs have grown in a context of a de-institutionalized private sphere, then the surge of new movements might be expected to subside in the face of present indicators of an incipient re-institutionalization of normative patterns in the private sphere, such as a slight dip in the divorce rate, declines in sexual promiscuity, or the resurgence of traditional affiliative structures such as college fraternities. Re-institutionalization of the private realm has undercut the 'cults of the 1970s' (Levin and Alan, 1985).

Sex Roles within NRMs. A key aspect of the de-institutionalization of the private realm has been the rapid erosion of traditional sex-role expectations and the resulting normative ambiguity in the realm of interpersonal and sexual intimacy (Aidala, 1984, 1985). According to Aidala (1985), increasing ambiguity regarding gender roles is a key dimension of the contemporary 'culture crisis'. Religious movements respond to emerging gender confusions and uncertainties and 'typically

differ from their secular counterparts in offering a morally absolute set
of definitions and rules to follow concerning women, men, and their
relations. This . . . is an important part of their appeal to potential converts'
(Aidala, 1985: 288; see also Harder, 1974; Harder et al., 1976; Palmer,
1987b). NRMs provide 'ideological solutions to problematic sex and
gender roles' (see Neitz, 1988 and Stark, 1981 on lesbian–gay occultism).

Research conducted by Aidala and colleagues on communal living
groups from the middle 1970s through to the early 1980s revealed 'three
general approaches to sexuality within religiously inspired communes:
compulsory celibacy, group controlled marriage, and ''free-love'''
(Aidala, 1985: 292; see also Palmer, 1987b; Wright, 1986).

> Whether asceticism or hedonism was encouraged, sexuality was typically scripted down
> to details such as the positions and prerogatives of males and females, the appropriateness
> of kissing with the mouth open . . . Ideological redefinitions of sexuality in both religious
> and psychospiritual movements were such as to eliminate or minimize individual
> decision-making and interpersonal negotiation regarding both sexual relationships and
> sexual behavior (Aidala, 1985: 292).

Sexual norms established in religious groups, although occasionally
violated, appeared to enjoy wide consensual support. 'Charismatic
authority transforms what seem to the outsider as severe restrictions on
individuality into potentialities for full and complete personhood' (Aidala,
1985: 293; see also Parsons, 1986). In many groups support for sexual
norms seemed to exceed support for other group norms such as division
of labor or sharing income (Aidala, 1985: 293).

Psychological data indicated that both males and females in religious
communes manifested a *lower tolerance for ambiguity* than males and
females in secular communes (Aidala, 1985: 307). The results are
interpreted as supporting Aidala's hypothesis that religious communes
are attractive to 'those with low tolerance for the shifting interpretations
of masculine–feminine which confronted youth in the late 1960s' (Aidala,
1985: 307). The author concludes that rapid social change and consequent
cultural fragmentation are particularly manifested today as gender role
confusion and uncertainty. 'It seems reasonable to conclude an ''elective
affinity'' exists between doctrine and practice regarding sex and gender
found in religious groups and the desire or need of many young persons
for clear guidance in resolving gender related ambiguities and strain'
(Aidala, 1985: 311). Aidala's conclusions are quite consistent with
Hunter's (1981) formulation regarding the de-institutionalization of the
private realm as a setting for the emergence of NRMs and are also
evocative of variations of the culture crisis thesis which have viewed new

religions as responding to contemporary *moral ambiguity* (Anthony and Robbins, 1982b; Bird, 1979).

As Aidala's work indicates, the 'ideological' response of NRMs to gender role uncertainty has frequently entailed a regression to absolutist, sexist and patriarchial patterns which may involve elders or pastors who reinforce the abusive or exploitative prerogatives of husbands in quasi-fundamentalist groups or entail exploitative behavior in guru or therapy groups. A study of voluntary female defection from NRMs (Jacobs, 1984) indicates that initial conversion of women was facilitated by the developmental socialization of the latter in terms of expectations of surrendering to a dynamic male. Defection ensues when extreme 'unequal exchange' is perceived in terms of sexual intimacy and gender relations (see also Rudin, 1984). Areas of tension include: (1) leaders' patriarchal exploitation and 'harems'; (2) leaders' support for husbands' psychological and physical abuse of wives; and (3) role-conflict arising from the contrast between chaste and passive behavior expected from women within the group and aggressive and seductive behavior encouraged for proselytizing and public solicitation (Jacobs, 1984; see Ch. 3). Paradoxically, there is also evidence of women being *empowered* by NRMs (Haywood, 1983).

It is worth noting recent research on the involvement of women, often with countercultural or feminist backgrounds, in conservative groups manifesting clearly structured patriarchal gender-norms, such as orthodox Jewish and Hasidic groups (Davidman, 1988) and charismatic evangelicals (Rose, 1987). For further discussion of gender roles in NRMs, see Barker (1986), Harder (1974), Harder et al. (1976), Haywood (1983), Jacobs (1987), Palmer (1987b), Rose (forthcoming) and Rudin (1984).

Cults and Families. To date there has been relatively little research on the formation and histories of families *within* religious movements, although the extreme pattern of Unification arranged marriages and mass weddings has received some attention (Bromley et al., 1982; Fichter, 1979, 1985; Galanter, 1986; Grace, 1985; James, 1983). More attention has been focused on the tense relations between religious movements and their youthful devotees' families of origin (Beckford, 1982a; Kaslow and Sussman, 1982; Kilbourne and Richardson, 1982; Marciano, 1982; Schwartz and Kaslow, 1979, 1982; Wright and Piper, 1986). Particularly interesting is Beckford's (1982a) conclusion that there is substantial variation in familial response to a member's involvement in a stigmatized cult and the argument of Kilbourne and Richardson (1982) that there is no clear causal relationship between involvement in NRMs and the weakening of family ties. Kilbourne and Richardson note that some persons attracted to new groups attest to a prior alienation from their families preceding movement affiliation (Galanter et al., 1978; Petersen and Mauss, 1973; Richardson et al., 1979). Moreover, some involvements with NRMs actually tend to increase affective ties between the devotee and family members (Richardson et al., 1978; Snow and Phillips, 1980). Kilbourne and Richardson (1982) see strain upon the institution of the family arising from structurally induced changes in American society preceding and facilitating the growth of NRMs, such that 'cult conversion' may be more a *symptom* of the decline of the American family (Doress and Porter, 1981; Galanter et al., 1979; Kilbourne and Richardson, 1982; Robbins and Anthony, 1982a,b), although other writers view it as a significant *cause* of familial disintegration (Clark et al., 1981; Delgado, 1977; Enroth, 1977; Galper, 1982; Singer, 1979). On group control of intimate dyads in three NRMs, see Wright (1986, 1987).

The findings of a recent study of the decisions of young persons to leave or remain in deviant religious movements 'suggest that cult involvement is neither a cause nor a symptom of family disorganization' (Wright and Piper, 1986: 22). Wright's data indicate that 'a convert's feeling of satisfaction with family is not directly related to [movement] affiliation'. Neither the reported prior closeness of the convert to his family nor the convert's self-reported smoothness of his relationship to his parents seem to be significantly related to the level of parental disapproval of the convert's involvement, i.e. 'parental disapproval is not a function of deteriorated parent–child relationships' (Wright and Piper, 1986: 22). Parental approval of affiliation was related to decisions to remain in an NRM and parental disapproval was not effective in influencing decisions to disengage among converts reporting closeness to their families.

According to Wright, his findings *attest to the strength and durability of the American family rather than to its weaknesses*. The researcher further interprets his findings as undercutting the 'family deprivation hypothesis' which sees young persons joining NRMs to compensate for unfulfilled needs arising from weaknesses of family life. Though widely affirmed (Galanter and Buckley, 1978; Kilbourne and Richardson, 1982; Marciano, 1982; Robbins and Anthony, 1972; Richardson et al., 1978; Schwartz and Kaslow, 1979, 1982; Zerin, 1985), the evidence for the thesis, argues Wright, is 'largely anecdotal and theoretical, or derived from isolated case studies' (Wright and Piper, 1986: 16).

In the view of this writer, data such as Wright's contravene the thesis that weaknesses in the American family are related to young persons joining religious movements only if this thesis is arbitrarily translated into a narrow proposition that NRM converts are consciously dissatisfied with their familial upbringing or consciously alienated from their families prior to conversion. But the 'weakness' of the American family may be unrelated to subjective alienation from families, e.g. memories of prior familial closeness may motivate adult individuals who have left their original families to seek family surrogates in adult milieux (Gordon, 1980). On the other hand the posited present 'weakness' of the family may be so multifaceted that the theory that family weakness is related to the rise of NRMs is empirically irrefutable and thus arguably not of substantial scientific value.

Further study of sex roles and family life *within* NRMs is imperative. Attention should also be given to gender discrimination and to alleged child abuse within new movements (Brooks, 1986; Markowitz and Halperin, 1984; Rudin, 1984).

NRMs and Secularization

In recent decades occult beliefs and practices have become increasingly conspicuous and have sometimes appeared to burst the confines of cultural rationality. A scientist laments, 'Indeed in the present antirational climate, it is difficult to determine whether an amendment to repeal the Enlightenment might not fare better than the ERA' (Weissman, 1985: 95).

The theory of secularization has appeared to some scholars to be the chief casualty of the growth of new religions and/or the current surge of evangelical Christianity. The growth of NRMs seems to have engendered among some sociologists of religion a mood of *triumphalism*, which is associated with strident rhetoric which thematizes the ever-present well-springs of religion and the consequent superficiality of secularization theory (discussed below). New forms of the sacred emerging in the last decades are seen to pinpoint the fundamental reality of *Unsecular Man* (Greeley, 1973). The experience of 'Youth in Search of the Sacred' convinces Joseph Fichter that 'secularity, not religion is in crisis' (Fichter, 1981: 22). Stark and Bainbridge argue forcefully in a number of publications that the growth of cults is evidence that secularization is really a 'self-limiting process'; when dominant traditions secularize and wither away, new faiths are generated to take their place (Stark, 1981; Stark and Bainbridge, 1985; see also Hadden, 1987a). Richardson writes:

Long ago Feuerbach said 'The secret of theology is anthropology'. Perhaps the research on conversion to new religions cited here suggests that 'The secret of sociology of religion is also anthropology', and the 'secret' reveals secularization theory to be ill-founded. Hundreds of thousands of youths in America and elsewhere, who are members of the most educated and affluent generation ever, are making conscious decisions to 'convert' to new religions, even if for relatively short times for many. These events are often of individual import, but cumulatively they also have considerable cultural significance. Sociologists of religion would do well to recognize this major anomaly in the secularization theory and seek more fruitful theoretical perspectives with which to address the continuing 'species specific' interest in religion among human beings (Richardon, 1985c: 115).

Notwithstanding all of this eager gravedigging of secularization theory, alternative formulations have been developed which proclaim the compatibility of an explosion of new movements with ongoing secularization processes, or go further and employ secularization as an *explanation* for the rise of cults (Bell, 1977; Turner, 1983; Wilson, 1976, 1982, 1985).

Bryan Turner's Analysis. For Bryan Turner, the present 'diversity of modern religious forms' arises in 'an economic context in which religious behavior has become divorced from the system of property ownership' (Turner, 1983: 201). The basic function of religion has been the *social control of reproduction and sexuality* and hence the maintenance of the integrity of the family units through which wealth is accumulated and transmitted. 'In late capitalism, where there is a degree of separation of ownership and control . . . the importance of the family for economic accumulation declines, and there is less emphasis on the importance of legitimacy and monogamy' (Turner, 1983: 9). The imperative for normative restraint of sexuality therefore diminishes, which in turn decreases the premium on religious orthodoxy. As the need to enforce familial integrity diminishes, religion retreats from the public realm and becomes increasingly diversified and exotic. Sexuality also becomes increasingly variegated and, like religion, becomes a commercialized item of mass consumption. Turner's analysis thus explains the *concomitance of enhanced religious diversity and the 'sexual revolution'*: parallel 'liberations' permitted by the economic peripheralization of family life!

Turner does not refer to the evangelical political surge in the United States; nevertheless, from his perspective it is rather fitting that the most powerful American movement which is attempting to reappropriate the public realm for religion, the New Christian Right, should articulate 'family' themes and connect its political activism to a call to recreate a favorable sociopolitical climate for wholesome traditional family life. The existence of dynamic movements stridently asserting religious claims in the public realm does not discredit Turner's analysis. However, there would be negative implications for Turner's view if conservative religio-political movements should manage to *succeed* in turning back the clock and re-establishing controlling Christian norms in various areas including sexual and reproductive behavior or education.

Bryan Wilson's Analysis. The idea that secularization has caused (and thus 'explains') the cultic upsurge is widespread. For Daniel Bell, cults appear 'when religions fail . . . when the institutional framework of religions begins to break up, the search for direct experience which people can feel to be 'religious' facilitates the rise of cults' (Bell, 1977: 443). Bryan Wilson concurs but places additional stress on the status of the growth of esoteric NRMs as a manifestation of inexorable secularization rather than a sign of the frailty or reversal of secularization.

Bryan Wilson argues that the number and variety of spiritual movements *increase* under the impact of secularization and a general decline in religious commitment. Modern society is characterized by a hegemony of impersonal bureaucratic patterns of social control, which preclude an authentic 'great awakening' capable of transforming society and culture. Today's new religions actually reduce religion to a *consumer item*. Spiritual 'shoppers' choose from a variegated and provocatively packaged array of mystiques in the 'spiritual supermarket'. But each shopper's personal consumption has 'no real consequences for other institutions, for political power structure, for technological constraints or controls'. The new movements essentially 'add nothing to any prospective reintegration of society and contribute nothing towards the culture by which a society might live' (Wilson, 1976: 96). In today's cultural milieu diverse and exotic structures of meaning are able to coexist and be tolerated precisely because of the pervasive secularization which reduces spiritual systems to trivial consumer items. By contrast Wilson sees new Christian and Islamic sects in Africa and Latin America as yet capable of exerting a powerful influence on social institutions, culture and nation-building processes. For Wilson the *transformative* potential of a religion is augmented by its location in a person-based rather than a modern role-based social system (Wilson, 1982) where social control is no longer anchored in interpersonal relationships. The Euro-North American new religions, however, represent the reduction of religion to an exotic consumer product and a vehicle for stylistic expressivity which has no significant consequences for dominant social institutions, political power dynamics, techno-economic processes, or bureaucratic administration. The basic trend is *rationalization*, 'against which the cults are likely to be no more than transient and volatile gestures of defiance' (Wilson, 1976: 12; see also Wallis, 1984, 1987b).

In modern society *charisma* is peripheralized and restricted to 'unserious' realms such as entertainment and sports (Wilson, 1975). Elsewhere functional reality is dominant. Discussing Pentecostal groups, Meredith McGuire comments:

> Although members of such groups appreciate nonrational styles of cognition in certain aspects of life, they desire and utilize rational modes in other aspects. They would be upset if the airplane in which they were riding were piloted by a person in a trance, if the job for which they had applied were allotted by divination, if the judge for their case were not in interested in rational evidence and intuited the resulting decision. Thus there is an interesting tension between believing that the supernatural realm does impinge on the events of everyday life (including safe arrival from a journey, getting jobs, and winning court cases) and, on the other hand, the overwhelming lack of certainty as to whether any given situation is so influenced (that is, 'of the Lord') (McGuire, 1982: 212).

More recently, in *The Politics of God's Funeral* (Harrington, 1983), Michael Harrington has also affirmed the relative sociological insignificance of contemporary NRMs. 'But the new religions that the social scientists are so fond of are, almost without exception, personal rather than social' (Harrington, 1983: 4). They epitomize the retreat of religion to the private realm where spiritual authority is exercised over isolated knots of devotees but not over any other spheres of the polity and society. Today's gurus and cults 'confirm the truth. . . that deities and churches cannot be invented simply because there is a need for them. They must grow out of the shared experience of a people' (Harrington, 1983: 57).

The institutional perspective of Turner and Wilson on secularization is very different from the conception of secularization implicitly affirmed by Greeley, Richardson and to a lesser extent Stark and Bainbridge, for whom the 'secularization thesis' denotes *more people becoming less religious or ceasing to need religion*. Bryan Wilson's 'model of secularization is concerned with the operation of the social system — it is the *system* that becomes secularized' (Wilson, 1985: 19). Religion may still be vital to individuals, but it is uncoupled from the basic control and policy-making institutions of the society and peripheralized.

Wilson, Turner and others (Wallis, 1984) are decidedly *not* maintaining that people no longer believe or need to be religious. Indeed, in the context of a secularized *system*, in which religion no longer permeates other institutions such as education or politics, popular spiritual hunger may *increase*! Nor are the theorists of institutional or systemic secularization denying that the 'privatized' constraint of religion has disruptive or destabilizing consequences. Wilson (1976) more or less makes this explicit, and his theory of secularization is quite compatible with the argument that the banishment of religion from 'the naked public square' is dangerous and socially unsettling (Neuhaus, 1984). What Wilson and others affirm is that a modern *linear transformation* in the institutional significance of (at least theistic) religion has transpired in the West. This thesis cannot be refuted by appeals to spiritual flux indicative of persisting religious needs and feelings.

Stark and Bainbridge's View. The general theory of religion which Stark and Bainbridge (1985) have largely extrapolated from their studies of NRMs has much to say about secularization and its relations to spiritual innovation. While in some ways the approach of Stark and Bainbridge shares the atomistic, non-institutional focus of Richardson (1985c) and Greeley (1973), in other ways Stark and Bainbridge's formulation might be viewed as a *synthesis* of perspectives which affirm secularization and perspectives which cite recent spiritual ferment to repudiate the secularization thesis.

Stark and Bainbridge 'acknowledge that secularization is a major trend in modern times, but argue that this is not a modern development and does not presage the decline of religion' (Stark and Bainbridge, 1985: 1–2). A unique and distinctively modern transformation in terms of the (diminished) importance of religion has *not* taken place. Stark and Bainbridge see secularization as a 'self-limiting process' because it 'generates two countervailing processes' (Stark and Bainbridge, 1985: 2). *Revival* entails the schismatic formation of new *sects*, which emerge from decaying religious traditions which have become tame and worldly. The second 'countervailing process' is *religious innovation*, i.e. 'new religions constantly appear in societies' (Stark and Bainbridge, 1985: 2), replacing the enfeebled older faiths. Mighty oaks can grow from tiny and disreputable acorns, e.g. Jesus 'leading a handful of ragtag followers in a remote corner of the mighty Roman Empire'.

> How laughable it would have seemed to Roman intellectuals that this obscure cult could pose a threat to the great pagan temples. In similar fashion, western intellectuals scorn contemporary cults. Yet, if major new faiths are aborning, they will not be found by consulting the directory of the National Council of Churches. Rather, they will be found in lists of obscure cult movements. Thus, to assess the future of religion, one must always pay close attention to the fringes of religious economies (Stark and Bainbridge, 1985: 2).

Notwithstanding the references to the unanticipated triumph of the original Palestinian 'Jesus Movement', Stark and Bainbridge (1985: 108) would not accept the problematic emergence of a new dominant faith — 'another Christianity' — as a criterion for evaluating their claim as to the intrinsic limits of secularization. Rather, they affirm that competitive pluralism is 'the natural state of the religious economy'. No one church can meet the needs of all persons. No single organization 'can offer the full range of religious services for which there is substantial market demand'. Given religious freedom, 'there will be many organized faiths, each specializing in certain segments of the market...with a constant influx of new organizations and [a] frequent demise of others' (Stark and Bainbridge, 1985: 108).

Neither the absence of a dominant consensual religious orientation nor the lost vitality of the churches is indicative of a real decline of religion:

> Faith lives in the sects and the sectlike denominations, and in the hearts of the over-whelming majority of persons. New hopes enter the marketplace of religion with every new cult movement, and a comprehensive census would probably reveal a birth rate of potential messiahs higher than one an hour. Far from marking a radical departure in history and an era of faithlessness, secularization is an age-old process of transformation. In an endless cycle faith is revived and new faiths born to take the place of those withered denominations that lost their sense of the supernatural (Stark and Bainbridge, 1985: 529).

Two critical points can be made here. (1) Because of its essentially *atomistic* focus on individuals choosing faiths in a market and needing still to believe, the Stark-Bainbridge theory does not clearly relate to the arguments of the institutional school which claims that a linear transformative process has culminated in a distinctively modern peripheralization of religion in terms of political, economic and educational processes. While acknowledging an enhanced modern separation of church and state, Stark and Bainbridge (1985: 529) argue that 'final separation...will be healthy for a religion, for what it loses in coercive power it will gain in spiritual virtue'. In other words, *arguments about secularization must always be resolved in terms of inquiries into the quantity and quality of individual faith*. Transformations on the institutional level are somewhat beside the point.

(2) Some critics have assaulted Stark and Bainbridge's analysis on its own (atomistic) level. Despite Stark and Bainbridge's major finding that the growth of cults (NRMs) varies inversely with the church membership rate (Stark and Bainbridge, 1980c, 1985), which is demonstrated for both the 1970s and the 1920s (Stark and Bainbridge, 1981, 1985), critics have argued forcefully that new cults are hardly *replacing* faltering churches, because the exodus from the latter significantly exceeds the movement

into the former (Bibby and Weaver, 1985; Wallis, 1984: 59–62; Wallis, 1986a; Wallis and Bruce, 1986: 47–80; Wallis, 1987a). Stark and Bainbridge's methodological reliance on ingenious calculations of the number of cults per million persons has been strongly criticized. What is really important, argues Roy Wallis, is 'the ratio of those recruited to new religious movements relative to the total lost by the old faiths. Outside the Bay area of California, the evidence suggests that the new faiths made negligible inroads into the mass of unchurched, who remain indifferent to religion of any sort' (Wallis, 1984: 61). This is particularly true for England (Wallis, 1984: 61), although Stark and Bainbridge's reliance on the ratio of cult groups per population allegedly distorts the true situation and incorrectly makes NRMs appear to be more prevalent and successful in Europe than in the United States (Bibby and Weaver, 1985; Wallis, 1984).

Recently Bibby and Weaver (1985) have used census data to analyze 'cult consumption in Canada' and criticize the assumption of Stark and Bainbridge that concentration of cults represents an actual numerical growth of NRMs. The data do not support the claim of Robbins et al. that NRMs 'have grown at the expense of mainline denominations' (Robbins et al., 1978: 113). Rather than embracing organized 'new religions', today's religiously detached persons are more likely to opt for *fragmentary a-scientific beliefs* (e.g. astrology, ESP, or magic). These beliefs may be held coincidentally with 'rational' beliefs, or even with orthodox religious beliefs (Campbell and McIver, 1987; Snow and Machalek, 1982). However, the 'a-science fragments' held by an individual are generally not integrated into a coherent belief system, nor are they likely to be organizationally objectified (Bibby and Weaver, 1985).

Thus, secularization in Canada has not produced a robust new religious market (Bibby, 1987), as Stark and Bainbridge's theory would predict, but rather a 'durable a-science market'. A-rational fragments are chosen over integrated systems because the former 'are more conducive to life in our present age' (Bibby and Weaver, 1985: 458), as well as the ('secular') context of life in a highly differentiated and pluralistic society.

Until it can be shown that NRMs 'actually reclaim people lost by conventional religion, there is no evidence that the secularization pattern has been altered' (Bibby and Weaver, 1985: 452). Even on the non-institutional level of individual options, the triumphalism of Richardson, Fichter and others would appear to be flawed. More substantial may be the claims by Hadden (1987a,b) and others that the contemporary politicized revivalism of the American 'New Christian Right' (NCR) has negative implications for conceptions of a linear secularization process.

The NCR aims at a reimposition of Christian norms on practices in the political and educational realm as well as over intimate familial and gender-role behavior. Should the NCR and the televangelists 'succeed', it would appear that the inexorable rationalization of social control affirmed by Wilson or the inevitable cultural consequences of corporate domination of capitalist dynamics affirmed by Turner are not irreversible developments and can succumb to moral–spiritual regeneration. Can the 'anti-modern protest' of the new revivalism (Hunter, 1983) challenge institutional or systemic secularization on its own level?

But what will constitute 'success'? Lechner (1985) has suggested that the new revivalism may have unanticipated consequences of enhancing religious pluralism, individualism and privatization, as has been the case with former periods of revival in which it was hoped to impose moral and spiritual unity on the nation. 'The traditions of secularism have become too deeply engrained in American culture and institutional structure to permit anything but, at best, a large-scale, private-sphere [Christian] renewal' (Hunter, 1983: 133).

Conclusion

In evaluating the above morass of theories and occasional research findings, some interesting implications arise and some cautionary considerations should be kept in mind.

(1) Many of the theories relating the recent proliferations of NRMs to factors such as moral ambiguity, cultural confusion, communal dislocations, civil religious decline, or a linear secularization process tend to be *crisis theories* and/or *modernization theories*. They tend to pinpoint some acute and distinctively modern dislocation which is said to be producing some mode of alienation, anomie or deprivation to which Americans are responding by searching for new structures of meaning and community. There would appear to be some imbalance, however, in *explanations of historically specific episodes in terms of long-range structural trends*. A cautionary viewpoint would also highlight the constancy and continuity of movements of 'religious outsiders' throughout American history as an intrinsic quality of American cultural experience such that the 'newness' of the recent flux may have been overestimated (Melton, 1987; Moore, 1985; Pritchard, 1976; Stark and Bainbridge, 1985).

(2) By and large the theories we have reviewed are underresearched. Informed but still speculative theorizing has far outstripped systematic

empirical analysis in this area. And the quality of research may leave something to be desired, e.g. 'few empirical studies have made use of control groups for comparison' (Barker, 1986: 337). The interface of case studies of specific movements and broad theoretical formulations evoking cultural and social dislocations creates a facile effect:

> While those who have not read sociological accounts of the new religions might still be at a loss to understand why anyone joins the movements, those who have read some of the sociological literature could well be at a loss to understand why *all* young adults are not members, so all-encompassing are some of the explanations (Barker, 1986: 337–8).

(3) If examined carefully, some of the theories purporting to explain the surge of NRMs in the late 1960s and 1970s may yield clues to the waning of esoteric religious innovation in the 1980s. If communal dislocations in terms of family breakdown or ambiguities in gender-roles and norms governing intimacy have been salient in providing the impetus for new movements, then incipient social reintegration as indicated by a slight dip in the divorce rate, diminished promiscuity, or the revival of conventional affiliative structures such as college fraternities and sororities, may presage and explain the leveling off of NRM growth. If the undercutting of civil religion and messianic Americanism has provided a context for the proliferation of smaller messianic faiths, then perhaps the recent patriotic revival and general Anglo-American conservative drift has adverse implications for religious innovation (but not necessarily for religious revivalism).

(4) Most of the theories described above are parochial in one of two ways: they deal primarily with *intra-societal* sources of sociocultural transformation and ignore contemporary 'globalist' or 'world system' influences (Robertson, 1985b,c; Robertson and Chirico, 1985; Wuthnow, 1982); and/or they treat the sources of new *religious* movements in isolation from the sources of other contemporary movements. Hannigan (1987) suggests that the sources of NRMs should be considered in conjunction with the sources of 'NSMs' or new social movements such as feminism (Haywood, 1983; Neitz, 1988) and environmental and anti-nuclear activism, which overlap with NRMs in terms of both holistic symbolic properties and social bases. Influenced by Robertson (1979), Hannigan suggests that a key factor encouraging the growth of both NRMs and NSMs is contemporary erosion of the boundaries between private and public domains.

(5) If the membership of NRMs has presently stabilized or declined (Barker, 1986), it may be necessary to reconsider those explanations for

the surge of movements in the 1970s which implied that mystical holism, spiritual innovation or 'seekership' is inherent in advanced Western modernity (e.g. Campbell, 1982; Eister, 1974; Westley, 1978a,b).

(6) Some of the problems of meaning and community involving lack of familial and vocational integration which are alleged to have predisposed young persons in recent decades toward alternative religions also characterize the situation of *elderly* persons, who may presently be targeted by NRMs (Brooks, 1986; Rudin, 1984). 'New Age' movements have been reported to appeal largely to middle-aged people and disproportionately to women (Salvatori, 1987).

(7) Attempted explanations for the surge of NRMs in recent Euro-American experience plus analyses of particular contemporary movements have led to a new interest in past surges, e.g. early Christianity (Stark, 1987a,b). Perhaps the dynamics of the present ferment cannot be grasped if the latter is viewed in conceptual isolation from other historical episodes (Hall, 1987).

(8) Present trends in the mid 1980s seem ambiguous, e.g. a possible diminution of spiritual innovation and communal totalism coexisting with resurgent and overtly politicized charismatic and fundamentalist evangelicism. One factor which may have a powerful but now indeterminate impact is the frightening worldwide AIDS epidemic. Three particular relevances may be suggested: (a) a renewed 'need' for a religious rationale for social and self *control of sexuality*; (b) the spectre of pestilence may reinforce and intensify prophetic–apocalyptic excitation and *eschatological expectation* of the imminent 'Great Tribulation' preceding the Second Coming (Balch et al., 1983; Hexham and Poewe, 1986: 90–3; Martin, 1982); (c) *healing* movements and rituals may respond to the trauma of AIDS, particularly since afflicted individuals are likely to live longer due in part to new medications and to eventual adaptation of the virus to humans. Some NRMs are responding to the new 'plague' (Palmer, 1986a, forthcoming). But this report does not adequately deal with healing practices in NRMs and associated vital notions of religious *power* (Beckford, 1983a, 1984, 1985d; Bird, 1978; Foltz, 1987; Kilbourne and Richardson, 1988; McGuire, 1982, 1983b, 1985; Neitz, 1987, 1988; Poloma, 1987; Wallis and Morely, 1976; Westley, 1983; see Ch. 7).

3

CONVERSION, COMMITMENT
AND DISENGAGEMENT

It seems clear that a disproportionate amount of the research on new religions has involved studies of processes of conversion and commitment. In a recent review essay 'The Sociology of Conversion', Snow and Machalek (1984) write:

> An inspection of Beckford and Richardson's (1983) more recent bibliography on new religious movements similarly reveals a sharp increase in research on conversion since 1973. Of the 145 entries that can be classified as pertinent to conversion, 95% have appeared in the last 10 years. It is also worth noting that these 145 comprise around 40% of the works listed in this more general bibliography. Thus, not only has conversion stimulated considerable discussion and research in recent years, but it appears to be the phenomenon that students of new religious movements examine most frequently. (Snow and Machalek, 1984: 167–8)

There are perhaps two basic factors which underlie this preoccupation with conversion and commitment processes. One factor is clearly the concern of the popular press and the media over the alleged employment by movements of 'brainwashing' methods for effecting 'forced conversions':

> Governmental authorities at every level have had to deal with this issue. Thus, we find that the general public is not so concerned about societal conditions that led to the new movements or to the characteristics of individuals who join. Instead attention at the popular level has focused on the organization of recruitment efforts by the new groups (Richardson, 1978a: 6).

An additional factor is probably the assumption, prevalent in a 'secular' society, that *spiritual apotheosis is an unnatural and problematic phenomenon which entails esoteric processes*. There is a paradox here. Although religion is considered to be more significant and vital in the United States than in other 'Western' nations, for many Americans religion has a routine or even nominal quality. Persons who actually 'live' their religion in a thorough and totalistic manner, particularly when marginal exotic groups and deviant perspectives are involved, are perceived as having undergone an unnatural metamorphosis. This perception engenders a compelling inquiry: how did they get this way?

In this chapter we will review the highpoints of the formidably vast literature on conversion (and deconversion) processes in NRMs. We will rely in part on some existing excellent review essays, critiques and syntheses (Balch, 1985a; Barker, 1986; Greil and Rudy, 1984a; Lofland and Skonovd, 1983; Machalek and Snow, 1985; Rambo, 1982; Snow and Machalek, 1984).

Conceptual and Analytical Confusion

One result of the obsession with cultist conversion and commitment processes is the wealth of empirical research in this area. Unfortunately the research and theory in the area of conversion is redolent of multiple confusions related to the divergent premises, conceptual frameworks, nomenclature and behavioral referents which different researchers have employed. In consequence many studies are not strictly comparable. The mountain of research and analysis has produced rather little by way of cumulative knowledge (Balch, 1985a).

Several researchers have noted that a troublesome issue is presented by the pervasive tendency to confuse *conversion* and *recruitment* (Balch, 1985a; Greil and Rudy, 1984a) or conversion and *commitment* (Staples and Mauss, 1987). 'Recruitment refers to joining a group, while conversion implies a radical change in belief and personal identity' (Balch, 1985a: 28). In Balch's study of a UFO cult, recruitment tended to be rather sudden whereas conversion was a gradual evolutionary process (Balch, 1980, 1985a; see also Downton, 1979, 1980). But intensity of commitment may vary among 'converts' (Staples and Mauss, 1987).

'Conversion' has any number of behavioral and cognitive referents, including transitions from one religion to another, transitions within components of a religion, movements from low participation or commitment to an intensified involvement, or radical diminutions of participation or commitment (Rambo, 1982: 4–5). Conversion often refers to a *radical transformation of identity or orientation*, e.g. 'the process of changing a sense of root reality' or 'a conscious shift in one's sense of grounding' (Heirich, 1977: 674). Snow and Machalek (1983, 1984) have conceptualized conversion as a change in one's universe of discourse which 'entails the displacement of one universe of discourse by another or the ascendency of a formerly peripheral universe of discourse to the status of a primary authority' (Snow and Machalek, 1984: 170). 'Rhetorical indicators' of conversion include biographical reconstruction, the adoption of a 'master attribution scheme', a suspension of analogical reasoning, and explicit embracement of the 'convert role'.

There is a continuing debate among scholars as to whether conversion entails sudden, gradual, or multiple-serial changes (Bankston et al., 1981; Lynch, 1978; Richardson, 1980; Richardson and Stewart, 1978). The 'serial monogamy' analogy is reflected in the concept of *conversion careers* (Richardson, 1978a, 1980; Richardson and Stewart, 1978) which reflects scholars' observation of sequential conversion patterns among 'protean' young converts in the 1970s.

Some of the recent literature on the problems of conceptualizing conversion has been concerned with distinguishing between 'true' conversion and less comprehensive or less discontinuous movements (e.g. Gordon's, 1974, distinction between conversion and *consolidation*) and Travisano's earlier dichotomy (1970) of conversion and *alternation* which Pilarzyk (1978a) has applied to a comparative analysis of processes of orientational shifts in Hare Krishna and the Divine Light Mission, which are related to differences in group structure. These dichotomies somewhat resemble the earlier distinction between conversion and *adhesion* propounded by A. D. Nock in his classic *Conversion* (Nock, 1933). Discussing religious patterns in the Roman Empire, Nock noted that Christianity and Judaism (a proselytizing religion during part of this period) were characterized by an *exclusivity* whereby the convert was cut off from his past lifestyle and identity and from other religious groups. One was thus *converted* to the intolerant faiths of Judaism and Christianity while one merely *adhered* to the cults of Isis, Orpheus, or Mithra. Participation in a particular 'mystery cult' was not incompatible with involvement in another mystery religion or with Roman civic piety. Nock's distinction between conversion and adhesion has always seemed to this writer applicable to differences between patterns of involvement with 'totalistic' groups such as the Unification Church and Hare Krishna and participation in more 'limited liability' groups such as Transcendental Meditation or est (e.g. Enroth, 1977; Snow et al., 1980). But Shepherd (1979) argues that participants in seemingly totalistic groups such as the UC are really only 'adhering' to such groups and are not really being 'converted', i.e. their involvement, while seemingly intense and total, tends to be ephemeral and ultimately shallow.

The common notion that totalistic movements manifest more intense converts or entail more profound conversion experiences than less exclusive or less communal movements has been challenged by Balch (1985b), who notes the substantial drop-out rate in the UFO cult he studied. Substantial defection has also been observed in the Unification Church (Barker, 1984) and Hare Krishna (Rochford, 1985).

Particularly pervasive has been the assumption that conversion constitutes a *unitary, qualitatively distinct social process* such that a general theory or model of conversion is possible. This assumption underlies the purported 'causal process models' of conversions such as that of Lofland and Stark (1965) and Downton (1980). Such models are, however, according to Machalek and Snow (1985), mere 'ideal typical natural histories' rather than true causal models. Arguably, a wide range of different processes may produce 'conversion', such that conversion can really only be 'explained by evoking general principles that apply to other kinds of social psychological changes as well' (Machalek and Snow, 1985: 124). Thus Long and Hadden (1983) deny that conversion constitutes a qualitatively unique phenomenon which requires concept-specific explanation; rather, conversions are understandable as instances of the more general process of *socialization*.

A similar pervasive assumption holds that 'conversion is something that happens to *individuals*...most conversion researchers treat the individual as the appropriate unit of analysis' (Machalek and Snow, 1985: 127, our emphasis). However, there is another tradition of looking at conversion as a form of collective behavior, e.g. revivalist 'mass conversion'. Machalek and Snow (1985) propose a concept of conversion as a 'social fact' to be analyzed in terms of rates and treated as a 'function of the properties of social structure, not simply individual circumstances and subjective states' (Machalek and Snow, 1985: 127). The recent growth of NRMs has thus stimulated a substantial theoretical and methodological literature on conversion as a sociological problematic. An ironic fruit of these discussions has been the growing awareness of conceptual and methodological confusion and the resulting incomparability of voluminous research reports and the resulting lack of cumulative knowledge (Balch, 1985a; Greil and Rudy, 1984a).

A hotly debated methodological and epistemological issue entails the analytic status of converts' verbal accounts of their conversions, which are said to be retrospective, temporally variable and socially constructed in terms of the ideology and vocabulary of the movement which entails standards of 'appropriate' conversions and 'correct' attributions (Beckford, 1978a; Preston, 1981; Snow and Machalek, 1984; Snow and Rochford, 1983; Wallis and Bruce, 1986: 11–46). Converts' retrospective accounts, like apostates' accounts, 'tell us more about the converts' current experience and orientation than about his or her past...much of the literature on conversion confuses retrospection and introspection ...and therefore treats converts' accounts as explanations of conversion rather than as phenomena requiring sociological explanation' (Snow and Machalek, 1984: 177–8). Nevertheless, this 'common sense heresy' has its staunch defenders (Bruce, 1982; Wallis and Bruce, 1986: 11–46).

Finally, the convert's account represents only the 'first order of abstraction'. Additional levels entail what people (family, friends, etc.) say about the conversion, and finally the researcher's standpoint, which is thus two levels removed from the 'real' event (Richardson, 1985a).

'Motifs' of Conversion

Lofland and Skonovd, in an important formulation (1981, 1983), appear to take a middling position between those who affirm a single conversion process and those who would seemingly eliminate conversion as a meaningful social science concept and substitute a broader notion such as socialization (Long and Hadden, 1983). Differences among conversion experiences have been reported by different researchers who have stressed 'affective bonds', 'programming', 'mind control' and self-induced or externally 'coerced' conversions. For Lofland and Skonovd these variations do not reflect merely 'the "theoretical goggles" worn by researchers . . . rather, such differences are inherent in the central or key features of the conversions themselves' (Lofland and Skonovd, 1983: 2–3). The authors propose the existence of several major 'types' of conversions, each type being characterized by a defining 'motif experience'.

Drawing on their own research experience and that of other students of NRMs, the authors develop a typology of five *conversion motifs* (Lofland and Skonovd, 1981, 1983), which are compared in terms of five variables: (1) degree of social pressure involved in conversion; (2) temporal duration of conversion experience; (3) level of affective arousal involved in conversion; (4) affective tone or content of conversion experience; and (5) the belief–participation sequence. Each 'conversion motif' is characterized by a particular profile in terms of these variables, although it is not entirely clear as to whether motifs are really defined in terms of their profile on the five dimensions.

The *intellectual* pattern of conversion entails an individual who privately investigates the possibility of 'new grounds of being' or is inspired through contact with 'disembodied' media such as books, pamphlets, television, or even lectures. Today 'it is increasingly possible sans social involvement to become acquainted with alternative ideologies and ways of life' (Lofland and Skonovd, 1983: 6; see also Shupe, 1976, 1982). A prototypical case is afforded by the retrospective self-report of sociologist Roger Straus (1979a) who 'substantially converted himself to Scientology through extensive reading' (Lofland and Skonovd, 1983: 6). The importance of the intellectual conversion motif is probably increasing in the contemporary 'media drenched' but 'underinstitution-alized' social environment in which religion is largely 'privatized' and *disembodied modes of communication* such as specialized newspapers and magazines or video and audio cassettes are increasingly prominent (Shupe, 1976, 1982). Intellectual conversion is thus characterized by little or no social pressure, 'medium' duration (a few weeks or months), medium arousal and an experiential–emotional tone of *illumination*. A 'reasonably high level of belief' is attained prior to actual participation in organized activities (Lofland and Skonovd, 1983: 6). Stark and Bainbridge's (1985) concept of the 'audience cult' may be pertinent here (see Ch. 5).

Mystical conversions are characterized by high subjective intensity and trauma. There is little or no social pressure, and there is usually a very short critical period of conversion preceded by a longer period of stress. 'The level of emotional arousal is extremely high – sometimes involving theophanic *ecstasies*, awe, love, or even fear' (Lofland and Skonovd, 1983: 9). Belief then ensues, which is followed by participation in organized actions. The self-reported born-again apotheoses of Charles Colson, Eldridge Cleaver and (ex-Manson Family member) Susan Atkins appear to Lofland and Skonovd to embody mystical conversion, which may function to alleviate guilt.

Experimental conversion, or rather the experimental motif, is present when individuals consciously decide to participate in a movement without yet having accepted (or totally discerned) the movement's worldview. Such 'converts-in-process' may exhibit a pragmatic 'show me' attitude. Straus (1976: 260) refers to an 'experimental rationale' on the part of a devotee of Yogi Bhajan. In his report on UFO cultists Balch concludes that participants initially learn to *act* like a convert. 'Genuine convic-tion develops later. . .after intense involvement' (Balch, 1980: 142). The role-theory model of conversion proposed by Bromley and Shupe (1979b, 1986) and arising from their study of 'Moonies' also manifests similar themes.

Lofland and Skonovd note that experimental motifs are found in many groups such as Jehovah's Witnesses (Beckford, 1975a) and Scientology (Straus, 1979a), which more or less 'insist that the prospective convert take an experimental attitude toward — and participate in — the group's ritual and organizational activities' (Lofland and Skonovd, 1983: 10). The authors feel that 'relatively low degrees of social pressure' are involved here since 'the recruit takes on a "try-it-out" posture' (Lofland and Skonovd, 1983: 11). Nevertheless, a lengthy passage quoted from Straus (1979a: 19) indicates a highly directed and managed sequence of structured interactions designed to move the participant toward a redefinition of personal goals and interests in terms of the group's definition of the situation, although Straus also emphasizes creative management of the interactive sequence by the subject, who partly 'accomplishes' his own conversion (Straus, 1979b). The temporal duration of experimental conversion may be rather lengthy, lasting months or even years. The level of arousal is low and its initial content is often mere curiosity. Lofland and Skonovd note that the symbolic interactionist analysis of situational adjustment–commitment as a terminus of continuing adaptation and the proliferation of 'side-bets' (Becker, 1960; Skonovd, 1981) is relevant here.

The '*affectional*' conversion motif highlights the importance of affective bonds to the conversion process (Lofland and Stark, 1965). Interpersonal bonds are now widely viewed as providing 'fundamental support for recruitment' (Snow and Phillips, 1980: 389). The prominence of this motif in discussions of conversion is seen by Lofland and Skonovd as reflecting the prevalent 'reality constructionism' of the 1960s and 70s and the posited grounding of social knowledge in underlying social support systems. Affectional conversion de-emphasizes the cognitive dimension. Participation precedes belief and medium social pressure operates but 'functions more as "support" and attraction than as "conducement" to convert' (Lofland and Skonovd, 1983: 13). As a process, affectional conversion may often be prolonged, but does not seem to entail extreme intensity.

Revivalist conversion refers to managed or manipulated ecstatic arousals in a group or collective context. Notwithstanding a recent tendency to debunk adulterated revivalist conversion in the style of Billy Graham (Wimberly et al., 1980), Lofland and Skonovd (1983: 14) insist that scholarly rationalism must not be allowed to obscure 'the very real fact that crowds *can* be brought to ecstatic arousals that have a critically transforming effect on people' (see also Lofland, 1985). Profound orientational experiences arising in the context of an emotionally aroused crowd are very much of a reality throughout the modern world, but 'real' revivalism has declined in significance in the United States in the twentieth century, although a mild revival of revivalism may have transpired in the 1970s with the surge of NRMs. 'The Unification Church. . .appears to have resurrected the revivalist experience in highly effective modern garb. Prospective converts recruited literally off the streets are taken on weekend retreats that involve a whirlwind round of singing, chanting, hand-holding, preaching, and diffuse, loving camaraderie' (Lofland and Skonovd, 1983: 15). The authors quote David Taylor's important ethnographic study of a Unificationist indoctrination workshop:

All aspects of the training session blend together with exhilarating momentum. [The members'] enthusiasm requires prospects to invest their entire beings in the participatory events. Jumping up to sing tumultuous songs; running from place to place in hand with a buddy; cheering and chanting, and clapping in unison with dozens of others inevitably make a deep impression on prospective members...possibly no participant escapes feeling intense excitement, even if he regards the performance as inauthentic (Taylor, 1978: 153–4; see also Taylor, 1982a, b).

Revivalist conversions entail intense social pressure but are of fairly short duration. There is a high level of affective arousal and the affective content is primarily positive — 'loving' — with a possible undertone of fear and guilt. The experience is perhaps particularly potent with American youths because it seems novel: 'Unacquainted with crowd arousal as a generic and powerful human experience known throughout history...prospects easily construe a special and causal relationship between the experience of emotional contagion and the religion producing it' (Lofland and Skonovd, 1983: 16).

True brainwashing or *coercive* conversion 'takes place only in extremely rare and special circumstances but which has been alleged by some to be rampant among the new religions of the Western world' (Lofland and Skonovd, 1983: 16). Lofland and Skonovd argue that the model of 'thought reform' developed by Lifton (1961) which is frequently applied to cultist processes (Lifton, 1985; Richardson et al., 1972) really embodies the rather broad and ubiquitous phenomenon of *ideological totalism* (see also Weightman, 1983: 154–60) which tends to characterize any communal ideological movement. True 'brainwashing' or 'coerced' conversions are embodied in the more restrictive model of Albert Somit (1968; see also Lofland and Skonovd, 1983: 17–18 and Weightman, 1983: 154–60), which is based on the forcible extraction of confessions by European and Chinese communists.

NRMs generally lack the kind of social organization for conversion described by Somit, which entails large amounts of space and time, personnel and other resources required to achieve an individual's sincere transformation (Lofland and Skonovd, 1983: 18). Similarly, Weightman (1983: 154–60) argues that the doomed settlement at Jonestown manifested the state of ideological totalism but not the dynamic process of brainwashing as restrictively conceptualized by Somit. But Lofland and Skonovd acknowledge that revivalist conversion may provide a setting in which 'social–psychological coercion' may arise (Taylor, 1978: 153–4) such that there may be 'crossovers between revivalist and coercive conversion' (Lofland and Skonovd, 1983: 19). The authors' tabular comparison of conversion motifs (1983: 4) suggests that revivalist and

and coercive conversion differ only in terms of the longer duration of the latter and the primacy of fear over love in the affective content of coercive conversion. The two motifs share the high levels of social pressure and affective arousal and the sequential priority of participation over belief.

While extremely provocative, Lofland and Skonovd's treatment has conspicuous elements of ambiguity. It seems uncertain whether one is to interpret 'conversion motifs' as types of individual conversions, as patterns of conversions predominating in particular groups at given times and places, or as a set of themes characterizing social scientists' analyses of conversion. The authors' discussions of each motif seem to highlight one or another use of the 'motif' concept; thus the different discussions and extrapolations of each motif do not seem to be strictly comparable, except in terms of the five variables employed for a tabular comparison (Lofland and Skonovd, 1983: 4) which are sometimes muted in the actual extended discussions. The different motifs do not always appear to be mutually exclusive, e.g. why cannot a given conversion process be either simultaneously or sequentially both affective (persons drawn in through social bonds) and experimental, and perhaps also revivalist?

Nevertheless, conversion motifs may provide a handle not only for studying conversion and commitment processes, but also for understanding a sociocultural change. In 'advanced' Western society, intellectual and experimental conversions may be increasing while revivalist conversion motifs have declined. The growth, development and decline of particular movements may be linked to shifts in typical conversion motifs, e.g. the rise to prominence and controversiality of the Unification Church (Bromley and Shupe, 1979a; Lofland, 1977) was clearly related to its 'move from affectional to revivalist conversions' (Lofland and Skonovd, 1983: 20). However, inferences about shifts in types of conversion are tricky, as the locus of change may really be in the way researchers are viewing conversion (Richardson, 1985a). Gartrell and Shannon (1985) have sought to 'explain' variations posited by Lofland and Skonovd in terms of converts' perceived payoff matrix and a rational choice/exchange theory of religion (Stark and Bainbridge, 1980a).

In general the literature on conversion processes in contemporary NRMs has been dominated by two models: the brainwashing model (not really a single model), and the early causal process model developed by Lofland and Stark (including the ultimately derivative social network research).

Conversion as Brainwashing

The present writer's view of the coercive conversion motif is somewhat similar to that of Lofland and Skonovd (1981, 1983; Robbins, 1984; Robbins and Anthony, 1980, 1982a). Snow and Machalek summarize the basic 'brainwashing' model:

> The 'brainwashing' or 'coercive persuasion' model is the most popular explanation for conversion [to NRMs] outside of sociological circles. The basic thesis is that conversion is the product of devious but specifiable forces acting upon unsuspecting and therefore highly vulnerable individuals. This proposition rests on the conjunction of elements from both physiological psychology and psychoanalytic theory. . . Induced physiological dysfunctioning of the brain is thus seen as the key to conversion. When this proposition is combined with psychoanalytic theory, we have a picture of the convert as an individual who has been made receptive to new ideas because his or her critical facilities and ego strength have been eroded by information control, overstimulation of the nervous system, forced confessions, and ego destruction, among other factors. . .
> (Snow and Machalek, 1984: 178–9).

The brainwashing explanation of conversion has gained currency among the public in part because, 'It provides a convenient and "sensible" account for those who are at a loss to explain why individuals are attracted to "deviant" and "menacing" groups. Moreover, it exempts both "the victim" and his or her significant others outside the movement from any responsibility, thereby preserving the integrity of their worldviews and lifestyles' (Snow and Machalek, 1984: 179). Since the Korean war it has been used to explain seeming desertion of one's family or nation (Robbins and Anthony, 1982a).

With several exceptions (Enroth, 1977; Levine, 1980a; Ofshe and Singer, 1986) sociologists have tended to be critical of 'mind control' and 'coercive' explanations for conversion to deviant perspectives and sustained commitment to deviate religiotherapeutic movements (Barker, 1984; Bromley and Shupe, 1981; Downton, 1979; Kilbourne and Richardson, 1984a,b; Lewis, 1987; Richardson, 1983, 1985d; Robbins, 1984; Robbins and Anthony, 1980, 1982a; Rochford et al., 1988; Stark and Bainbridge, 1985: 417–21). Medicalistic and 'brain control' variants of the mind control theme (Appel, 1983; Conway and Siegelman, 1978; Verdier, 1980) are particularly scorned (Kilbourne, 1983, Robbins, 1986d; Robbins and Anthony, 1982a) and have been compared to premodern demonology and conceptions of spirit possession (Hargrove, 1983; Shupe et al., 1978). '"Brainwashing". . .may be seen as the "evil eye" theory appropriate to modern scientific culture. Psychological technology is something we understand a little about and we understand to be amenable to counteraction by improved technology' (Hargrove, 1983: 303). The linkage of cult/mind control debates to intense and emotional controversy over the 'counter-technology' of 'deprogramming' has probably distorted scholarly discourse and pushed scholars (reacting against coercive deprogramming or speculative psychophysiological models) into downplaying manipulative and coercive elements in some movements, cf. Balch's (1985a: 26) comments on Bromley and Shupe (1981). On the other hand, not all clinicians who have studied converts have looked favorably upon brainwashing analyses (Coleman, 1985a,b; Levine, 1984; Maleson, 1981; Ungerleider and Wellisch, 1979). Ofshe and Singer (1986) delineate a less medicalistic and more social psychological model of coercive processes in religiotherapeutic groups (see also Keiser and Keiser, 1987).

The absence of the extreme stress qua physical coercion and brutality characterizing 'classical' brainwashing settings (e.g. POW camps, forced confessions) has been cited by social scientists critical of mind control explanations (Anthony, 1979–80; Barker, 1979, 1984; Richardson et al., 1972). Much has also been made of the substantial evidence that even highly authoritarian and 'totalistic' groups such as the Unification Church, as well as less austere groups, manifest a *strikingly high rate of voluntary defection* (Barker, 1984; Beckford, 1978b, 1985a; Bird and Reimer, 1982; Jacobs, 1984, 1987; Levine, 1984; Ofshe, 1976; Skonovd, 1981; Wright, 1987). It may also be relevant that only a tiny proportion of potential converts who are approached actually become seriously involved (Galanter, 1980; Levine, 1984). 'If recruitment techniques are so sinister, why do they so rarely work?' (Levine, 1984: 27). At best the Unification Church practices 'resistible coercion' (Barker, 1981).

Skeptical sociologists have had little difficulty identifying the invidious, reductive or 'anti-religious' premises underlying some brainwashing formulations (Anthony et al., 1983; Kilbourne and Richardson, 1984a,b; Robbins and Anthony, 1980, 1982a; Robbins, 1984, 1985b). Bizarre movements may be assumed to be so 'inherently repugnant to people in possession of their rational faculties' that sustained involvement must really be 'imposed on a reluctant clientele' (Snow and Machalek, 1984: 179). More subtle is the 'atomistic bias' whereby 'it is assumed that authentic spiritual experience or ideological commitment is exclusively personal and not mediated by social reinforcement such that an apparent dependence of belief upon social support may, on this premise, be taken as prima facie evidence of inauthenticity' (Robbins and Anthony, 1980: 30). It has been noted that the models of brainwashing, thought reform and coercive persuasion which are applied to cults originated in a 'cold war' anti-communist setting and have a distinct anti-collectivist bias (Richardson and Kilbourne, 1983a). Robbins (1984, 1985b) argues that both 'sides' in the controversy over cultist brainwashing tend to talk past each other since they employ differing interpretive frameworks, epistemological rules, definitions (e.g. of 'coercion') and underlying assumptions.

Finally, it has been noted that the empirical base of brainwashing allegations tends to entail the testimony of ex-devotees and particularly deprogrammed ex-devotees. 'Accounts of apostasy are no less retro- spective or transformative than accounts of conversion, and they are therefore no more reliable as sources of data' (Snow and Machalek, 1984: 179). Affirming their prior passivity and lack of deviant motivation may be rewarding to apostates in terms of reintegration into conventional roles, re-unification of sundered families, insulation from deviant stigma or management of guilt feelings (Bromley and Shupe, 1981; Lewis, 1986; Robbins and Anthony, 1980, 1982a; Shupe and Bromley, 1980a). Some data on recriminatory testimonies arise from very specialized 'network samples' of ex-devotees who have become involved in a social network of deprogrammers, counselors, ex-convert support groups and 'concerned' (or 'anti-cult') organizations (Robbins, 1985b). Many ex-converts do not claim to have been largely passive victims of mind control (Beckford, 1978b, 1985a). Those who *do* make this claim are more likely than other ex-converts to have undergone deprogramming and/or to have had contact with counselors, rehabilitation groups, deprogrammers, ex-convert support groups and organizations concerned with cult problems (Lewis, 1986; Skonovd, 1981; Solomon, 1981; Wright, 1984). These findings are susceptible to different interpretations.

Recently one study has reported an absence of significant differences between the accounts of deprogrammed and non-deprogrammed ex- devotees; however, the sample was drawn from the anti-cult network (Conway and Siegelman, 1982). There has also been debate about the statistical methods employed in an earlier tabulation based on the same study (Kilbourne, 1983, 1986a; Maher and Langone, 1985).

Toward Synthesizing Formulations. Despite the general critical stance which sociologists have taken toward brainwashing explanations, the existence of manipulative, deceptive and coercive pressures in some movements has been widely acknowledged (Bromley and Shupe, 1981; Downton, 1979; Lofland and Skonovd, 1981, 1983; Richardson et al., 1972; Robbins and Anthony, 1980; Taylor, 1982a,b). Richard Ofshe's (1980b) study of the Synanon leadership's manipulative managerial strategy for organizational transformation has been widely cited. The work of the sociologically oriented psychiatrist, Marc Galanter (1978, 1980, 1982, 1983a,b, 1985, 1986; Galanter and Buckley, 1978; Galanter et al., 1979), has attempted to draw insights from researchers in both 'camps'. Particularly interesting is a recent (Galanter, 1985) attempt to point the way toward a *systems theory* formulation which would inter-relate the transformative conversion experience of devotees with the pre-conversion emotional distress of some devotees, their post-conversion 'relief effect' (Galanter, 1978; Galanter and Buckley, 1978; Galanter et al., 1979), social cohesiveness in the group and the group's systemic imperative of 'boundary control'. This approach also attempts to syn-thesize the contributions of operant reinforcement theory, sociobiology, 'thought control theory' and attribution theory (Galanter, 1985). The latter psychological model has previously been employed to analyze the manipulative process of induction into religious movements and the perceived therapeutic efficacy of such involvement (Galanter et al., 1979; Proudfoot and Shaver, 1975).

An important synthesizing formulation has been developed by Long and Hadden (1983), who see analyses of conversion to NRMs polarized between the brainwashing model and a *social drift model* (Balch and Taylor, 1978; Downton, 1979, 1980; Lofland, 1977, 1979; Lofland and Stark, 1965; Lynch, 1978; Richardson and Stewart, 1978; Richardson et al., 1979). The latter 'suggests that people become converts gradually through the influence of social relationships, especially during times of personal strain. Conversion is viewed as precarious and open to change in response to shifting patterns of association' (Long and Hadden, 1983: 1). Each model pinpoints 'a central, but only partial, aspect of cult conversion processes. Neither model by itself is capable of com-prehending the apparent duality of cult life, for each is built on a fundamental denial of the reality perceived by the other' (Long and Hadden, 1983: 2). A synthesis is urged which 'integrates the seemingly contradictory phenomena of brainwashing and drift'. See also Gordon (1984a) who suggests that drifting into collectivist 'self-abandonment' can paradoxically enhance inner autonomy.

Long and Hadden argue that a more general and synthesizing model is available if conversion is viewed as a subtype of *socialization* activity. It can then be seen that the brainwashing and drift model embody the two key dimensions of the socialization process: group tactics employed to mold new members, and the sometimes idiosyncratic, gradual and problematic development of members' often transitory involvement. Conversion to NRMs seems to be characterized by *both* 'techniques of thought reform' *and* an overall pattern of drifting in and out of particular groups. Some drift theorists have in fact acknowledged the presence of commitment mechanisms such as 'mortification rituals' in cults, which, however, *are not seen as effectively overwhelming converts' capacity for choice* (Barker, 1984; Downton, 1979: 169–78); Richardson et al., 1979; Robbins and Anthony, 1980).

Long and Hadden illustrate the utility of their socialization emphasis with a discussion of problems of commitment to the Unification Church (Bromley and Shupe, 1979a; Lofland, 1977) in which manipulative patterns appear to produce fervent but ephemeral commitment. Social bonding and collective ecstasy are stressed in the UC but *cognitive socialization is weak*. Beliefs are not central to many recent converts (Bromley and Shupe, 1979b); thus, 'When affective bonds become uncertain, converts' moral commitment to the group has no backing in cultural belief; they have no taken-for-granted ontology to sustain them' (Long and Hadden, 1983: 10). Recently indoctrinated Moonies sent to raise funds 'in the world' exhibited high defection rates (Bromley and Shupe, 1979a). Eager to quickly *deploy* recruits in proselytization and fundraising, the Moonies overstressed tangible group encapsulation; their 'failure to create strong cognitive worlds among their members appears to be a significant factor which has undermined their retention' (Long and Hadden, 1983: 13). Socialization has also been preferred to brainwashing as a guiding concept for Moonist indoctrination by an anthropologist who has published an ethnography of a Moonist communal retreat and intensive indoctrination program (Galanti, 1984).

It is important to realize that there are a number of *different* models pertaining to 'thought reform', 'coercive persuasion', 'brainwashing', 'menticide', etc. (Richardson and Kilbourne, 1983a; Lofland and Skonovd, 1983; Robbins, 1984). These models vary in the stringency of the operational criteria (i.e. in the scope of their applicability) and in the degree to which they depict the persuadees as passive victims who lose their free will and become a bit like puppets or robots. The more sophisticated models (Lifton, 1961; Schein et al., 1961) are broadly applicable; moreover, their creators appeared to be trying to transcend the sensationalist 'robotist' demonology of some of the earlier writings. Thus Robert Lifton decries the connotation of brainwashing as an all-powerful, irresistible and quasi-magical technology for gaining total control over human beings; this 'loose usage makes the word a rallying point for resentment, urges toward submission, justification for failure, and for a wide gamut of emotional extremism' (Lifton, 1961: 4; see Lifton, 1979 for an application of his 'thought reform' model to Jonestown, and Lifton, 1985 for a general application to cults). Mind control models may also vary substantially with respect to a dominant focus on physiological, depth-psychological, or social psychological factors (Richardson and Kilbourne, 1983).

The multiplicity of models has led to a certain confusion and inadvertent rhetorical exploitation on the part of both 'anti-cult' writers and alleged 'cult apologists'. Critics of the application of brainwashing metaphors to religious movements have had an easy time demonstrating that 'classical' brainwashing contexts qua forcible confinement and 'forced confessions' are really absent from formally voluntary movements (James, 1986). Scholars making this point have not always been quick to point out that some broader models of 'thought reform' (Lifton, 1961, 1979, 1985) and 'coercive persuasion' (Schein et al., 1961) are indeed applicable to many cults, although Weightman (1983: 154–60) presents a detailed comparative evaluation of the applicability of Lifton's thought reform model and Somit's more restrictive model to the Jonestown community (see also Lifton, 1979, 1985; Richardson et al., 1972). Some of the more vehement critics of cults, particularly in court testimony, have sometimes made formal references to broadly applicable models while describing the nature and consequences of cultist indoctrination in terms which evoke more restrictive models or special cases of broader models associated with brutality.

The Barker Study. A careful analysis of the alleged coercive quality of cultist conversion should take account of the following: (a) the existence of, and distinctions between, different modes and models of pressured persuasion; (2) the existence of strong pressures and manipulative tactics in some movements; and (3) the reality of the 'revolving door' of substantial voluntary defection. In this respect Eileen Barker's study of the indoctrination and conversion of British 'Moonies' represents an empirical and theoretical tour de force.

Dr Barker rejects absolutist perspectives (e.g. we are all brainwashed; no one can really be brainwashed; persons adhering to such bizarre notions must be brainwashed) which define away the problem. She also discards the dichotomy of *free will vs. determinism* and substitutes *coercion vs. choice*. Choice is grounded in man's innate capacity for reflection, including the capacity to imagine alternative futures and recall the past. A decision is involuntary if the actor is prevented from considering the context of his recent experiences or from considering an alternative line of action.

Dr Barker distinguishes carefully between *deception* and *coercion* and then develops a typology of situations in which the individual's dispositions, the social context, the positive appeal of the movement and the actual indoctrination process (seminars) interact and are differentially weighted to produce a convert. Barker distinguishes among chemico-biological *brain control*, *physical control* through *bodily constraint* and control through *mental coercion* (the latter would entail total manipulation of a person's memories of the past and imaginings of the future). In all three situations the intense indoctrination process would become the key independent variable which overshadows the effects of individual dispositions, the broader social and cultural environment and the attractiveness of the spiritual ideal. In contrast there are three types of *suggestibility*, plus the situations of the cult as *refuge from society* and the cult as *promising utopia* (embodying the movement's self-understanding), which all entail different kinds of interactions between the individual's dispositions, society, the 'pull' of the spiritual ideal and the managed indoctrination process.

Dr Barker's English data plus the American data compiled by Galanter (1980) allow Barker to conclude that 'from the number of those who get as far as visiting a Unification center, a generous estimate suggests that no more than 0.005 percent will be associated with the movement two years later' (Barker, 1984: 147). This fact plus other considerations (e.g. indications that different potential converts react very differently to the indoctrination stimuli) arising from observational, interview and questionnaire data, allow Barker to *eliminate those formulations which stress the overwhelming efficacious coerciveness of the immediate indoctrinational environment*. Barker's analysis also indicates that those persons who would appear most suggestible — young adults who are drifting, socially isolated and having difficulties in occupational and educational performance — tend either to not join or to join temporarily and leave. Persisting converts compare favorably with 'the ones that got away' on various measures of susceptibility and psychological stability (Barker, 1981, 1983, 1984). While acknowledging and analyzing deception and manipulation in Unificationist recruitment, Barker concludes that most recruits make their affiliative decision voluntarily and are aware of the messianic claims of the movement, although these latter claims are only slowly revealed to initiates.

Final Considerations on Coercive Models. In the view of Robert Balch (1985a: 17) 'social scientists have spent altogether too much time haggling over the merits of the brainwashing metaphor. What we need is reliable data linking recruitment and socialization techniques with objective measures of effectiveness.' The whole mind control issue really 'boils down to a hypothetical causal relationship between resocialization techniques and subsequent levels of commitment' (Balch 1985a: 29). Abundant case studies fail to really establish cause and effect. 'It is commonly assumed that totalism produces highly committed followers' (Balch, 1985a: 29), but this notion has yet to be tested properly with totalistic and control samples of groups. What about high defection rates among Moonies (Barker, 1984) or a notorious UFO cult (Balch, 1980)? Is 'commitment' unidimensional? Totalism may produce fervent but not persistent commitment, as a schedule of continuous operant reinforcement produces a high rate of response which is easily extinguished by non-reinforcement. Of course non-totalist groups also exhibit substantial defection (Bird and Reimer, 1982).

The brainwashing thesis has been enormously influential, even among sociologists who tend to reject it and for whom it has set the agenda of inquiry and discourse (Robbins, 1986b). Thus Richardson (1985a) seems to be reacting against the brainwashing notion when he urges a more *activist* model of conversion which will stress the creative, 'seeking' role of the convert. The brainwashing analysis is viewed by Richardson as an extreme subtype of the (obsolete) classical 'Pauline' model which sees conversion as something which happens to someone — a sudden, irrational, overpowering experience impacting on a passive subject from an ego-alien source. Richardson assimilates various recent formulations to his activist model (e.g. Bromley and Shupe, 1979b; Downton, 1980; Lofland, 1978; Straus, 1976; Taylor, 1976; see also Gartrell and Shannon's rational choice model, 1985). On the other hand, the role-theory model of Bromley and Shupe (1979b, 1986), which is intended in part as an alternative to the mind control model, is partly convergent with the latter in *downplaying the prior motivations or predispositions of converts*. The movement is seen as shaping recruits' needs and motives (Bromley and Shupe, 1979b).

The Lofland–Stark Process Model

Aside from brainwashing and allied constructs, the most influential sociological model of conversion–commitment processes in religious movements has been the Lofland–Stark (1965) 'process model', which arose from an influential study of early American followers of Sun Myung Moon (Lofland, 1977; Lofland and Stark, 1965). The Lofland–Stark 'value-added' model identified seven sequential stages through which converts proceeded en route to full commitment. Conversion is accomplished when a person (1) experiences *acute and persistent tensions*, (2) within a *religious problem-solving perspective*, (3) which leads the individual to define himself as a *religious seeker*, (4) after which he encounters the movement at a crucial *turning point* in his life, (5) and forms an *affective bond* with one or more converts, (6) after which *extra-cult attachments become attenuated*, and (7) the convert is exposed to *intensive interaction* within the group and ultimately becomes the group's 'deployable agent' (Lofland and Stark, 1965: 874). Richardson and Stewart (1978) have published an early evaluation of the model's applicability to NRMs.

The pervasive influence of the Lofland–Stark model may be related in part to the fact that it appears to encompass so many factors, e.g. felt tensions, predispositional variables, affective bonds and encapsulation. Subsequent discussions have aimed at discriminating the relative weightings and universality of these factors. However, as Greil and Rudy (1984a) note, Lofland and Stark never made any claims for their formulation as a universally applicable general model of conversion (see also Lofland, 1978). Nevertheless, Greil and Rudy (1984a) note that a number of subsequent researchers and writers have applied the Lofland–Stark model to conversion processes in diverse groups such as Hare Krishna (Judah, 1974), the Divine Light Mission (Downton, 1980), Nichiren Shosha Buddhism (Snow and Phillips, 1980), a UFO group (Balch and Taylor, 1978), the 'Church of the Sun' (Lynch, 1978), fundamentalist 'Crusade House' (Austin, 1977), the 'Christ Communal Organization' (Richardson et al., 1978, 1979), Mormons (Seggar and Kunz, 1972) and a Mormon schismatic sect (Baer, 1978). More recently the model has been applied to a comparative study of Catholic Charismatics, Christian Scientists and Bahai converts (Ebaugh and Vaughn, 1984). Some of these and other analyses have given rise to suggested modifications and qualifications of the Lofland–Stark model (Baer, 1978; Ebaugh and Vaughn, 1984; Greil and Rudy, 1984a; Richardson, 1978a; Snow and Phillips, 1980; Volinn, 1985).

The Greil and Rudy Analysis. In attempting to evaluate the Lofland–Stark process model on the basis of ten earlier empirical case studies which had addressed the model, Greil and Rudy (1984a) encountered certain difficulties. The various studies had not been conducted with an eye to comparison and each researcher supplied his own operational criteria for the process variables. Although the original Lofland–Stark study (1965) analyzed conversion in terms of individual background factors interacting with situational properties, Greil and Rudy felt compelled to take each *group* as the focus of the analysis. Most researchers on conversion have done this 'on the apparent assumption that all individuals who join a particular group bring with them the same background characteristics, join for the same reasons and go through the same changes. There is good reason to doubt that this is always so' (Greil and Rudy, 1984a: 311; see also Austin, 1977: 284–5; Balch, 1980; Gordon, 1974; Pilarzyk, 19787a; Richardson, 1978a; and Wallis, 1977).

A related problem involved the implicit equation of 'conversion' with recruitment by many of the researchers, who did not attempt to gauge the actual degree of *identity transformation* involved. But recruitment qua deciding to participate and 'play the role of convert' is often separate from and temporally discontinuous with 'conversion' in the sense of identity and worldview reconstruction (Balch, 1980; Judah, 1974; Lofland and Skonovd, 1981, 1983; Straus, 1976, 1979b; Zygmunt, 1972).

Greil and Rudy note that since conversion is generally 'conceptualized as a radical reorganization of experience, the converts' accounts of their past experiences may best be seen as products of their new identity-transformation processes', rather than reports of antecedents (Greil and Rudy, 1984a: 312; see also Beckford, 1978a; Lofland, 1978; and Snow and Phillips, 1980). Ideological pressure often leads converts to construct testimonials of the 'I once was lost, but now I'm found' variety (Heirich, 1977), hence the status of the retrospective accounts of converts is a particular problem with respect to the process variables of *felt tensions* and decisive *turning point*. Predictably most of the studies reviewed by Greil and Rudy entail accounts which affirm high levels of *pre-recruitment tensions*, but there is 'no way of knowing whether experiencing tensions distinguishes converts from non-converts' (Greil and Rudy, 1984a: 313). Heirich (1977) reports that the high levels of tension reported by his Catholic Pentecostal converts did not significantly differentiate them from a matched sample of non-Pentecostals. Snow and Phillips (1980) suggest that reports of pre-conversion tension should be viewed as indicative of converts' biographical reconstruction rather than as identifying actual prior feeling-states. Several studies have found that converts to communal movements report high levels of pre-conversion *drug use*, although no control group levels of use were reported (Johnson, 1976; Judah, 1974; Lynch, 1978; Nordquist, 1978).

With regard to the alleged precondition for conversion of a *religious problem-solving perspective*, all but one of the studies reviewed by Greil and Rudy report some degree of disposition to accept a group's ideology prior to encountering the group. Other writers have emphasized the importance of prior ideological backgrounds and dispositions (Gordon, 1974; Harrison, 1974; Richardson, 1978a; Richardson et al., 1978). However, Greil and Rudy downplay the significance of their finding; it is hardly surprising 'that people join movements whose ideologies make sense to them' (Greil and Rudy, 1984a: 314). Galanter (1978, 1980) and Barker (1981, 1984) report some differences regarding emotional and cognitive variables between 'Moonie' converts and persons who attended indoctrination workshops but did not join.

In six out of ten cases there is evidence 'for some pattern of religious seekership' (Greil and Rudy, 1984a: 314). A pattern of *seekership* preceding conversion appears to be associated with stigmatized communal groups in which participation entails discontinuity of social roles. However, 'the "seekers" described in the case studies are not anomic fanatics frantically chasing after meaning, but rather people who seem curious about religious and/or occult matters' (Greil and Rudy, 1984a: 315; see also Balch and Taylor, 1978; Downton, 1979, 1980; Richardson et al., 1978). But other sociologists have claimed that 'addictive' personality types (Simmonds, 1978) or disoriented persons with character disorders (Levine, 1980b) are 'susceptible' to conversion to cults (see also Snow and Machalek, 1984: 180).

Most of the respondents of all but one of the studies (Seggar and Kunz, 1972) reported that contact with the group coincided with a *turning point* in their lives, but Greil and Rudy also suspect retrospective biographical reconstruction here. 'In the convert's eyes it is the fact of the experience of conversion that defines the turning point as a turning point' (Greil and Rudy 1984a: 315–16). Greil and Rudy conclude that, there are 'conceptual weaknesses with the formulation of three of Lofland and Stark's seven prerequisites for conversion (e.g. "tensions", "religious problem-solving perspective" and "turning point")', which disincline them to give much credence to the studies' data relating to these issues (Greil and Rudy, 1984a: 317).

In eight out of ten studies the formation of *affective bonds* appeared to be a significant aspect of the conversion process. In six out of Greil and Rudy's ten cases conversion appeared to be associated with the *neutralization* or absence of extra-group affective ties. 'Neutralization of extra-cult attachments seems most important in groups where conversion involves a radical transformation of social roles and where conversion involves the sacrifice of social respectability' (Greil and Rudy, 1984a: 316). Greil and Rudy (1984: 16) note that their analysis supports the argument of Snow and Phillips (1980: 442) that 'neutralization of extra-cult attachments will be an important part of the conversion process primarily in the context of "deviant" groups' (Greil and Rudy, 1984a: 316) when significant others will likely oppose the convert's new commitment (see also Richardson and Stewart, 1978).

All ten studies reviewed by Greil and Rudy indicated that *intensive interaction* was a vital element of the conversion process, with a partial exception of a study of a UFO cult (Balch and Taylor, 1978).

Greil and Rudy conclude that the Lofland–Stark model appears to have its strongest applicability to *deviant* groups which entail a radical transformation of the new members' social roles. 'Thus the Lofland–Stark model seems to describe accurately the religious conversion process as it occurs in *one organizational context*' (Greil and Rudy, 1984a: 317) (our emphasis). Groups such as Crusade House, the Levites, and Nichiren Shoshu, which are not highly stigmatized and do not drastically transform the social roles of converts, are able to recruit new members from pre-existing social networks. Conversion of prior 'seekers' and neutralization of extra-cult attachments are manifested less by such groups than by communal groups such as the Unification Church or Hare Krishna, which are perceived as highly deviant and involve a radical discontinuity of social roles (see also Greil and Rudy, 1984b; Rochford, 1982; Snow et al., 1980).

Boundary control between members and non-members is a crucial imperative for what Greil and Rudy elsewhere (1984b) call identity transforming organizations (ITOs). Such groups, which include rehabilitation programs and deprogramming operations as well as some NRMs, endeavor to create 'social cocoons' through patterns of physical and/or social and/or ideological *encapsulation* which promotes intensive interaction among members and limits the potential effects of interaction between members and non-members (Greil and Rudy, 1984a,b). ITOs may thus be seen as *systems* in which the system property of boundary maintenance is crucial and is supported by an intensive indoctrinational process (Galanter, 1985). Neutralization of extra-group bonds is a crucial component of encapsulation, e.g. Galanter (1980) reports that joiners of the Unification Church are differentiated from persons who flirted with joining but ultimately chose not to make a commitment by the latter's larger number of 'outside affiliations'. Greil and Rudy suggest that the high defection rate in the Unification Church, which Long and Hadden (1983) explain in terms of inadequate cognitive socialization, 'may be due rather to the difficulties inherent in trying to maintain the boundary between members and non-members' (Greil and Rudy, 1984a: 318; see also 1984b). Nevertheless, Long and Hadden's analysis illustrates Greil and Rudy's argument that effective encapsulation of converts is inhibited by simultaneous organizational needs to obtain funds and recruits, e.g. the Moonist emphasis on quick *certification* and *deployment* of participants interfered with effective indoctrination and led to high defection rates when devotees were deployed outside of (intensively interacting) communal centers (Bromley and Shupe, 1979a; Long and Hadden, 1983).

Greil and Rudy (1984a: 318) affirm the dictum of Snow and Phillips (1980: 444) that 'the interactive process holds the key to understanding conversion'. To 'convert' is to come to see oneself as a particular reference group sees one, 'to see that reality is what one's friends say it is' (Greil and Rudy, 1984a: 318; see also Lofland and Stark, 1965: 871, and Stark and Bainbridge, 1980a). Notwithstanding the difference between what Greil and Rudy (1984a) call 'type one' groups, which entail role-discontinuity, communal totalism and deviant stigmatization, and less radical 'type-two' groups, 'the essential dynamic of the conversion process remains the same. . . any religious group which is to be successful in facilitating the conversion of recruits will need to be structured in such a way as to foster intensive interaction among group members' (Greil and Rudy, 1984a: 318).

As an alternative to the causal process or state-sequential approach, Greil and Rudy discuss an *organizational approach* which 'emphasizes the way in which organizational patterns of interaction are structured so as to encourage the acceptance of a new world' (Greil and Rudy, 1984a: 319; see, as examples, Balch, 1980; Bromley and Shupe, 1979b; Gerlach and Hine, 1970; Greil and Rudy, 1984b; Harrison, 1974; Kanter, 1972). Another alternative to process theory is the 'subject-centred' (Straus, 1976, 1979b) or 'drift' (Long and Hadden, 1983) perspective, which focuses on how social actors *creatively construct for themselves the role of the convert* and thus 'accomplish' their conversion. A third alternative is medicalistic brainwashing theory, which explains conversions in terms of the use of unorthodox and powerful psychological techniques. Greil and Rudy contrast the organizational and brainwashing approaches and criticize the latter's somewhat *non-sociological* orientation; 'the difference between conversion and other kinds of socialization lies not in the psychological processes involved but in the organizational context in which it takes place' (Greil and Rudy, 1984a: 319–20). Greil and Rudy criticize Long and Hadden (1983) for implicitly equating the organizational and brainwashing approaches.

Wilson (1983) also evaluates the Lofland–Stark model and stresses the importance of *deconditioning* supplementing positive socialization in 'Becoming a Yogi'. A number of reports have emphasized the key significance of *ritual* in creating or reinforcing commitment (Bird, 1978;

Halloman, 1974; Jacobs, 1986; Kanter, 1972; McGuire, 1977, 1982; Palmer, 1986a, 1988; Preston, 1981; Volinn, 1985; Westley, 1978b).

Social Networks

Some of the studies reviewed by Greil and Rudy (1984a), particularly that by Snow and Phillips (1980), explore the role of social networks in explaining recruitment to social movements and social movement organizations (SMOs). Social network studies of NRM recruitment are related to the current broader vogue for social network analysis in sociology. However, the ancestry of the Lofland–Stark model and its stress on affective bonds is also generally recognized by analysts studying 'networks of faith' (Stark and Bainbridge, 1980a) and NRMs (Snow and Phillips, 1980; Snow et al., 1980).

There are a number of important social network analyses of NRM recruitment (Jorgensen, 1982; Rochford, 1982; Snow and Phillips, 1980; Snow et al., 1980; Stark and Bainbridge, 1980a). A paper by Snow et al. (1980) is particularly provocative. Snow and his colleagues conclude that 'the probability of being recruited into a particular movement is largely a function of two conditions: (1) links to one or more movement members through a pre-existing or emergent interpersonal tie; and (2) the absence of countervailing networks' (Snow et al., 1980: 798). In effect one is likely to be recruited to a movement to the degree that one is already linked to members through extra-movement social networks and to the degree that one is not inhibited by countervailing influences including alternative social networks which do not involve members as well as 'extraneous commitments such as spouse, children, debts and occupational reputation' (Snow et al., 1980: 794). To the degree that an individual is detached from such commitments and from 'countervailing networks', he or she is *structurally available* for recruitment to a social movement. Volinn (1985) uses the concept of structural availability to analyze recruitment to a meditation group.

It follows from the above that movements which are connected to potential recruits through interpersonal networks are likely to grow faster and larger than 'movements which are structurally more isolated and closed' (Snow et al., 1980: 797). The latter tend to be movements which require the *exclusive participation of members* such that the latter are encouraged to cut themselves off from extra-movement networks and involvements., Such 'totalistic' groups will tend to employ proselyti-zation strategies which entail an *outreach to strangers and social isolates* who are contacted in public places such as airports or bus depots. More 'inclusive' movements which do not require members to cut themselves off from prior and extra-movement involvements will be more likely to rely upon extra-movement interpersonal associations and social networks, i.e. members will bring in their prior associates, friends and kin.

Snow et al. support their theory with data from a comparative analysis of recruitment to Hare Krishna and Nichiren Shoshu Buddhism. The latter attempt public proselytizing but do not carry it off successfully and end up recruiting primarily from existing social networks. The more stringently communal and totalistic Hare Krishna have tended to pressure recruits to sever extra-movement ties, and are thus compelled to seek their recruits in public places and recruit a larger proportion of 'alienated' and socially unattached persons (Snow et al., 1980). A more recent analysis by Rochford (1982, 1985), however, reports that the pattern of Hare Krishna recruitment has actually varied significantly from city to city as the Krishnas have exploited local opportunity structures. In some locations there has indeed been substantial recruitment from social networks. The role of social networks in ISKON recruitment is growing as the movement increasingly relies on financial and other supports from part-time devotees and sympathizers (Rochford, 1985: 166). But Snow et al.'s point concerning the greater efficacy of social network recruitment is supported by Stark (1984), who compares Mormon recruitment via existing networks with the tendency of the 'Moonies' to target social isolates (often persons new to a given area) with whom intense attachments can rapidly be built up. Stark's subsequent investigation of Mormons 'has revealed the superiority of recruitment strategies based on gaining access to new social *networks*. For then, much more sustained and rapid growth is possible as conversion spreads through *preexisting* social bonds' (Stark, 1984: 26; see also Stark and Bainbridge, 1980a; Stark and Roberts, 1982; Stark, 1987a). The heavy recruitment of social isolates may have a delayed negative feedback effect on further recruitment as prior social isolates, unlike the charismatic founders of movements, are likely to lack the social skills to function as effective recruiters (Stark and Roberts, 1982).

A forceful critique of Snow et al.'s alleged mechanistic approach to movement recruitment has been mounted by Wallis and Bruce (1982, 1986). 'Snow et al. fail to appreciate that recruitment strategies are not independent of movements' goals and beliefs about the world' (Wallis and Bruce, 1982: 104). Hare Krishna's conspicuous ethos of 'world-rejection' (Wallis, 1978c, 1984) provokes hostility and places them at a disadvantage with regard to recruitment of persons tied to conventional commitments and networks. Differential Hare Krishna and Nichiren Shoshu patterns of recruitment cannot therefore be said to be '*"largely"* a function of networks rather than of what. . . [Hare Krishna] has to offer, and of the cultural distance between potential constituency and movement membership' (Wallis and Bruce, 1982: 104).

Wallis and Bruce mount a broad conceptual assault on the 'variable' of *structural availability*. 'Availability is not a fixed quality. Whether we are *available* for adultery despite our wives, children, and loan payments will often depend upon who exactly offers us their company' (Wallis and Bruce, 1982: 106). A married man with a family might be 'available' for a romantic liaison with Brooke Shields but not with Margaret Thatcher.

> Similarly, whether we are available for recruitment to a social movement will depend upon its aims, legitimacy, personnel, methods, etc. In short, network ties and commitments are strong or weak *only in retrospect* when we see whether they have been countervailing factors or not. . . recruitment to a social movement cannot in any sense be understood without exploration of the meaning-endowing activity of the pre-recruit, his active construction of the movement, its aims and importance and his reconstruction of his biography, commitments and relationships in this light (Wallis and Bruce, 1982: 106; see also Wallis and Bruce, 1986).

Wuthnow (1981a, 1987) has criticized the current 'sociometrical reductionism' whereby interpersonal bonds are treated as the underlying 'objective' factor which 'explains' putatively subjective beliefs.

Notwithstanding the above, it appears to this writer that the concept of 'structural availability' may be useful if it is not treated reductively as a simple substitute for analysis of meaningful motivation and predisposition. Imaginatively 'controlling for' the latter, some persons are objectively less socially anchored and thus more 'available' for recruitment. Why have NRMs recruited primarily young persons (Snow and Machalek, 1984: 181–2)? 'Being young, single, free from occupational ties, or a student makes for a kind of structural availability that affords people the discretionary or unscheduled time to participate in religious movements' (Snow and Machalek, 1984: 182). Recently some concern has been expressed over the (putatively exploitative) recruitment of elderly persons to cults (Rudin, 1984). Are not elderly persons now 'available' in the somewhat similar sense that young persons are, i.e. they are becoming detached from former social networks, occupational commitments and familial responsibilities? Interestingly, Wallis and Bruce seem to employ an implicit notion of structural availability in analyzing the recruitment of affluent autonomous professionals to the Bhagwan movement (Wallis and Bruce, 1986: 202–3).

Defection and Deconversion

At this time there appears to be a shift of scholarly attention from processes of conversion and commitment to processes of deconversion and disengagement. Perhaps this reflects a perceived waning of the surge of NRMs (see Ch. 1). Nevertheless, at this writing much of the relevant analytical material is in press or in preparation (see Beckford, 1985a: 135–48 for a review and analysis of early studies). This section presents a very preliminary report on available materials.

It has been noted earlier in this chapter that the pervasive implicit equation between conversion and recruitment has been a source of confusion in the scholarly conversion literature. The analogous *equation of deconversion and disaffiliation* is common in the literature reviewed here. See Brinkerhoff and Burke (1980), however, for a theoretical distinction between personal commitment to belief and communal commitment and a discussion of different paths of disaffiliation from total (communal plus personal) commitment to total apostasy.

A typology or formal comprehensive classification of modes of disaffiliation has been developed by Richardson et al. (1986). The authors distinguish among *exiting* or disaffiliation initiated by a member, *expulsion*, in which the organization initiates disaffiliation, and *extraction*, in which the disaffiliative process is initiated by an external agent (e.g. relative, spouse, friend, or counselor). Extraction is subdivided into coercive and non-coercive extraction. Richardson et al. suggest that the likelihood of a particular mode of disaffiliation being attempted and being successful will depend upon whether the movement is communal or non-communal, and whether it embodies an amorphous and poorly bounded 'cult-like group' or a more cohesive and doctrinaire 'sect-like group'. Richardson et al. (1986) use labeling theory and existing research reports to delineate the patterning of each mode of disaffiliation in each organizational setting. The categories formulated by Richardson et al. will be used to organize our review.

It may be questioned, however, whether in actual cases it is always clear which mode of disaffiliation is being enacted. Solomon (1981) argues that 'intervention' of some sort (e.g. counseling, therapy, rehabilitation, or deprogramming) is so ubiquitous that the distinction between 'voluntary' and 'involuntary' (i.e. coercive and non-coercive) disaffiliation is often unclear. Moreover, in terms of the attitudes and retrospective interpretations of ex-members, what is important is not so much the tenuous voluntary/involuntary distinction but the *degree of intervention* and the putatively correlated factor of assimilation to a supportive network of ex-members and an anti-cult social movement. It is also likely that the pressures operating in 'extractive' situations may blur the distinction between coercive and non-coercive extraction, or between extraction and exiting. 'Actually, the line of demarcation distinguishing voluntary and involuntary "aids" to exiting (exit therapy, counseling, rehabilitation) has become blurred at times and problematic' (Wright, 1985: 1). But the distinction between extraction (coercive or non-coercive) and spontaneous exiting can also be problematic, as when an already discontented devotee is rendered susceptible to the communications of extractive agents seeking to extract him. Finally, a discontented member may express his dissidence in such a manner that his disaffiliation is suggested by other members or leaders, i.e. the line between exiting and expulsion can thus be indistinct. The situation is further complicated by the temporal or sequential factor. A person who is forcibly removed from a group may later voluntarily decide whether to return; coerced physical removal may or may not lead to inner deconversion. The latter might be conceived as a sequential process with coercive and non-coercive or extractive (pressured) and spontaneous phases.

Exiting. Sociologists have continually maintained that contemporary NRMs, whether 'totalistic' or embodying a non-residential 'limited liability' pattern, usually exhibit *high rates of spontaneous defection* (Barker, 1981, 1984; Bird and Reimer, 1982; Bromley and Shupe, 1981; Jacobs, 1984; Ofshe, 1976; Rochford, 1985; Shupe and Bromley, 1980a; Skonovd, 1981, 1983; Wright, 1984, 1987). This insight undercut the stereotypical belief that 'young people who are entrapped by a cult generally do not come out by themselves. They need to be deprogrammed' (Hershell and Hershell, 1982: 131). Are voluntary leavers generally persons who have only been in a group for a short time (Hershell and Hershell, 1982)? Ungerleider and Wellisch (1979) report that the successfully deprogrammed subjects in their sample (i.e. those who did not return to their NRM) tended to have been involved for less than one year, while voluntary leavers tended to leave *after* the first year (see also Richardson et al., 1986).

Wright (1985, 1987) has reviewed studies of 'purely voluntary' exits. Unfortunately, 'research on the mechanics of leave-taking has raised more questions than it has answered' (Wright, 1985: 1). Existing studies have produced conflicting findings. Beckford reports that persons departing from the Unification Church in Great Britain rarely made explicit plans for leaving: 'the decision to leave was usually taken on the spur of the moment and was not followed by any careful planning for the move' (Beckford, 1985a: 159). In contrast Skonovd (1981: 122, 1983) talks about 'strategies of leave-taking' and suggests that most departures tend to be covert.

Wright's sample, developed through 'snowballing' from initial respondents who responded to posters and newspaper ads on university campuses, entailed forty-five in-depth interviewees, who seemed to have enacted *three basic patterns of exiting* (Wright, 1985, 1987). Forty-two percent of the interviewees appear to have enacted *covert* departures involving stealth and secrecy. Forty-seven percent of the departees were *overt* leavers whose departures were quiet and 'without fanfare' but not distinctly secretive. A few of the ex-members, however, had made *declarative* departures in which they demonstratively affirmed their intentions and presented their reasons, thereby clearly and decisively settling the issue of disaffiliation. Overt/declarative disengagement seemed to be significantly associated with *length of membership*, e.g. most of the covert departees had been members for less than a year:

> We can generalize the observed patterns of leave-taking by saying that covert defectors tend to be novices who demonstrate a proclivity to wrestle with vague, unfocused discontents or deep emotional attachments which may be difficult for them to manage or articulate in an open confrontation with leaders. These individuals express a greater inability to cope with dissonance that accompanies an overt mode of exit and consequently, they choose to leave by the back door. Overt defectors are more likely to be seasoned members who become involved in conflicts over explicit policy-related issues which prompt a direct approach to conflict-resolution through open confrontation or negotiation. Declarative defectors are veterans who confront, but do not wish to negotiate. There is no longer anything they wish to gain (Wright, 1985: 14–15; see also Wright, 1987).

Thus each mode of exiting is said to manifest its own inner logic and is associated with a distinctive complex of individual and social factors (Wright, 1985, 1987).

Richardson et al. (1986) suggest that exiting from a communal group will be significantly different from exiting from a non-communal group. Balch (1985b) suggests that organizational totalism has a far greater impact on the nature of defection than does belief system. Departees from non-communal groups may resemble 'denomination switchers' who glide in and out of various groups (Richardson et al., 1978, 1986; Wallis, 1977: 183–9). On the other hand, members of communal organizations are likely to have a lot more 'investments' of varying types within the group, which is likely to exercise substantial control over its members (see Beckford, 1978b). 'Such a situation is one of *limited viable alternatives*. The group could find ways to bring subtle (and perhaps not-so-subtle) pressures to bear on such a person to discourage thoughts of leaving, thus prolonging the process of disaffiliation' (Richardson et al., 1986: 9). 'Some groups have special counseling for persons who are considering defecting and/or members are expected to report potential defectors to leaders, i.e. there is an "early warning system" which allows rapid activation of procedures to deter the defection' (Richardson et al., 1986: 104).

The issue of defection can sometimes be traumatic for a close-knit communal group, particularly with a charismatic leadership. Anxiety and 'paranoia' about past and future defections was central to the escalating tension which led up to the mass suicide/homicide at Jonestown in 1978 (Hall, 1981, 1987; Weightman, 1983).

Often, however, 'the pressure to remain in the group may derive in part from the simple fact of not having anything of value to take with one, or anywhere to go that seems better' (Richardson et al., 1986: 104). Members' level of 'investment', their dependency on the group and the multiplication of 'side bets' such as friendships, work roles, or food, clothing and shelter obtained through involvement with the group and presupposing further participation may be so great as to make exiting very difficult (Kanter, 1972: 80–2); Ofshe, 1982; Richardson et al., 1986; Skonovd, 1981: 103–12). Thus the dependency of the devotee on the organization may be tangible and structural as much as (or more than) 'psychological'. But when the continued involvement of individuals with a cult is explained in terms of 'brainwashing', voluntary exiting tends to be explained in terms of inadvertent 'weak points' and imperfections bedeviling the brainwashing process such as ' "incomplete suppression" of undesirable thoughts' through repetitive chanting and other mind control techniques (Appel, 1983: 145; Clark et al., 1981). This model would appear to imply that, were it not for glitches in the brainwashing process, all converts would be totally socialized and docile.

Motivational Dynamics of Exiting. A fascinating study by Jacobs (1984) examines the voluntary departure of female devotees as it relates to *sexual exploitation* in religious movements. Jacobs' conclusions are based on in-depth interviews with forty former religious devotees to a variety of groups including Hindu, Buddhist and Charismatic Christian groups. Jacobs maintains that any religious organization sustains an 'emotional economy' for its participants which is particularly vital for women members. In joining NRMs Jacobs' respondents appear to have been influenced by romantic idealism arising from a familial socialization which disposed them to seek an overpowering but 'loving' male to submit to. Over time this idealism tended to be undermined by a growing perception of a substantial *unequal exchange* characterizing the organization's 'economy of love' (see also Ch. 2). Defection occurred when this perception clearly crystallized.

There were three kinds of issues which tended to generate a perception of unequal exchange: (1) sexual exploitation of the devotee by a guru or cult leader, particularly in a 'harem' context (but defection tended to occur only after the leader had rejected and replaced the once favored devotee); (2) the tendency for psychological and (occasionally) physical abuse of women devotees by devotee-husbands to be positively sanctioned by movement leaders; and (3) role conflict related to the sharp contrast between the emphasis on chaste and passive feminine behavior within the group and the expectation that women should act aggressively and seductively outside the group to solicit funds and lure young males to join (see also Wallis, 1978a,b). Thus the romantic idealism of the devotee could be destroyed by direct exploitation, physical or psychological abuse, or being locked into an extreme variant of a traditional domestic sex role. See also Wright (1986, 1987) who compares defection and control of interpersonal dyads in three groups.

In an analysis of 'deconversion from authoritarian movements' based on the same study, Jacobs (1987) re-examines the relationship between defection and growing disaffection mediated by the severing of socioemotional ties to the movement and the charismatic leader. The primary complaint of defectors was restrictions on their social life. A two-stage separative process is delineated in which first the bonds to the group are broken and subsequently there is emotional disengagement from the leader. It is the latter bond between leader and follower which is particularly crucial for sustaining continued commitment to the movement (Jacobs, 1987b). The leader–follower bond derives its strength from the capacity of the former to gratify the basic needs of the latter through the role of 'god the father' and 'god the ego ideal'. Doubt and disillusionment emerge as the leader's actions suggest not godliness but arbitrariness, betrayal, abuse and deception. Disaffiliation will likely ensue if the devotee has an alternate source of spiritual satisfaction available.

Balch (1985b) found that defectors from a UFO cult, whom he directly observed during their defection, tended to *reconstruct reality in preparation* for defection, in effect constructing a new 'vocabulary of motives' legitimating their exodus from the group. This 'symbolic bridge-building' functioned to ease the transition back to a world which they had previously abandoned. Large-scale defections can arise from prophetic disconfirmation (Balch et al., 1983) or other developments (Downton, 1979; Ofshe, 1980b).

Mediated Disaffiliation. Whether or not coercion is employed, the convert's biological family is often actively involved in their child's disaffiliation. 'Under conditions in which converts grow disillusioned with a cult and seek to reenter the cultural mainstream', comment Wright and Piper (1986: 17), 'it is reasonable to assume that the family serves as an important link in this transition'. 'Moreover, parental disapproval was particularly effective among youth who reported a smooth adolescent experience and to a lesser extent a closeness to family before joining' (Wright, 1986: 22). Favorable parental attitudes toward the NRM were related to remaining in a movement among those devotees who reported a pre-entry familial closeness. Non-leavers were four times as likely as leavers to report parental approval. Wright and Piper conclude that whether a convert chooses to remain in a movement or leave 'is to some degree influenced by that person's parents and the quality of family life in the years preceding conversion' (Wright and Piper, 1986: 22).

When mediation by parents and/or other agents is very active, disaffiliation would be classified by Richardson et al. (1986) as *extraction*; although, as we have suggested, the operational boundary between extraction and exiting may be ambiguous, as is the boundary between non-coercive and coercive extraction. Coercive deprogramming, a topic surrounded by sensationalism, will be discussed in the next subsection. However, Shupe and Bromley (1980a) have discussed a less coercive variety of deprogramming or very actively mediated disaffiliation which does not entail physical force and which they term *re-evaluation*. The term *exit counseling* has also been used when persons claiming special expertise and professional or paraprofessional status (frequently ex-members) are involved. Such 'counselors' are usually not well-integrated into professional psychotherapy (Sullivan, 1984a).

The re-evaluation process usually involves someone with affective ties to the member raising objections to his membership and thereby commencing 'a dialogue or interaction that involves a reassessment of that membership' (Richardson et al., 1986: 102). Physical coercion is generally dispensed with, although strong psychological pressures may

be mobilized. As 'a more benign alternative' to abrasive and confrontational procedures based on physical coercion, two clinicians suggest the
following procedure, to be instituted once a family can convince a devotee
to visit home and can then 'convene the entire family and friends as we
do when undertaking network family therapy' (Schwartz and Kaslow,
1982: 24):

> Instead of using a deprogrammer, a team of well-qualified network therapists, who
> are familiar with the various cults and their modus operandi, can be invited to be in
> charge. Familiarity with the specific cult involved in and its jargon would be advan-
> tageous. Networks share numerous properties with cults, and this should introduce
> a familiar and treasured part of the cult atmosphere into the session — thus making
> the transition a little easier. The lead therapist is usually a powerful figure who emits
> a sense that he can heal those in his charge, and help them garner the strength and
> motivation to make the requisite changes in their lives (Schwartz and Kawslow, 1982:
> 24–5).

Effective re-evaluation, deprogramming and exit counseling will
thus be more likely to succeed when the process *furnishes an alternative affiliative and support structure for the extractee*. But such
procedures are only possible if contact and communication are possible
between the member and those who question his involvement. Some
groups discourage contacts and may try to block communication. Extraction may thus be more difficult when the individual is involved in a
tightly knit communal group (Richardson et al., 1986), and in this
case relatives seeking to extract a devotee will be most likely to resort
to physical coercion. However, an evaluation study (Eichel et al., 1984)
reports greater 'success' attained by a non-coercive anti-cult counseling
program compared to either deprogramming or conventional psychotherapy.

Coercive Deprogramming. Deprogramming refers to intensive sessions
of 'information-giving' aimed at facilitating the extraction and inner
deconversion of a devotee. 'Voluntary deprogramming' may be indistin-
guishable from re-evaluation or exit counseling. Coercive deprogramming
entails the physical seizure of a devotee who becomes a captive audience
for re-evaluative communications. Brutality and 'third degree' trauma
are less common now than in the 1970s (Robbins, 1979; Shupe et al.,
1978). Coercive deprogramming is usually extra-legal but particular
deprogrammings were frequently legalized through the granting of tempo-
rary guardianships and conservatorships to parents in the 1970s (Robbins
and Anthony, 1982a; Shupe and Bromley, 1980a). Attempts to explicitly

legalize deprogramming on a general basis through amendment of the guardianship and conservatorship statutes almost succeeded in several states in the early 1980s, but were blocked ultimately (Robbins and Anthony, 1982a), although the legal situation with regard to prosecution and civil action against deprogrammers is very murky (Bromley, 1983; Robbins, 1985g, 1986c). Coercive extractions have been more prevalent in the United States than in Europe or Canada (Beckford, 1981b, 1985a; Wallis, in press). Deprogramming has been much studied by social scientists (Beckford, 1985a; Bromley and Perry, 1986; Bromley and Shupe, 1981; Galanter, 1983b; Kim, 1979; Langone, 1984; Levine, 1980a; Shupe and Bromley, 1980a; Shupe et al., 1978; Solomon, 1981; Ungerleider and Wellisch, 1979; Wright, 1983).

Notwithstanding the element of physical coercion there are clearly elements of *negotiation* in the deprogramming process which produces relatively 'successful' deprogramming outcomes:

> In order for a person to agree with the deprogrammers and decide to leave a group of which they were a member, a *justificatory* or *excusatory account* must be developed to explain why a person joined in the first place. It is not in the interest of the deprogrammers and parents to promote the idea that the person was stupid and made a dumb mistake when they joined the movement. This type of approach would not be acceptable to many deprogrammees. Instead, *an account must be negotiated that is acceptable to all concerned*, the member, the parents, and *other significant others* (Richardson et al., 1986: 110).

A similar point is made by Skonovd (1983) who studied defectors from totalistic movements and who discusses how deprogrammers promote the social reintegration of the ex-devotee of an unconventional communal group by providing the deprogrammee with an *alternative interpretive framework* for his involvement with a stigmatized movement:

> After inducing dissonance . . . deprogrammers typically present a 'brainwashing model' of conversion and membership in religious 'cults'. This is a type of 'medical model' which absolves individuals of responsibility for their own conversions, for remaining in the group, and for behaving in 'abnormal' ways while in, based upon the argument that they were brainwashed into converting and then manipulated by mind control. The 'brainwashing model' also holds out the promise of 'health' — the promise of a viable existence apart from the movement in which the individual can experience independence and intellectual freedom once again. This facilitates apostasy in a way similar to that of adopting a competing religious world view. Such a model or paradigm provides a cognitive structure with which individuals can interpret the cultic world view and their respective experiences in it, as well as anticipate a life outside it (Skonovd, 1983: 101).

The accounts of various social scientists who have studied deprogramming, 'imply a labeling of all the principals in the deprogramming situation. This labeling focuses on the agency' (Richardson et al., 1986: 110). The authors analyze the role of labeling in the various modes of disaffiliation, particularly extraction and expulsion. Kim (1979) uses related symbolic interactionism as well as Schein et al.'s (1961) coercive persuasion model to analyze the sequence of deprogramming–rehabilitation.

What proportion of deprogrammings 'succeed'? A study (Langone, 1984) based on questionnaires printed in a 'concerned citizens' or anti-cult journal indicates that 37 percent of deprogrammings resulted in the convert returning to the NRM. 'Hence it seems reasonable to conclude that, on the average, one-fourth to one-third of forced deprogrammings result in the converts returning to the cult' (Langone, 1984: 74). Langone's data suggest that 39 percent of the sample of questionnaire respondents left a movement voluntarily without any deprogramming (40 percent left after physically coercive, i.e. abductive deprogramming, and 21 percent left after voluntarily undergoing deprogramming). Langone (1984: 74) suggests that 'the true voluntary departure rate' including ex-members 'who do not come in contact with the concerned citizens network' may be significantly higher, given his methodology.

There is presently some dispute as to whether deprogramming traumatizes devotees and threatens their mental health (Barker, 1984; Judah, 1974; Kilbourne, 1983; Lewis, 1986; Lewis and Bromley, 1988; Levine, 1980b; Ungerleider and Wellisch, 1979) or is helpful to converts damaged by cults (Conway and Siegelman, 1978; Carmichael, 1986; Levine, 1985; Conway and Siegelman, 1982). It seems likely that the practice of coercive deprogramming is now declining as a result of: (1) some degree of legal deterrence (Bromley, 1983; Robbins, 1985f, 1986c); (2) the falling recruitment rate of notorious 'destructive cults' such as the Unification Church or Hare Krishna; and (3) the professionalization and consequent moderation of the ACM, which has moved away from legitimation and advocacy of deprogramming (Bromley and Shupe, 1987; Shupe, 1985). Barker (1983d, 1984) argues that the threat of deprogramming has enhanced solidarity among Moonies.

The recrimination against cults for brainwashing converts has derived much of its popular plausibility from the accounts of ex-members, who have often become ACM activists. Research by sociologists has revealed that there is really a wide range of attitudes to be found among ex-converts, and recriminative attitudes are exhibited primarily by ex-members who have been deprogrammed or have otherwise been involved in ex-member support groups and therapeutic programs linked to the ACM (Beckford, 1985a; Lewis, 1986; Skonovd, 1981; Solomon, 1981; Wright, 1984). Voluntary defectors sometimes appear confused or ambivalent and unwilling to contribute to public discourse over cults (Beckford, 1985a), in contrast to deprogrammed ex-devotees who may appear to confidently 'know the answers' and to be themselves committed to working as deprogrammers or exit counselors and to speaking out against cults, etc.

An interesting study of ex-converts is that of Solomon (1981), who interviewed and distributed questionnaires to 100 former adherents of the Unification Church. Solomon's sample was obtained through contacts with the concerned citizens or ACM network and thus 67 percent of her respondents had been deprogrammed. Nevertheless, she found that how much 'intervention' the ex-devotee had experienced during or before his exit correlated with whether the respondent was now antagonistic to the UC and whether he or she accepted the brainwashing explanation of his or her involvement. Intervention meant 'deprogramming', 'rehabilitation', or 'therapy'. The latter could be situation-centered, in which case it tended to focus on cultist mind control, or person-centered, i.e. focusing on the individual's personality. Deprogramming and rehabilitation, which are often orchestrated in sequence (Kim, 1979), tend to entail counter-indoctrination about mind control. Solomon feels that the amount of intervention a person experiences can be treated as a measure of the individual's *exposure to a supportive ex-member social network linked to an anti-cult subculture*:

> It can readily be seen that contact with the anticult movement, either at the point of exit or subsequent to that time, serves an important reference-group function for former members searching for a framework within which to view their experiences. It is also influential in defining postexit attitudes and values. It is indeed ironic that this function is in many ways similar to the role played by the [Unification] Church in providing recruits with a new view in which to perceive their past and present lives (Solomon, 1981: 293).

A systematic replication of Solomon's study has been attempted by Lewis (1986) using a sample ($n=157$) 'snowballed' from contacts with both cult and anti-cult groups. Extent and duration of involvement with the ACM as well as involuntary mode of exiting were significantly correlated with negative and 'stereotypical' attitudes toward cults.

Expulsion. As Richardson et al. (1986) note, it is not common knowledge that some NRMs actually compel the disaffiliation of some members by expelling them. 'When a new group is organizing, its leaders might be less careful about who is allowed to affiliate. After the group has established itself and acquired some resources, one would expect more care in allowing people in to share limited resources' (Richardson et al., 1986: 101). Issues involved in expulsion from NRMs generally tend to involve the following: (1) dissidence, insubordination and challenges to authority (Rochford, 1985; Straus, 1986; Wallis, 1977); (2) rule-breaking (Straus, 1986); and (3) the incapacity of those devotees who cannot care for themselves, or who may embarrass the group or be unable to contribute to enhancing the movement's resources (Beckford, 1985a).

Dissidence and intragroup conflict also motivate voluntary exiting (Rochford, 1985). Rule-breaking may entail the refusal of members of a close-knit communal group to break ties or identification with other groups and bonds (Richardson et al., 1986). Thus expulsion is probably more frequent and easier to accomplish (i.e. harder for a devotee to fend off) in a *communal* group (Richardson et al., 1986). Cults have been accused of 'dumping' incapacitated members, whose problems may be partly due to the traumatic intensity of indoctrination. On the other hand, it has been claimed that cults tend to recruit maladjusted individuals (Levine, 1980b; Maleson, 1981; Simmonds, 1978). The UC has definitely expelled some incapacitated individuals (Beckford, 1985a: 207–9).

It is probably not always possible to discriminate between expulsion and voluntary defection (exiting). Defections may be sparked by the sudden imposition of austere commitment rituals such as vasectomies at Synanon (Ofshe, 1980b) or traumatic recruitment tactics such as sexualized 'flirty fishing' in the Children of God (Wallis and Bruce, 1986). In the case of commitment rituals and other sudden impositions, the leadership may seem to be instituting de facto mass expulsions of certain devotees who are deemed to be not totally loyal or opposed to new directions and are thus being forced to defect (Ofshe, 1980b). Intra-movement conflict and policy disputes as well as attenuation of leadership charisma can suddenly increase the rate of defection (Rochford, 1985). Some defections may be related to movement splintering or schisms (Rochford, 1987).

Unlike exiting and deprogramming, there has been little systematic theory or research on expulsion. There is a substantial amount of research on voluntary defection just published or forthcoming, including a monograph (Wright, 1987) and a reader (Bromley, 1988a). The latter contains a section on disaffiliation from mainline churches, including a paper on Mormon defection (Albrecht), and a section on 'Disaffiliation from Alternative Religious Groups'. The latter also includes papers on defection from the Unification Church (Barker), defection from contemporary communes (Zablocki), a review essay on recent research (Wright), a paper on 'Social and Emotional Problems Associated with Leave-Taking' (Rothbaum), a paper on deprogramming (Bromley) and an analysis of 'The Impact of Apostates on the Trajectory of Religious Movements: The Case of Jonestown' (Hall).

4

ORGANIZATION AND TRANSFORMATION
OF MOVEMENTS

This chapter deals largely with the growing literature on the institutionalization and transformation of NRMs over time. This is an increasingly
significant topic as two facts are becoming apparent. Firstly, some current
NRMs appear to be highly *volatile* and to undergo institutionalization
or other transformational processes more rapidly than have past movements. Movements such as the Bhagwan Movement of Rajneesh are
'manufactured' in the sense that 'beliefs, practices, corporate identities
and physical location may be changed quickly to suit necessities and
convenience of the moment. . . Their social systems and legal identities
are very impermanent' (Carter, 1987: 149). Secondly, the survival of some
current movements appears to be precarious (Bromley and Hammond,
1987; Wilson, 1987), and continuous adaptations to shifting environmental forces and properties are vital (Richardson, 1985b). Such
adaptations have substantial implications for organizational and doctrinal
properties of evolving NRMs as well as internal social control practices.
The present chapter thus deals with *change* in NRMs, which is ubiquitous,
such that any account of a particular movement at a given point in time
constitutes at best a 'snapshot' of a fluctuating entity whose properties
may indeed be quite different several years hence.

The present chapter also deals with the *organizational* patterns of
NRMs. Wilson (1982: 131) has noted that, as largely 'lay' movements
operating in a modern capitalist milieu, present NRMs are freer than
either conventional churches or past movements to adapt rational
organizational techniques for fundraising, recruitment and communication, although such rational instrumental organization may undermine
the public perception of the movements' authentic 'religious' nature
(Robbins, 1985a).

The evolution of a given movement represents an accumulation of
adaptive responses to environmental pressures and opportunities, which
interact with 'internal' factors such as leadership and initial organizational and belief patterns to produce transformations of a range of
organizational, leadership, recruitment, financial and social control
practices (Richardson, 1985b). Although Richardson's (1985b) general
model provides a preliminary conceptual model of these patterns, this
subarea would appear to be underdeveloped. No application of the

organization–environment theories (e.g. Aldrich and Pfeffer, 1976) which flourished in the 1970s has been made. Although there is no extended discussion here, mention should be made of the literature applying 'movement organization' concepts to NRMs (Beckford, 1977; Gordon, 1984a; Harper, 1982; Lofland and Richardson, 1984).

Formation of New Movements

A small literature exists dealing with the emergence of 'cults' through a process of differentiation from a broader 'cultic milieu' (Campbell, 1972, 1977, 1978; Wallis, 1974, 1975a,b, 1977). The most provocative discussion of spiritual movement formation is by Bainbridge and Stark (1979; Stark and Bainbridge, 1985: 171–88). According to Bainbridge and Stark the formation of non-schismatic NRMs or 'cults' (see Ch. 5) is a two-step social process in which innovators both invent new religious ideas and then 'transmit them to other persons in exchange for rewards' (Bainbridge and Stark, 1979: 283). Bainbridge and Stark identify *three* models of cult formation.

The Psychopathology Model. This model has been well publicized in discussions of NRMs, e.g. 'it is closely related to deprivation theories of revolutions and social movements' (Stark and Bainbridge, 1985: 173). The model sees cults being invented by disturbed persons, who 'typically achieve their novel visions during psychotic episodes' (Stark and Bainbridge, 1985: 174). The meanings developed by the prophet-psychopath meet his own needs and appear compelling to him because of the intensity of his needs and/or demonstrative hallucinatory experiences. Should his society contain many other individuals suffering from problems similar to those experienced by the prophet, the latter will be likely to succeed in forming a cult around his vision; thus, 'such cults most often succeed during times of societal crisis, when large numbers of persons suffer from similar unresolved problems' (Stark and Bainbridge, 1985: 174). If a cult centering around the prophet and his ideas does emerge, the social legitimation of the prophet's vision and the rewards he receives from followers may significantly mitigate his mental illness, although others (Johnson, 1980; Lifton, 1979, 1985; Wallis, 1984) stress the role of absolute power and the adoration of followers in psychologically destabilizing a leader.

Stark and Bainbridge note that biographies of cult founders and prophets frequently contain material supportive of clinical attributions of paranoid-schizophrenic and manic-depressive syndromes. Such disorders may provide the founder with the stamina and energy to propagate and socially organize his vision in the face of strong opposition or indifference (Stark and Bainbridge, 1985: 175). A recent analysis of today's NRMs by two Christian scholars converges in some respects with the psycho-pathology model (Hexham and Poewe, 1986: 131–66).

Entrepreneurial Model. While the psychopathological model posits a prophet who develops new meanings initially to meet his own inner psychic needs, an alternative entrepreneurial model posits cult founders who develop new meanings with the definite intention of propagating them and receiving substantial rewards in *exchange* for their ideas. 'Perfectly normal' persons may thus be attracted to the enterprise of cultist innovation.

The entrepreneurial model thus views cults as 'businesses which provide a product for their customers and receive payment in return' (Stark and Bainbridge, 1985: 178). Cults are primarily in the business of selling seemingly novel *compensators* (beliefs and prescriptions which substitute for immediate rewards). 'Therefore, a supply of novel compen-sators must be manufactured' and 'both manufacture and sales are accomplished by entrepreneurs', who are seeking profit from 'exchanging compensators for rewards' (Stark and Bainbridge, 1985: 178). Cultist entrepreneurs are likely to have had prior involvement (as a devotee/ employee) with a successful cult and have thereby both perceived that the 'cult business' can be remunerative and acquired pertinent 'business' skills. Entrepreneurs create marketable compensators largely 'by assembling components of pre-existing compensator systems into new configu-rations or by further developing successful compensator systems'; therefore, 'cults tend to cluster in *lineages*' (Stark and Bainbridge, 1985: 179; our emphasis). Different cults thus 'bear strong "family resemblances", because they share many central features' (Stark and Bainbridge, 1985, 179).

Since cult formation is an entrepreneurial operation aimed at evolving a profitable new organization exchanging novel cultural items, concepts originally developed to analyze technological innovation can also be applied to the study of cults. The Church of Scientology is the cult equivalent of the Massachusetts Institute of Technology, whose employees have founded numerous high technology companies:

Cultic entrepreneurs have left Scientology to found other cults based on modified Scientology ideas, including Jack Horner's Dianology, H. Charles Berner's Abilitism,

Harold Thompson's Amprinistics, and the flying saucer cult described in the ethnography *When Prophecy Fails* (Festinger et al., 1956). Scientology, like M.I.T. is a vast storehouse of exotic culture derived from many sources. Social scientists studying patterns of cultural development should be aware that an occasional key organization can be an influential nexus of innovation and diffusion (Stark and Bainbridge, 1985: 181).

'Cults can, in fact, be very successful businesses' (Stark and Bainbridge, 1985: 179). Stark and Bainbridge cite the sizeable financial intake of Mankind United (Dohrman, 1958), the Washington DC branch of Scientology (see Behar, 1986 for a more recent look at Scientology finances) and a Scientology offshoot, The Process (Bainbridge, 1978). Vulgar approximations of Stark and Bainbridge's entrepreneurial model have been employed in current commentary on 'messianic capitalism' (Grafstein, 1984) and in exposés of putatively exploitative cultist commercial operations (Behar, 1986; Grafstein, 1984; Robbins, 1988b). Later sections of this chapter will present more material on both the competitive 'marketing' of NRMs and on their specific financial and commercial practices.

The Subculture-Evolution Model. Unlike the previous two models, which 'stress the role of the individual innovator, the subculture-evolution model emphasizes group interaction processes' (Stark and Bainbridge, 1985: 183) and questions the necessity of single authoritative leaders to create cults.

The subculture-evolution model views cults as expressions of *novel social systems* composed of intimately interacting persons. 'Cults are the result of sidetracked or failed collective attempts to obtain scarce or non-existent rewards' (Stark and Bainbridge, 1985: 183). Cults emerge when persons who are working together to obtain certain rewards gradually 'begin exchanging other rewards as well, such as affect. As they progressively come to experience failure in achieving their original goals, they will gradually generate and exchange compensators as well (Stark and Bainbridge, 1985: 183). When the intragroup exchange of rewards and compensators attains a threshold of intensity, the collectivity 'implodes' or becomes relatively encapsulated. Given a degree of autonomy, a cult will emerge and evolve a *novel culture* which will legitimate and facilitate the continuing exchange of rewards and compensators. Ultimately a novel religious culture will be objectified in a distinct social group which, like a business or any other organization, must face problems related to extracting resources and replenishing its membership from the environment.

As Stark and Bainbridge note, some of the literature on the development of deviant subcultures appears to formulate a similar model, e.g. Cohen's (1955) analysis of processes of 'mutual conversion' through which interacting individuals evolve a deviant normative structure. 'Thus, mutual conversion can describe the social processes through which people progressively commit each other to a package of compensators that they simultaneously assemble' (Stark and Bainbridge, 1985: 184). It appears to this writer that approximations of the subculture-evolution model have been crudely formulated by several earlier sociological studies of recent NRMs which have downplayed psychopathology and (to a lesser extent) entrepreneurialism and have highlighted collective problem-solving, responses to felt deprivations and spiritual legitimation of communal life and interpersonal rewards (Anthony and Robbins, 1974; Downton, 1979; Johnson, 1976; Robbins and Anthony, 1972; Snelling and Whitely, 1974; Tipton, 1982a). Some of these writers have not focused sufficiently on the *processes* through which the legitimating, gratifying or problem-solving cult emerges. These 'implosive' processes are highlighted in the important study by Bainbridge (1978), from which the formal subculture-evolution model appears to be largely generalized. As problem-solving exchange groups:

> Cults are particularly likely to emerge wherever numbers of people seek help for intractable personal problems. The broad fields of psychotherapy, rehabilitation, and personal development have been especially fertile for cults. A number of psychotherapy services have evolved into cult movements...Other independent human services organizations may also be susceptible to cultic evolution (Stark and Bainbridge, 1985: 185).

Cults can also evolve from traditional religious sects, e.g. The People's Temple was a Christian sect which 'evolved into a cult as Jones progressively became a prophet with an ever more radical vision. Either the psychopathology or entrepreneur models may apply in this case, but the committed members of the sect probably contributed to the transformation by encouraging Jones step by step and by demanding that he accomplish impossible goals' (Stark and Bainbridge, 1986: 187). Thus, Stark and Bainbridge's (1986: 187) three models of cult formation are really complementary rather than mutually exclusive, 'and can be combined to explain the emergence of particular cults'.

Nevertheless, there are salient differences between the distinctive emphases of the models. The entrepreneurial model and the psychopathology model focus on a single prophet-producer of new meanings, who ultimately exchanges them with followers. The entrepreneurial model highlights the likelihood of *cultic lineages*, i.e. the innovative cultural items which are produced as compensators tend to be novel primarily in the sense of being *new combinations of existing cultural elements*. Bainbridge (1985) has extrapolated this point in the direction of analogies with biological mutation and genetic recombinations via DNA. He proposes a new science of *cultural genetics*, 'based initially on concepts borrowed from biology and on information about these exotic micro-organisms, religious cults' (Bainbridge, 1985: 194).

Determinants of NRM 'Success' and 'Failure'

Recently some sociological literature has probed the question of what enabled new religious movements throughout history to 'succeed' and why so many NRMs 'failed'. Of course, 'success' is somewhat of a subjective concept; it cannot be simply assumed 'that growth means success and that decline means failure. Not all movements seek unconditional or unlimited growth, and those that do may pay for it at the cost of abandoning pristine teachings and organization' (Wilson, 1987: 31).

In *The Future of New Religious Movements* (Bromley and Hammond, 1987) various eminent scholars ruminate on the survival of particular movements and the evolution of the collective NRM scene. In a key article Rodney Stark develops a theoretical model of 'How New Religions Succeed' which draws on the experience of Pauline Christianity, early Islam, Mormonism, Christian Science and contemporary NRMs (Stark, 1987a). Mormonism represents 'a priceless gift to sociologists of religion' as it is arguably in the process of becoming 'a major world faith over the next century' (Stark, 1987a: 11; see also Stark, 1984).

Stark defines 'success' as '*the degree to which a religious movement is able to dominate one or more societies*'. Such domination may be the result of conversion of the masses, or elites or both' (Stark, 1985a: 12). In effect, Stark defines success in terms of *influence*. It is arguable that the influence of some movements such as the Unification Church is disproportionate to their limited numbers as a result of wealth and political contacts (Bromley, 1985; Horowitz, 1978, 1981; Robbins and Anthony, 1984). Stark specifies nine conditions which, if fulfilled, enhance the likelihood of a movement's success.

(1) *Cultural continuity* with existing conventional faiths is a key factor, e.g. 'Christians did not ask Jews to discard their traditional scriptures, but to add to them' (Stark, 1987a: 13). Similarly, Islam presented itself as the culmination of the Jewish–Christian prophetic tradition, while 'Allah' was initially a superior deity of the pre-Islamic pagan Arab

pantheon. These founders of NRMs 'whose revelations are rooted in familiar cultural material are the ones likely to succeed' (Stark, 1985a: 15). Contemporary Buddhist and Hindu groups in the United States 'suffer from asking converts to reject their whole religious heritage and thus risk being defined as too deviant' (1985a: 15).

According to Stark (1985: 15), 'imported faiths appear to do best when they are taken over by locals and modified to include familiar cultural elements', e.g. local pagan deities becoming medieval Christian saints. But must such adaptive modification always be explicit and acknowledged? Arguably, 'Eastern' mystical teachings popular in the United States are now being implicitly 'Americanized' and adapted to various cultural motifs such as materialism, hedonism and the success ethic, as well as being combined with Freudianism and other therapeutic frameworks, i.e. *implicit syncretism* is emerging (Anthony and Ecker, 1986; Anthony et al., 1978; Tipton, 1982a; Wuthnow, 1985).

(2) Stark's second criterion is *medium tension* with the environment. If tension and conflict between an NRM and environmental forces is too intense and a group is too deviant, the costs of membership are likely to become too high such that a violent explosion may ensue and/or many people will defect. Yet new movements must maintain 'a substantial sense of difference' and tension with the environment if the movement is to have a basis for successful conversion; 'Thus, it must maintain a delicate balance between conformity and deviance' (Stark, 1985a: 16). But Wilson (1987: 31) comments that 'what constitutes "medium tension" may be discernible only retrospectively', such that Stark's analysis may contain a tautological element. Moore (1985) argues that it is a recurrent pattern in American religious history for the founders of new sects such as Joseph Smith (Mormons) and Mary Baker Eddy (Christian Science) to employ an 'outsider strategy' which motivates converts and heightens cohesion by accentuating tension and/or downplaying underlying cultural continuities. Galanter's social system model of 'charismatic groups' (Galanter, 1985) explicates the functional significance of maintaining a level of tension via boundary definition for internal solidarity and motivation of devotees.

(3) *Effective mobilization* is another key factor contributing to success. 'Ineffective mobilization is chronic among new religious movements' (Stark, 1987a: 16). Wagner's (1983) study of 'a virtual non-organization', The Spiritual Frontier Fellowship, 'could be applied to many new religious movements' (Stark, 1987a: 16). Effective mobilization requires effective organization which is precarious in charismatic guru systems (Rochford, 1985; Shinn, 1985a; Stark, 1987a: 16; Wallis, 1984). Elitist

inward-turning mysticism inhibited effective mobilization among ancient Gnostic Christian movements (Pagels, 1981), whose 'loose networks of individual adepts could not withstand the mobilized might of the Pauline church' (Stark, 1987a: 18). Various contemporary 'New Age' and mystical groups may share the problems of the Gnostics.

Some contemporary NRMs have indeed generated high mobilization levels (e.g. the 'Moonies'). Yet, unlike the quintessentially 'successful' Mormons, groups such as the Unification Church attain and sustain their mobilization by *withdrawing members from the conventional secular world*. 'This procedure results in isolation and in reliance on collective economic activities (which may deflect from religious goals); often such a high level of mobilization inhibits fertility and family life' (Stark, 1987a: 17). With regard to the Moonies, encapsulative indoctrination contributed to a high defection rate, as mobilized devotees had difficulty functioning in 'the world' (Bromley and Shupe, 1979a; Long and Hadden, 1983).

(4) *Demographic factors* also influence the likelihood of ultimate success, which is facilitated if a movement's membership manifests 'a normal age and sex structure' (Stark, 1987a: 18-19). The effect of a limited, demographically circumscribed appeal may be the creation of 'a population composition incapable of sustaining its ranks' (Stark, 1987a: 18). Given the likelihood of an eventual falling-off in the conversion rate (Stark and Roberts, 1982), movement growth will ultimately depend heavily on intragroup fertility rates. Outstanding demographic 'losers' in American religious history include the Shakers, who prohibited sex and initially attracted more women than men, and Christian Science. The latter exhibited a sensational rate of growth in its early years, but 'the massive overrecruitment of older females, who either did not have children or whose children were already grown before their mothers' conversion resulted eventually in an extraordinary mortality deficit' (Stark, 1987a: 18) which exceeds the continuing gain from significant conversion rates. In contrast, the Mennonites have not declined because their balanced demographic structure and high fertility rate compensates for insignificant conversion and substantial defection. 'The great majority of new religious movements resemble the Shakers more than the Mennonites' (Stark, 1987a: 18).

As Bryan Wilson notes, 'The new religious movements of recent times have appealed very largely to middle class youth' (Wilson, 1987: 39). This limited demographic range foreshadows future maintenance problems:

The age-based sect becomes a feature of a stage in the life cycle of adherents, having as its primary source of further recruitment only the pre-conversion friends of its votaries or those of their generation. When adherents age, they drop out as sect experience becomes less congruent, or, within sects recruiting the middle-aged and elderly, they die. The mood and tone of the movement, becomes somewhat less than congenial to others. The movement, resting on a narrow social base, has limited viability socially, no matter what measure of internal coherence its homogenous constituency confers upon it (Wilson, 1987: 39).

Other demographic aspects of today's NRMs darken the horizon. The general rapid turnover will inhibit stabilization. Many or most groups recruit individuals; they 'do not embrace whole families, and...are unlikely to enjoy the natural recruitment of the next and subsequent generations' (Wilson, 1987: 40). Stark and Wilson appear to concur in predicting that successful movements will be demographically and organizationally normal, i.e. possessing a population structure similar to that of the society and organized in terms of the conventional units of social organization (e.g. families).

(5) NRMs will be more likely to succeed, in Stark's view, if they operate in the context of *a favorable ecology*. A key subdimension of this condition is 'the degree to which the religious economy is *regulated*' (Stark, 1987a: 19). Supposedly in the United States, all religious groups, large or small, enjoy equal legal privileges, e.g. tax exemptions:

American tax laws induce new religious movements to become formally organized at a very early date and thus may make them visible sooner than is true of similar groups in Europe. As a result, the primary regulators of our religious economy are state and federal tax collectors. This situation is reflected in the fact that founders and leaders appear to be the single highest risk group in terms of prosecution for tax viola- tions. Unwittingly perhaps the IRS serves as a functional equivalent of the Holy Inquisition in the officially unregulated religious economy of the United States (Stark, 1987a: 19; see also Richardson, 1985b; Robbins, 1985a).

(6) An additional dimension of ecological favorability involves the *condition of existing faiths*. Sects are continually tamed and transformed into churches, which makes them vulnerable to replacement by new 'high-tension' movements. The ongoing secularization of older traditions grants new religions 'the opportunity to take over the market' (Stark, 1987a: 20). Additionally, periods of 'grave crises and social disorganiza-tion' can 'produce market opportunities for new faiths' either by placing '*demands* upon a conventional religion which it *appears unable to meet*' or by disrupting the social ties 'by which most people are bound to social institutions, including religion' (Stark, 1987a: 20). Thus, a high level of

geographical mobility, such as characterizes California, 'prevents substantial social integration in the Far West and accounts for the very high rates of involvement in new religions' (Stark, 1987a: 21). Finally a profound 'crisis of confidence' generally 'awaits most new religions as members of the founding generation reach the end of their lives . . . Unless the movement achieves a persuasive appearance of major success within the first generation, the founders will [likely] lose hope and turn the movement inward — adopt a new rhetoric that deemphasizes growth and conversion' (Stark, 1987a: 21; see also Stark and Roberts, 1982).

(7) The importance of *network ties* to conversion and commitment has been discussed in an earlier chapter. Effective mobilization requires 'a dense network of internal attachments among its followers' (Stark, 1987a: 22). 'A common failure of new religious movements' is the relative absence of social relations among followers, as observed by Wagner (1983) in one diffuse movement. Weak networks constrain the effective mobilization and growth in Scientology:

> The basic unit of Scientology is the dyad: the auditor and the person undergoing therapy. The movement has failed to discover organizational means to create bonds among those undergoing auditing; hence, whenever members suspend their therapy sessions (which most do periodically because of the great expense involved), the risk that they will drop out altogether is high — there is nothing to tie them to the group (Stark, 1987a: 23).

Some movements attempt to maximize and intensify internal network ties by developing 'internal networks that are too all-embracing and impede the ability of members to form or to maintain attachments with outsiders' (Stark, 1987a: 23). Totalistic encapsulation may impede recruitment and fundraising (Greil and Rudy, 1984b; Long and Hadden, 1983; Stark, 1984, 1987a) as well as maximize stigmatization and legal vulnerability (Beckford, 1985a; Robbins, 1985d).

(8) Under the rubric of *secularization* Stark treats the necessity for a successful movement to maintain a balance between worldly accommodation versus uncompromising sectarianism, i.e. both sectarian isolation and extreme accommodationist pliability will undercut the actual influence exerted on social institutions by a movement (Stark, 1987a: 23; Yinger, 1946). 'During their rise, successful religious movements do not abandon their original content' (Stark, 1987a: 24), although some might challenge this view, e.g. did Paul shift the original message of Jesus? Further growth after an initial spurt may require some accommodation. A growing NRM appears to the present writer to be somewhat like an American presidential candidate going after his party's nomination, i.e. he initially attracts loyal supporters and funding by taking strong

stands which distinguish him from a crowd of blander competitors. Subsequently he will 'move toward the center' to appeal to different groups in a pluralistic culture.

(9) Finally, there must be *adequate socialization* of persons born into the faith. 'Lacking this, a movement will develop powerful internal pressures toward secularization' (Stark, 1987a: 24), as generations born into a movement will tend toward tension-reduction vis-a-vis the social environment. Effective socialization will implant a sense of superiority to outsiders among followers. Large-scale defection of adult movement progeny will ensue if effective socialization is not provided for. Successful movements often reinforce socialization with a special commitment-building role for youth; here 'the Mormon practice of basing its primary missionary effort on teenage volunteers' stands out and has a positive effect 'on the commitment of the best and brightest of its young people in each generation' (Stark, 1987a: 25).

Bryan Wilson's essay in the Bromley and Hammon (1987) volume comments on Stark's model and analyzes the conditions underlying the 'failure' of NRMs under five headings: ideology, leadership, organization, constituency and institutionalization. Much of Wilson's chapter deals with *institutionalization*, broadly conceived, and which has been pioneered by Wilson's student, Roy Wallis (1981, 1984; Wallis and Bruce, 1986). This is a topic to which we shall soon turn later. However, there appears to be a recurring theme in Wilson's essay to the effect that *contemporary NRMs are particularly likely to 'fail'*, in part because they have recruited primarily young people, who have no experience of permanent commitment. Today's NRMs are vulnerable 'to the fact that in contemporary society abiding relationships are much less the norm than they were' (Wilson, 1987: 44), as indicated by the high divorce rate, etc. Some of the same sociocultural factors which enhance the appeal of NRMs to modern 'protean' young persons who continually exchange and shift attachments and identities and thus manifest 'conversion careers' (Richardson, 1978b), also operate to destabilize commitments, such that *movements easily proliferate but generally lack staying power*.

Institutionalization Patterns

We have noted the manipulatively protean quality of many 'manufactured' movements, e.g. 'with the Rajneesh, a "clergy" was invented and discarded within a two year span' (Carter, 1987: 150). This volatility may constitute a limiting factor with regard to the discussion below of recurrent or typical patterns and fundamental processes.

From several analyses and perspectives it can be inferred that the institutionalization of contemporary NRMs is often a two-phase process. In *phase one* a rudimentary movement ('cult' in Wallis's terms, 'audience cult' or weak 'client cult' in Stark and Bainbridge's terms; see Ch. 5) evolves into a more clearly bounded, formally organized and authoritatively led movement. In *phase two* the movement develops a hierarchical authority structure, a differentiated membership which includes both activists and less involved 'lay' members, a dilution of the charismatic authority of the guru or prophet with rational-legal elements and a pattern of tension-reduction and accommodation vis-a-vis the sociocultural environment.

Rudimentary movements emerge from a broader *cultic milieu* (Campbell, 1972, 1977; Wallis, 1974, 1975b, 1977). Organization may be minimal, membership shifting and barely committed, and its group boundaries ambiguous. Doctrine may be poorly developed. Examples of such groups are Meher Baba (Anthony and Robbins, 1974; Robbins, 1969; Robbins and Anthony, 1972), a 'Ouija board cult' (Quarantelli and Wenger, 1973) and the diffuse and minimally organized Spiritual Frontiers Fellowship (Wagner, 1983).

At some point the rudimentary NRM either fades back into the broader cultic milieu, i.e. its rudimentary organizational and doctrinal boundaries dissolve and its followers drift away, or it emerges as a more cohesive *sect*, or in Stark and Bainbridge's terms a *cultic movement* such as Hare Krishna (or a relatively strong and firmly organized client cult such as Scientology). Such groups possess the capacity to mobilize resources because they have a firmer organization and because their membership evinces a higher commitment relative to a rudimentary movement. Leadership may still be charismatic, but it is more clearly channeled through concrete organizational forms.

Schismatic movements (or 'sects' in Stark and Bainbridge's terms) do not emerge from a cultic milieu but from another religious organization (Stark and Bainbridge, 1985). Such groups omit the initial phase and may emerge immediately as dynamic, cohesive organizations.

Organized sects or cultic movements are capable of sustaining a certain degree of tension with the surrounding sociopolitical environment. Indeed, such tension may be functional in terms of the commitment of members and the appeal of a novel movement to 'alienated' or discontented persons (Bromley and Shupe, 1979a; Stark, 1987a). However, tension may sometimes escalate until there is an explosion such as occurred at Jonestown, or until the costs of participation become prohibitive. The People's Temple, the Bhagwan Movement of Shree Rajneesh and Hare Krishna are movements which have either become defunct or are declining in North America in part due to reciprocated hostility to the broader society (Carter, 1987; FitzGerald, 1986; Hall, 1987; Palmer, 1988; Rochford, 1985).

Further adaptive movement evolution in the direction of 'denominational' stability and legitimacy is likely to involve accommodation or mitigation of tension with the social environment. Other changes often associated with the second phase or sect-to-denomination transformation involve an emergent differentiation of clerical and lay positions, the professionalization of clergy, the elaboration of administrative hierarchy and a mitigation or 'routinization' of charismatic leadership and authority in a rational–legal direction. A reduction of the intensity and emotional fervor of commitment also frequently accompany the above changes and the lessening of tension with the social environment (see Rochford, 1985: 214–20 for a brief summary of the sect-to-denomination 'institutionalization model'; see also Wallis, 1981).

Some First Phase Studies. The classic study of cult-to-sect (or amorphous 'audience cult' to highly organized and authoritarian 'client cult') evolution is Roy Wallis's monograph on Scientology (Wallis, 1977). A diffuse cult based on L. Ron Hubbard's bestseller, *Dianetics*, arose in the 1950s but eventually faded and splintered. It was reorganized in an authoritarian direction as a hierarchical 'church' subservient to Hubbard as infallible prophet and guru. Wallis (1974: 308) notes that the 'crucial factor' in negotiating the transformation from cult to sect 'lies in the successful arrogation of authority. Typically this is effected on the basis of a claim to unique revelation of a transcendent kind. If the claim is accepted, it provides charismatic legitimation for organizational and doctrinal adaptation' (Wallis, 1974: 308).

James Richardson (1979) has elaborated Wallis's model further and applied it to the 'Jesus Movement' groups flourishing in the late 1960s and early 1970s, particularly 'Christ Communal Organization' (Richardson, 1979; Richardson et al., 1978). Summarizing Wallis's and Richardson's findings, McGuire (1986: 138) notes, 'In the transformation from cult to sect...certain members successfully claim strong authority, thereby enabling them to clarify the boundaries of the group belief system and membership. The successful claim to strong authority gives leaders a basis for exercising social control in the group and for excluding persons who do not accept the newly consolidated belief system.'

Second Phase Studies. There are many classic studies of 'denominational-ization' processes in the past (e.g. Niebuhr, 1929). But 'second phase' studies of contemporary NRMs are understandably rarer. A significant article by Wallis (1981) discusses some 'accommodative' tendencies on the part of the highly stigmatized Children of God movement. The latter part of this article develops a comparative analysis of incipient institutionalization among a number of groups including the Unification Church, Hare Krishna, the COG, and the (not yet denominationalized) Jehovah's Witnesses sect. Wallis draws various provocative inferences about the process of denominationalization.

Wallis emphasizes the mitigation of *exclusivity*: 'there is a shift from a self-concept as possessors of sole access to the truth or salvation to one more tolerant of the claims of other groups' (Wallis, 1981: 117). Exclusivity or intolerance may actually increase during phase one or cult-to-sect evolution. The Children of God became more exclusive in the 1970s, but now, in the early 1980s, 'they no longer so roundly curse the hellish system and its churches. They have accepted that others, who do not maintain all their beliefs and loyalties, are none the less doing God's will, if only to a limited extent' (Wallis, 1981: 120). The persistence of exclusivity is a barrier to the full denominationalism of the Jehovah's Witnesses.

Denominationalism, according to Wallis, is a *relational* process, i.e. it does not occur 'simply as a consequence of the attitudes and behavior of members of the group' (Wallis, 1981: 118). The public must cease to regard the evolving group 'as a deviant organization and begin treating it as one group among many, competing equally with other religions' (Wilson, 1987: 142; see also Hampshire and Beckford, 1983). Persisting public hostility may undermine the denominationalization of a number of contemporary groups, particularly Hare Krishna (Rochford, 1985). Of course, public hostility interacts with and responds to movement properties and behavior. Aside from particular deviant acts by cults, there may be notable media hostility to charismatic leadership (Wilson, 1987).

Bureaucratization, in Wallis's view, has been over-emphasized by Wilson (1978) and others as a key internal element in denominationalization:

Some sects, such as Jehovah's Witnesses and Scientology, became highly bureaucratized without leading to denominationalization. Bureaucracy is largely a function of the size and spread of the collectivity rather than of its denominational character. It is, in many cases, a way of *implementing* its denominationalism rather than being *constitutive* of it (Wallis, 1981: 118).

Internal *differentiation* between clerico-monastic activists and an incipient 'laity' is important to denominationalization. Yet differentiation, even when accompanied by *accommodation* to diminish tension with the social environment, does not, in Wallis's view, entail denominationalization. An aspect of accommodation is de-totalization (our term) or the diminished physical encapsulation of the devotee. Wallis sees accommodative tendencies in the COG responding to four developments: (1) the disappearance of the movement's original bohemian and 'alienated' ('hippie') recruitment base; (2) the aging of members, who increasingly desire to settle down to a more normal and stable lifestyle; (3) the rising hostility to 'cults', which puts a premium on the physical dispersal of members and the reduction of organizational visibility; and (4) the movement's premillennial but post-tribulationist conception of an imminent reign of Antichrist, who will persecute the movement (this view reinforces the perceived premium on member dispersal and low visibility).

Wallis discusses tendencies toward differentiation and de-totalization in Hare Krishna, which 'is encouraging more limited forms of attachment than the early complete transformation of life required of its young devotees' (Wallis, 1981: 127), and the Unification Church. The latter developed a 'Home Church' program for those whose interest in or commitment to the Church is less than that of the early disciples (Wallis, 1981: 127); see also Hampshire and Beckford, 1983: 226). Robbins and Anthony (1984) see the UC as *over-institutionalized* in the sense that while recruitment in the United States is down, many auxiliary institutions including media, educational programs, banks, political groups, forums, seminars and businesses linked to the UC and its leaders are proliferating. As the 'community of the faithful' shrinks, the various political, educational, publishing, financial and commercial institutions now linked to the UC may attain varying degrees of functional autonomy. Wallis (1981: 128) sees 'a relatively early transition to denominationalism' as a possible consequence of its distinctively accommodative strategic response to the familiar late 1970s 'syndrome' of the disappearance of its original constituency, the aging of members and social stigmatization.

For Wallis, the keys to denominationalization are the shedding of *exclusivity* and the attainment of public *respectability*. Hampshire and Beckford (1983) have analyzed the 'external' dimension of sect-to-denomination processes through a comparison of the experience of the Mormons in Illinois in the 1840s and the 'Moonies' in England in the 1970s. The authors stress the *transactional* or relational quality of the accommodative/alienative process and the *contingent* quality of the interaction between a sect and its social environment. A key variable is the degree to which the unconventional beliefs and practices of a group are perceived as *social* deviance which threatens vital institutional norms rather than esoteric doctrinal elements detached from the everyday world (Hampshire and Beckford, 1983; see also Harper, 1986).

Rochford (1985: 214–20) evaluates the fit between the 'institutionalization [denominationalization] model' and the evolution of ISKON. The apparent 'features of denominationalism' which have emerged within ISKON 'do not point to denominationalism', which may not be possible for the movement 'in the foreseeable future because of. . .its public definition as a threatening movement' (Rochford, 1985: 217). ISKON, a declining movement in the late 1970s and early 1980s, did move somewhat in the denominational direction 'as a strategy to avoid organizational failure' (Rochford, 1985: 217). It employed 'certain protective strategies (e.g. becoming structurally more open to the outside, inclusive in its membership, and maintenance oriented at the expense of missionary objectives)'; yet 'the sectarian lifestyle and practices of the devotees remained largely intact' (Rochford, 1985: 218). The leaders of Hare Krishna were simply operating organizational maintenance strategies directed more to raising money than to gaining public acceptance. Their basic exclusivity remains and the ultimate consequences of some of their economic strategies may be inimical to public acceptance (Huber and Gruson, 1987).

Organizational maintenance strategies and accompanying re-orientations of goals, practices and devotee lifestyles may produce dissidence and defection (Ofshe, 1980b; Richardson et al., 1986). Rochford discusses *ideological work* (Berger, 1981) which responds to the emerging disjunctions between devotees' professed beliefs and their daily routines. Ideological work rationalizes apparent goal displacement and soothes alienated feelings arising from increasing commercialization and the necessity of deviant practices (Rochford 1985; Michael, 1988).

According to Rochford, Hare Krishna is becoming a less encapsulative lay movement, in part as a response to the movement's economic decline. Communal groups can no longer support all of their members, thus compelling some devotees to leave the communal network and seek secular employment, return to school, etc. This development enhances the likelihood of erosion of commitment. For Hare Krishna, increasing differentiation and de-totalization may signify not the path to denominationalism but the path to extinction.

It is important to realize that de-sectarianization is not inevitable; moreover, the process is *reversible*. The People's Temple (Hall, 1987) is a tragic case in point. Some movements respond to tension with the social environment by retreating to an isolated communal enclave where they can construct a 'pure' spiritual life without interference.

The early study of a 'California Cult' by Dohrman (1958) provides the prototype of a close-knit movement which responds to environmental stresses by decamping and reconstructing communal totalism in a remote enclave. Lofland (1977) speculated on the possibility of Unificationism taking this direction. The Mormon settlement of Utah is an earlier example of radical sectarian withdrawal. Had this option not been available for the Mormons, as it may not now be easily available for most contemporary NRMs, the movement might have been extinguished amid strife and violence (Moore, 1985). FitzGerald (1986) describes a process of escalating tension leading to the demise of the Rajneesh community in Oregon. The affairs of this once wealthy enclave were wound up without major violence, though there had been speculations that increasing tension and the imposition of controls by public authorities would produce 'another Jonestown'. Ofshe (1980b) describes a process of increasing exclusivity, authoritarian totalism, tension with the environment and proclivities toward violence characterizing the evolution of Synanon and culminating in episodic violence, legal reprisals and movement decline.

Charismatic leadership appears to enhance volatility and deviant proclivities which in turn inhibits accommodation (Johnson, 1980; Lifton, 1979; Ofshe, 1980a,b; Regan, 1986; Rochford, 1985; Wallis, 1984; Wallis and Bruce, 1986). Internal factionalism in a context of charismatic leadership may enhance violent proclivities, and thus inhibit accommodation by eliciting renewed tension. Charismatic leadership per se, regardless of its inherent deviant or violent proclivities, may encourage the mobilization of popular and media hostility (Wilson, 1987) which can inhibit institutionalization and accommodation.

Precariousness of Charisma

In the 1980s Roy Wallis appears to have substituted a new typology of world-affirming, world-accepting and world-rejecting groups for the cult–sect–denomination–church conception he developed in the 1970s (see Ch. 5). Replacing the cult-to-sect-to-denomination trajectory of institutionalization was a conception of religious movements embodying at a given moment unstable combinations of world-rejecting, world-accepting and world-affirming elements, although one tendency may overshadow the other. The instability of a movement's momentary combination interacts with environmental pressures to stimulate change processes which shift the movement's position along the continua of world affirming/accommodating/rejecting. Movement away from the world-rejecting pole is referred to as conventionalization (Wallis, 1984: 79), a tendency which responds to various stimuli, including the disappearance of an alienated or radicalized constituency, a desire to stabilize financial support and a desire to achieve respectability or placate authorities. Accommodative responses interact with movement crises and internal factionalism, and can sometimes provoke internal conflicts and schisms. Some movements, particularly if charismatic leadership is present, may follow a lurching or zig-zag course. Wallis (1984: 79–85) discusses the evolution of and eventual schism in The Process as described by Bainbridge (1978), the zig-zag course of the Divine Light Mission (Downton, 1979; Pilarzyk, 1978a,b) and the evolution of a Kundalini Yoga group (Parsons, 1974).

The most trenchant analysis of the problems of institutionalization in Wallis's synthesizing monograph (1984) involves the discussions of the precariousness of the market and the precariousness of charisma. These are problems or types of problems which most movements face, but which are said to generally impinge differentially upon world-rejecting and world-affirming movements.

Some movements such as The People's Temple (Hall, 1981, 1987; Johnson, 1980), the Children of God (Wallis, 1976, 1982a, Wallis and Bruce, 1986). Synanon (Ofshe, 1980b), and the Charles Manson group have followed a very erratic trajectory culminating (for three of these four groups) in sensational violence. These groups have been compared by Wallis (1984: 103–9) and Wallis and Bruce (1986: 115–27), who point out that they are all world-rejecting movements with pronounced charismatic leadership. World-rejecting movements' 'sharp break with the world around them can only be legitimated by extraordinary authority' (Wallis, 1984: 107). However, movements possessed of a clearly charismatic leadership face 'a distinctive precariousness' arising from the nature of charismatic authority (Weber, 1947, 1948; Wilson, 1973) and its tendency to undercut the stability and predictability of methodical procedures associated with the institutionalization of 'rational–legal' authority. The decision-making of charismatic leaders is often arbitrary since little value is necessarily placed on rationality and precedent; moreover, the supreme leader is 'exposed to highly selective information, as he relies on favored disciples to channel opinions and reactions to him' (Wilson, 1973: 205).

'Charisma is inherently unstable and tends to become institutionalized' (Wallis, 1984: 110); moreover, such institutionalization is essential to preserve or expand the movement and meet 'the need for mechanisms of coordination, supervision, and delegation' and the imperative of securing a stable financial base. As these needs are met, 'mundane structures' emerge and entail a network of legitimated rules, regulations and subordinates' rights to office which 'constrain the leader and trammel his capacity for arbitrary behavior and dramatic unilateral changes in doctrine and policy' (Wallis, 1984: 110).

Wallis (1984: 110–13) delineates four patterns of responses to incipient rationalization on the part of charismatic NRM leaders:

(1) *Acquiescence*: the leader accepts the situation with more or less good grace, e.g. Guru Maharaj-ji of the Divine Light Mission accepted a diminished presentation of himself as a great humanitarian leader rather than a manifestation of God. This lesser presentation fitted the increasingly Westernized 'style' of the movement and its increasingly bureaucratized organization after 1973. Maharaj-ji reasserted his messianic status in 1976 (Downton, 1979; Wallis, 1984: 110).

(2) *Encouragement*: the leader 'embraces the possibilities involved in institutionalization and actively directs that process in such a way as to control it and utilize institutionalized structures to buttress his authority rather than allowing it to constrain him' (Wallis, 1984: 10; see also Khalsa, 1986). Examples are Mary Baker Eddy and Christian Science (Wilson, 1978) and L. Ron Hubbard and Scientology (Wallis, 1977). The latter elaborated a hierarchical structure involving routinized procedures which institutionalized the position and absolute authority of Hubbard and the position of an elite staff personally controlled by and devoted to Hubbard. Encouragement of institutionalization by the leadership is often associated with world-affirming movements (Wallis, 1984) and wordly success ethics (Khalsa, 1986). Johnson (1987b), commenting on Wallis, associates *encouragement* with a chief executive 'CEO' leadership style.

(3) *Displacement* involves the emergence of a pattern of institutionalization which 'proceeds without clear recognition by the charismatic leader of what is occurring...' (Wallis, 1984: 111). The leader may be hostile to institutionalization; however, he may awaken to what is unfolding too late and his belated opposition may elicit his ouster, as in the case of Robert de Grimston, founder of The Process. The latter was ousted by subordinates who desired to make accommodative alterations in the extreme theatrical style of group ritual and dress developed by de Grimston and in his elaborate theology, which had been socially

stigmatized as Devil worship (Bainbridge, 1978; Wallis, 1984: 111–12). Extreme displacement thus leads to *expulsion* of the prophet/guru. This requires unity among the staff and an organizational capacity to function and subsist without the charisma of its original founder (Johnson, 1987b).

(4) Finally, there is the effective *resistance* to institutionalization exhibited by Moses ('Mo') David Berg, founder of the Children of God (Wallis, 1976, 1982b), who employed a strategy of 'perpetual environmental change and the shifting of goals' (Hiller, 1975: 344), which 'brought down the institution-builders, the administratively inclined who sought to bridle the free reign of God's spirit through Mo, but it mobilized the following, freeing them from institutional controls, directing them away from mundane and routine considerations, ever more pressing as they produced children and grew older' (Wallis, 1984: 113). Perpetual flux renewed members' fervor and commitment.

Wallis's analysis of the leader's effective resistance to routinization in the COG evokes in the present writer the image of Mao-Tse-Tung instigating the Great Proletarian Cultural Revolution to shake up the Chinese Communist Party and overthrow a bureaucratized party leadership. Wallis and Bruce (1986: 115–27), however, develop a comparison between the COG and the erratic and volatile charismatic leadership styles of Charles Manson, Chuck Dedrich of Synanon and Jim Jones. World-rejecting movements are volatile to the degree that their leadership is *exclusively charismatic*, with other axes of authority and accountability demolished:

> Undermining institutional structures and patterns not only constitutes change and eliminates constraints upon further change, it also creates ambiguities and conflicts of policy and practice which leave the members without any clear guidelines to action. Only by constantly watching the leader, subordinating themselves totally to his inspiration of the moment and being willing to humble themselves for their failure to follow that inspiration closely enough, can they remain among the favored (Wallis and Bruce, 1986: 124; see also Johnson, 1987b).

Roy Wallis sees charismatic leadership with its particular volatility and precariousness as a key factor influencing the evolution of world-rejecting communal sects such as the Children of God. Johnson (1987b) also highlights the 'personal factor' and identifies movements with 'chief executive' (CEO) leaders as most likely to grow and groups whose leaders are effectively resisting routinization as most precarious and unstable. Movement growth has the consequence that the perspectives or 'worlds' of the guru/prophet, the staff and the general membership increasingly diverge, with consequences for future conflicts (see Palmer, 1988, on the leadership of Bhagwan Rajneesh, and Wallis, 1982a, for analyses of charismatic leadership in various controversial movements).

Hare Krishna Routinization Problems. A key dimension of the precariousness of charisma entails the related problems of replacing a revered
charismatic leader who has departed and of 'qualifying' a suitable
successor(s). Rochford (1985) describes the internal conflict and factionalism which has pervaded Hare Krishna since the death of its revered
elderly founder, Prabhupada, in 1977 (see also Bromley and Shinn, 1988;
Huber and Gruson, 1986; Shinn, 1987). The post-Prabhupada governance
of ISKON has been uneasily shared between eleven putatively charismatic
(but generally relatively young) gurus and the administrative Governing
Body Commission (GBC). The gurus' charismatic authority has been
precarious, because they are relatively young men who *now claim a
sanctity and deference almost equal to that of the departed Prabhupada.*
'Many of Prabhupada's disciples found it difficult to take seriously the
claim that their Godbrothers, whom they often knew rather intimately,
were "realized souls"...' (Rochford, 1985: 237).

The essentially bureaucratic authority of the GNC (whose members are
not gurus) is even weaker than that of the gurus, because, 'ISKON's beliefs
require that charismatic leadership be continued in the form of gurus'
(Rochford, 1985: 254). New devotees must be initiated by gurus and the
primary loyalty of a devotee thus tends to be largely directed to the guru
who initiated him, and not a putatively superordinate administrative entity
(Rochford, 1985; Shinn, 1985a, 1987). The GBC has thus encountered
substantial difficulties in asserting its authority over the gurus and in
disciplining and constraining eccentric gurus such as the paramilitarist
Berkeley guru whose foibles embarrassed ISKON and elicited unwelcome
attentions from public officials in 1980–1. At this writing the GBC is
attempting to expel and disassociate ISKON from Guru Bhaktipada, whose
organization controls Ohio Valley operations and who, along with some
close colleagues, is being investigated by several government agencies for
allegedly building the Golden Temple of Prabhupada in West Virginia with
profits from drug sales and for complicity in the murder of a dissident
(Bromley and Shinn, 1988; Huber and Gruson, 1987).

The 'centrality of the guru-disciple relationship' for Hare Krishna
makes it unlikely, in Rochford's view, that ISKON will follow the path
of Christian Science, in which the absolute personal authority of the
founder was quickly succeeded by the absolute personal authority of a
board (see Wallis, 1984: 118, for a somewhat different view). Unfortunately, 'guru authority systems are inimical to effective organization and
are subject to constant fission and schism since members are committed
to a particular guru, not to a larger organization' (Stark, 1987a: 16; see
also Michael, 1988; Shinn, 1985a, 1987).

Yet the authority of the post-Prabhupada Krishna gurus is challenged not only by the GBC, but also by an increasingly organized and strident *dissident movement*, which repudiates the guru system as antithetical to the real intentions of Prabhupada and demeaning to his spiritual primacy (Rochford, 1985). These dissidents have increasingly tended to accuse the gurus of serious improprieties and even crimes. The GBC, while seeking to assert its ultimate authority over the gurus, has yet defended them against the clearly 'anti-establishment' dissidents. Recently, escalating allegations of gurus' improprieties made by dissidents appear to have created the setting in which brutal violence both against guru Bhaktipada and allegedly by Bhaktipada's subordinates against a dissident has erupted (Huber and Gruson, 1987). The conflict between Bhaktipada and the GBC has also taken on a new urgency and intensity as the charges against the regional guru and his associates will surely bring the movement into disrepute. Although he has been expelled from the movement by the GBC, Bhaktipada now claims to be *the sole legitimate successor to Prabhupada* (Huber and Gruson, 1987; Michael, 1988).

Fierce factionalism and violence have thus erupted in one movement in the context of a three-way struggle between precarious charismatic guru authorities, a weak bureaucratic authority and a strident dissident group. The charismatic authority of the revered Prabhupada has not been effectively routinized (Rochford, 1985; Shinn, 1985a). The *interface of factional strife and the movement's economic decline* (Rochford, 1985) presented a threat to the group's survival even before public investigations and media stories concerning violence and crime in the movement emerged in 1986.

Precariousness of the Market

Roy Wallis (1984: 86–7) notes that 'world-rejecting movements' such as Hare Krishna, the Children of God, or the Unification Church emerged 'out of the specific historical conditions of the disintegration of the counterculture, and depended on the existence of a substantial constituency of young people sufficiently alienated from their society to be prepared to seek such drastic alternatives to it'. While the decline of political radicalism in the early 1970s may have initially augmented the growth of religious movements (Bromley and Shupe, 1979a), the further decline of the countercultural climate undercut the appeal of radically unconventional and demanding religious groups, as did an economic recession in the 1970s and the more precarious job market. 'Economic contraction was incompatible with a widespread sense of social progress and experimentation. . . As the economic order of their society became more precarious, fewer young people wished to abandon it, even temporarily' (Wallis, 1984: 87).

Numerical stagnation and decline characterized many world-rejecting movements in the mid to late 1970s and early 1980s, including Hare Krishna (Judah, 1974; Rochford, 1985), the UC (Bromley and Shupe, 1979a; Lofland, 1977), the COG, and The People's Temple (Hall, 1987). The same decline in recruitment also affected some of the non-totalist and world-affirming movements such as Transcendental Meditation (Bainbridge and Jackson, 1981) and the Divine Light Mission (Downton, 1979). The threat of extinction was more immediate with respect to the more deviant and totalist world-rejecting movements, which have therefore felt a need to 'change their styles and methods of proselytization' to articulate a more accommodative response to dominant cultural expectations and to seek 'greater access to less marginal sectors of society' (Wallis, 1984: 87). Pertinent developments in the late 1970s and early 1980s included the Unificationist 'Home Church' program, which de-emphasized the necessity of dropping out of conventional routines (Wallis, 1984: 88), and the development of collaboration between the Hare Krishna movement and the immigrant Indians in the West, whose Hindu traditions highlight pilgrimages to temples and shrines (Melton, 1987; Rochford, 1985). The relaxation of sectarian rigor in some groups and the growth of a 'householder' component of the Krishna movement also reflects an accommodation to movement decline and environmental tension (Rochford, 1982, 1985; Wallis, 1981, 1984: 88–9). Wallis finds some support for the proposition advanced earlier by Robbins et al. (1975: 58) that there is 'a general tendency for youth culture religions to evolve in a more adaptive direction' (Wallis, 1984: 90).

While all kinds of NRMs must cope with market problems, the factor of the precariousness of the market is particularly salient with regard to world-affirming movements (discussed below), while problems related to charisma are often associated with world-rejecting groups. An analysis somewhat similar to that of Wallis (see discussion below) is propounded more briefly by Wilson (1987: 41–2) who compares communal (world-rejecting) and therapeutic groups.

Market Dynamics of Less Radical Movements. 'World-affirming' movements, such as Scientology or Transcendental Meditation, 'seem as a rule in no danger of an early demise', but they are nevertheless, highly marketed and 'tend to construe themselves in terms of a consumer commodity market and are thus liable to its vicissitudes, and subject to fluctuations in consumer taste' (Wallis, 1984: 90; see also Johnson, 1987a and Wilson, 1987).

Transcendental Meditation has been called 'the marketed social movement' (Johnston, 1980). Woodrum (1977, 1982) divides the history of TM into three distinct stages involving continuing adaptation to broad cultural shifts. As summarized by Wallis (1984: 90–1), an initial *spiritual–mystical period* (1959–65) was succeeded by a *voguish self-sufficiency period* (1966–9) in which rapid expansion was attained by identification with countercultural mystical themes. From 1970 on, a secularized *popular religious phase* emerged in which other-worldly references were diminished and practical therapeutic and instrumental benefits were stressed.

Within the broad Human Potential Movement (HPM), economic trends have heightened the appeal of *instrumentalist* movements which promise 'worldly' material and social benefits and undercut the appeal of groups which highlight mainly expressive and ecstatic emotional release (Hoffman, 1977). Some persisting groups such as Scientology 'are able to combine elements of both philosophies' (Wallis, 1984: 91). A diversity of commodities 'are thus available in the world-affirming range, between which market preference may shift' (Wallis, 1984: 91). *Product diversification* has thus ensued and has been particularly 'notable in Scientology, which has generated a vast range of new courses and procedures' (Wallis, 1984: 92) and in the broader Human Potential Movement (Wallis and Bruce, 1986: 157–221). The same may hold for the 'New Age' constellation of the mid 1980s.

Commercialization and Transcendentalization. Various therapeutic groups appear to have evolved in terms of their conceptual foundations from naturalistic systems to a primacy of *supernaturalistic claims*. This has been the case with regard to Scientology (Wallis, 1977), The Process (Bainbridge, 1978), Synanon (Ofshe, 1980b) and other offshoots of Scientology (Wallis, 1984: 92–3). Stark and Bainbridge seek to explain this developmental tendency in terms of their general exchange/market theory of religion (Stark and Bainbridge, 1985). Their general theory of religion and their specific applications to naturalist-to-supernaturalist sequences (Bainbridge and Jackson, 1981; Bainbridge and Stark, 1981; Stark, 1981; Stark and Bainbridge, 1980b, 1985) have been criticized by Roy Wallis and Steve Bruce (1986: 42–102; Wallis and Bruce, 1984: 47–74, 157–90).

Stark and Bainbridge argue that frustration necessarily ensues for devotees of movements which promise tangible, verifiable rewards such as enhanced IQ, effective resistance to illness, or greater material success.

This frustration imperils the legitimacy of movements via devotees' disconfirming experiences. Over time, then, a given movement will tend to shift its emphasis from naturalistic rewards to supernaturalistic 'compensators', *which cannot be clearly and tangibly disconfirmed*. Thus Scientology, which has developed a system of 'modern magic', is likely to evolve in a more clearly 'religious' direction (Bainbridge and Stark, 1980; Stark and Bainbridge, 1985: 263–83). This analysis is extended to the growth of 'religious' claims in therapeutic movements such as Synanon (Ofshe, 1980b) and The Process (Bainbridge, 1978).

Wallis's interviews with ex-members of The Process indicate that those members who persisted in their commitment through the movement's transformation into a religion actually believed that the movement in its earlier phases 'had in fact been producing the goods', and that the new spiritual goals were accepted as *additional* motivators rather than as substitutes for earlier naturalistic goals and rewards (Wallis, 1984: 94; Wallis and Bruce, 1986: 64). An analysis of the biographies of followers of Dianetics, L. Ron Hubbard's naturalistic forerunner of Scientology, indicates that although drop-outs from Dianetics tended to believe that involvement had indeed failed to provide promised naturalistic rewards, 'Those who remained through the transition to Scientology either believed that they had received substantial naturalistic rewards, or they had been looking for something spiritual all along. . .' (Wallis and Bruce, 1986: 64). Although Wallis feels that these findings tend to refute the Stark–Bainbridge analysis, the theoretical possibility exists that persisting devotees and leaders who thought they had received naturalistic rewards began to stress supernaturalistic rewards *because they saw other followers leaving the movement in a state of disillusionment with the promise of naturalistic rewards*.

The transformation from a naturalistic reward orientation to an increasing emphasis on supernaturalism seems to have occurred repeatedly in the HPM (Stone, 1976; Wallis and Bruce, 1986: 183–5), both in terms of the transformation of movements such as Scientology (Wallis, 1977) and in terms of the alteration of individual orientations and shifts of affiliations, e.g. the recruitment of HPM veterans into the Bhagwan Movement of Shree Rajneesh (Wallis and Bruce, 1986: 183–5, 195–204). The continuous transcendentalization of the HPM has developed 'in consequence of factors quite contrary to the Stark–Bainbridge proposals' (Wallis and Bruce, 1986: 68). Many persons involved in the HPM found that its techniques did produce powerful and provocative effects on them:

The very success of its methods gave rise to new questions, awakened new interests, and thus provoked further search, again leading in a more spiritual direction as followers and practitioners sought to find a *general* explanation and plan behind the effects of diverse *particular* practices and remedies. The very diffuseness of the movement ideology encouraged a spiritual drift for many who found that rewards they sought *had* been produced. Just as Hindu philosophy can explain and justify the worship of thousands of different gods and spirits, so a religious ideology can bring together and make sense of a smorgasbord of secular therapies (Wallis and Bruce, 1986: 68; see also Anthony et al., 1978).

Perhaps an analogy might be made here with the earlier sequence of individuals who proceeded from psychedelic drugs to Eastern mysticism (Johnson, 1976; Robbins, 1969; Robbins and Anthony, 1972) not because hallucinogens did not produce powerful effects, but rather because *these effects appeared too chaotic, uncontrollable and ephemeral.*

In Wallis and Bruce's view, the transcendentalization of movements and personal identities evolving within the context of the HPM offered viable solutions, not to problems related to the failure of groups and practices to produce rewards, but to the *diffuseness* of the HPM ideology and the pervasive epistemological individualism within the HPM whereby each client or devotee is the ultimate arbiter of how he or she interprets experiences, what beliefs are accepted and what behaviors are sanctioned.

'Epistemological individualism', in Wallis and Bruce's view, is linked to market conditions when 'the customer is the final arbiter of whether he needs, or has benefited from, a particular service', such that a supplier must differentiate his product(s) 'to accommodate diverse interests and backgrounds' (Wallis and Bruce, 1986: 178). Instability is built into movements which ultimately depend upon the shifting whims of the 'salvational consumer', who 'may sample at will; buy something of what is offered from one producer and move on to another...' (Wallis, 1984: 97), altering his taste in accordance with transitory fads and fashion (Bird and Westley, 1985; Johnson, 1987a).

Wallis and Bruce's trend analysis of the broad Human Potential or Growth Movement indicates that those movements have prospered which have *explicitly organized themselves on commercial lines*, e.g. Scientology, est, Silva Mind Control and Lifespring. Concurrently the targeted clientele has shifted from countercultural youth to more respectable and conventional persons and institutions, e.g. corporations operating executive training programs. 'Developments of these kinds inevitably encouraged the adoption of a professional model of the relationship between practitioners and clients... The emergence of commercialism and professionalism as organizational principles are in direct consequence of the movement's precariousness, resulting from the location of authority with each member, that is, from its *epistemological individualism*' (Wallis, 1984: 100).

Religious trends in the HPM and specifically the recruitment of Human Potential veterans, including experienced group leaders, to the Bhagwan Rajneesh movement (Wallis and Bruce, 1986: 157–221) emerged in part as a reaction against commercialism, 'Those who could not adjust to the Growth Movement as a merely commercial or professional enterprise were often strongly attracted to a movement such as that of Bhagwan, which contained an extensive round of growth activities, within the framework of a life of spiritual devotion and a community of the like-minded' (Wallis, 1984: 100–1).

Transcendentalization of world-affirming therapeutic movements competing in a market context can also be viewed as a strategy to insulate a movement from demand fluctuations. 'To achieve this end, clients must be transformed into followers, undermining their authority to operate in the market as free agents' (Wallis, 1984: 101):

> The most readily available method of arrogating authority is through the proclamation of some spiritual revelation permitting the transcendentalizing of one's product, thereby giving it greater breadth of relevance and the promise of vastly greater efficacy, and providing the resources for demanding a higher level of involvement, commitment and loyalty than hitherto. Such is the logic of the transition which turned Dianetics into Scientology (Wallis, 1984: 101).

Transcendentalization in the service of demand control is accompanied by other devices such as 'laicization' or extension of the hierarchy of sanctification such that 'advanced' devotees are encouraged to strive to ascend to newly formulated, more advanced levels, e.g. Scientology's elevated *clear* status 'becomes merely the first step to O.T. [Operating Thetan]. Transcendental Meditation, once the complete answer to the world's ills, is relegated to the status of prerequisite for training to achieve the powers of the Siddhis' (Wallis, 1984: 102). Increasingly the felt imperative is not merely to encourage continued devotee/client loyalty, 'but to *demand* it through the implementation of methods of social control' (Wallis, 1984: 102) such as Scientology's stringent system of 'Ethics' (Straus, 1986). These developments are facilitated 'by a shift from offering a mundane or empirical product, to a more transcendentally based commodity or system of belief and practice' (Wallis, 1984: 102). The risk here is that enhanced '[product] differentiation, transcendentalization, and sectarian control may simply drive away the remainder of the declining original clientele' (Wallis, 1984: 102), or that legal complications may attend a greater reliance on manipulative recruitment and stringent social control (Beckford, 1985a).

Currently the HPM appears to have been assimilated to the broader

'New Age' subculture. The latter appears to be increasingly commercialized as well as increasingly redolent of supernaturalism, a key instance being the commercialized mediumistic practice of 'channeling' (Babbie, 1987). Applications of the concepts and analytical frameworks developed by both Stark and Bainbridge and Wallis and Bruce may prove fruitful here.

Financing the Millennium

Wallis's analysis of the 'precariousness of the market' deals with the 'economics' of NRMs broadly conceived. We turn now to the NRM economics in the narrow sense of the specific financial and commercial practices of NRMs. The above subtitle is taken from a penetrating report by Bromley (1985) on the financial structure and commercial operations of the Unificationist Movement (UM) of Sun Myung Moon. According to Bromley, an understanding of the financing of contemporary NRMs is indispensable to an appreciation of recent American religious experimentation. Although the growth of NRMs in recent decades has been attributed to various sociocultural factors involving shifting values and weakened families, nevertheless:

> ...new religions also articulate with economic components of contemporary society as well. The social landscape is dominated by advanced mass media technology and corporate style organization on an international scale. The New Christian Right, for example, has discovered the utility of harnessing the mass media to its religious purposes. Other new religious movements as well reflect and have adapted to this environment although the style of the adaptations varies. Transcendental Meditation and Scientology have merged economics and religion by detaching and marketing specific aspects or spin-offs of their religious practice (i.e., their meditation techniques and "technologies," respectively). The UM has taken a somewhat different but analogous tack. It has created an economic conglomerate to underwrite its theological agenda (Bromley, 1985: 272).

Although many churches have amassed substantial wealth throughout history, the UM appears somewhat unique in that 'international, corporate organizations have been established and nurtured to propel the movement' (Bromley, 1985: 272). Much of the 'success' of the Moon movement 'must be attributed to its economic base. This strategy, of course, has also been a major source of problems for the movement' (Bromley 1985: 273). Extreme economic diversification has rendered NRM 'empires' more vulnerable to state intervention (Robbins, 1985a). Other problems for the movement are likely to be created or aggravated by the nature and extent of its economic infrastructure, which will impact on its evolutionary prognosis. 'Since the UM's prominence in the United States is so heavily dependent on economic resources, the American UM is a drain on international movement resources, and the movement is dominated by Japanese and Korean leadership, the long term prognosis for the American branch of the UM is murky' (Bromley, 1985: 272).

Distinctiveness of NRM Economic Strategies. An important analysis of the 'Economic Strategies of New Religious Movements' (Bird and Westley, 1985), based on research on groups in the Montreal area, maintains that the economic strategies of contemporary new religious and para-religious movements tend to possess a distinctive character. They are characterized by (1) services provided for fees or donations by largely transient 'clients' or affiliates, and/or (2) essentially unpaid labor (in public solicitation or commercial projects) donated by highly committed adepts. The economic strategies of contemporary NRMs are also notable for their lack of dependence upon regular financial contributions from continuing lay members which has 'traditionally been the backbone of the political economy...of most religous movements' (Bird and Westley, 1985: 169).

Bird and Westley argue that the distinctive financing modes of contemporary NRMs render the latter *economically unstable*. Clients may never become strongly committed; they will come and go and offer transitory allegiance to various organizations in response to shifting fads and fashions in the 'spiritual supermarket' (Johnson, 1987a; Wallis, 1984: 86–102). Highly committed adepts, on the other hand, tend to become an 'ideologically closed group' which is likely to gradually lose connection with the broader culture and thus with the needs and predilections of the potential spiritual 'consumers'. 'Without [regular lay] members to act as mediators, adepts who become too insulated will be unable to market services to the clientele upon which they depend' (Bird and Westley, 1985: 169).

The analysis of Bird and Westley is highly provocative and may pinpoint a vital weakness in the recent spiritual 'awakening'. Nevertheless, there are several possible flaws: (1) many movements, particularly 'neo-Christian' groups, do have a large proportion of 'lay' members, who, moreover, are more likely to tithe than are members of more conventional churches; (2) many new churches throughout American and European history have begun as groups consisting disproportionately of totally committed adepts but have eventually developed a professional clergy differentiated from a less involved lay congregation (Niebuhr, 1929; Wallis, 1981); and (3) some groups appear to depend heavily on large gifts from a few wealthy adepts, e.g. the grandiose Detroit Hare Krishna Temple complex was originally built with money from a Ford family heir.

On the other hand, Bird and Westley's arguments regarding the instability of financing based on clients paying fees/donations for services and/or the unpaid labor of virtuoso adepts seem quite correct. In the United States certain legal factors are emerging which threaten both aspects of NRMs' economic strategies (Robbins, 1985a). It has been claimed that the fee-for-service exchange patterns entailed in some religiotherapeutic movements really embody professional–client relationships, which are subject to legal regulation in terms of preventing fraud (when promised benefits do not materialize) and applying criteria of informed consent to the use of psychologically intrusive techniques (Heins, 1981; Richardson, 1986, 1988a; Robbins, 1985a, 1988). Large civil awards have been granted by juries to ex-devotees of the Church of Scientology.

It has also been argued that the services donated by devotees to religious movements entail oppressive *exploitation* (or even de facto *slavery*) when devotee labor is remunerated in spiritual rather than material terms (Delgado, 1979–80; Ofshe, 1982; Robbins, 1981, 1985a). Kilbourne (1986b), however, reports that 'Moonies' do not *feel* exploited. In 1985 the US Supreme Court ruled that commercial operations transpiring under the auspices of a religious organization are subject to the minimum wage and overtime provisions of the Fair Labor Standards Act (Robbins, 1985a, 1988).

In general, non-bureaucratized churches without hierarchical levels and churches which draw their major funding from the public (i.e. from non-members) are: (1) more prone to financial mismanagement and 'corruption'; (2) have fewer internal mechanisms for accountability to donors; and (3) are therefore more susceptible to state intervention (Ofshe, 1980a; Regan, 1986; Robbins, 1988). The US Internal Revenue Service (and equivalent foreign agencies) constitute powerful environmental forces mediating the financial stability of NRMs and influencing shifts in their economic strategies and basic institutional patterns (Emory and Zelenak, 1985; Richardson, 1985a, 1986; Robbins, 1985a, 1988a; Stark, 1987a).

Economics and Ideology. In the mid 1970s, 'the counterculture ideal which supported alternative religions lost popularity' (Khalsa, 1986: 244; see also Rochford, 1985; Wallis, 1984). 'The loss in enrollment combined with a recessive national economy placed the new religions in a position that required the development of creative and practical techniques for group survival. Consequently funding methods were needed that did not depend on ever-increasing numbers' (Khalsa, 1986: 244). Ideological changes were then required to legitimate apparent goal-displacement entailed in a greater stress on economic activities and a diminished emphasis on missionizing and membership growth (Rochford, 1985; Khalsa, 1986). An increasing emphasis on a worldly success ethos seems to have been a significant dimension of the institutionalization of movements such as the Happy–Healthy–Holy (3HO) Sikh movement (Khalsa, 1986), the Vajradhatu Tibetan Buddhist church (Khalsa, 1986), and Hare Krishna (Rochford, 1985). In contrast to the Weber–Michels goal-displacement model of institutionalization, the development of hierarchical structures in 3HO and Vajradhatu has not emerged as an unanticipated result of group activity in behalf of expressed spiritual goals, but rather appears to represent a *deliberate policy* and an autonomous goal (Khalsa, 1986). Patterns of institutionalization in these movements are further linked to 'the turn toward worldly success', which 'must be understood as being initiated by the charismatic leadership' (Khalsa, 1986: 243).

Rochford (1985: 192–214) discusses the 'ideological work' which Hare Krishna devotees have found it necessary to engage in to rationalize their subjective perceptions of despiritualizing goal-displacement entailed in the heightened organizational emphasis on commercial pursuits and financial solicitation. The need to legitimate deviant instrumental behavior, e.g. 'stealing for Krishna' (Rochford, 1985: 198; Michael, 1988) has also spurred ideological work.

Like Khalsa (1986), Rochford (1985) has focused on the *linkage between a movement's institutionalization and its economic practices*. In particular, Rochford probes the interface between the financial strain on the ISKON and the recent factionalism arising from the failure to routinize the charisma of the revered founder of the movement, Swami Prabhupada (see earlier discussion). Economic imperatives have intensified the conflicts among regional gurus and between gurus and dissidents disenchanted with the post-Prabhupada regional guru system. In a context of financial stringency, regional gurus have invaded (operated commercial enterprises within) each others' assigned territories, competed for the allegiance of entrepreneurially skilled devotees, suppressed commercial operations organized by devotees not under their control and often followed divergent economic policies (Rochford, 1985: 224–7). Increasingly, the organizational emphasis has shifted from missionizing and sacred book distribution to selling commercial objects ('picking'), which may appear unrelated to the Hare Krishna creed, e.g. buttons with the Pope's picture on them! (Rochford, 1985: 227). Notwithstanding adaptive ideological work, many devotees became alienated from the emerging patterns and left the movement or transferred their allegiance from a regional guru who emphasized picking to one who still encouraged book distribution (Rochford, 1985).

Expanding the Focus on Economic Practices. We may now know more about the financial and commercial practices of 'cults' than of 'churches'. Both types of religious organizations tend to be secretive in this area, but the operations of NRMs are more visible (e.g. street solicitation, restaurants, boutiques); moreover, alleged abuses have spurred investigations. But most of the work on financing NRMs and the literature discussed above is fairly recent. A number of monographs on specific groups have contained significant information on financial patterns including the early 'resource mobilization' analysis of the Unificationist Movement by Bromley and Shupe (1979a), plus works by Wallis (1977) and Cooper (1971) on Scientology, Wooden (1981) and Hall (1987) on The People's Temple, Tipton (1982a) dealing in part with est, Bainbridge (1978) on The Process, Rochford (1985) on ISKON and Richardson et al. (1979) on Shiloh. Fairly early papers by Ofshe (1976, 1980b) on Synanon and Johnston on TM (1980) also focus on economic practices. The collection on the UM edited by Horowitz (1978) deals extensively with interpenetrating political and economic operations. *Strange Gods* (Bromley and Shupe, 1981) and articles by Bromley and Shupe (1980) and Richardson (1982a, 1983) discuss financial operations as do the later papers discussed above (Bird and Westley, 1985; Bromley, 1985; Khalsa, 1986).

A forthcoming special issue of *Sociological Analysis* (Richardson, 1988c) deals with economic and legal problems involving NRMs and will include a paper on the economics of The People's Temple by John Hall. James Richardson, the special editor of this issue, is also editor of *Money and Power in New Religious Movements* (1988d) which includes many significant papers among which are the original authors' extensions of Bird and Westley's earlier analysis of distinctive patterns of NRM financing and Bromley's analysis of the economic practices of the UC. There are additional chapters dealing with the Love Family (Balch), ISKON (Rochford), Transcendental Meditation (Johnston), est (Tipton), Rajneesh (Mullan), Mormons (Heinerman and Shupe) and 'a communal psychotherapy cult' (Oakes). Additional theoretical papers are offered (or reprinted) by Richardson and by Singh. This writer's chapter, 'Profits for Prophets', explores alleged abuses of NRMs and related legal issues arising in a number of areas, e.g. employment, social services (therapeutic and other), financial mismanagement, tax exemption and contested 'religious' authenticity.

Conclusion

In 'God's Little Acres' (Cawley, 1979) a journalist describes the extreme commercialization of the messianic Brother Julius sect in New England, which became heavily involved in real estate and other economic enterprises. Funds were shifted from spiritual projects such as revision of holy scriptures to commercial enterprises and finally Brother Julius was shunted aside by a new leadership manifesting an increasingly secular outlook. Devotees who did not appear to be commercially viable (i.e. skilled, disciplined and presentable in business suits) were forced out of the group. The pattern appeared to entail marked goal displacement.

The economic or financial dimension of NRMs increasingly seems to become significant as a stimulus determining the direction of movement evolution. A recent study of American communes reports that the communal period of many nineteenth century utopian social experiments was really fairly short, but the movements sometimes persisted as corporations pursuing economic rationality (Erasmus, 1977). Organizations may tend to persist even if their goals shift drastically in the process (Ofshe, 1980b). The competitive capitalist context of the American sociocultural environment may facilitate goal displacement in a direction of economic rationality.

Certain difficulties may arise to impede commercialization. FitzGerald (1986) reports how European followers of Shree Bhagwan Rajneesh spontaneously developed a variety of enterprises and contributed some of their profits to the guru's Rajneeshpuram community in Oregon. The economic complex rapidly declined, however, after emissaries from the guru imposed a ruthless but economically dysfunctional policy of centralized control and putative rationalization. The proclivity of authoritarian religious leadership to centralize, closely supervise and ruthlessly 'milk' businesses may demoralize local adherents, whose initiative and creativity are essential to the creation and maintenance of dynamic enterprises.

Another difficulty pertains to the advantages of maintaining a 'religious' designation as a 'church' and 'non-profit' organization to minimize regulatory intrusion and safeguard tax privileges (Ofshe, 1980a, 1986; Robbins, 1985a, 1988b). While a group such as Scientology clings to its a status as a church and uses it to obviate regulatory constraints (Robbins,

1988b; Straus, forthcoming), Transcendental Meditation has rejected a status which might inhibit the opportunities for legally inculcating its techniques in military, correctional and (public) educational contexts.

Finally, the commercial and financial diversification of NRMs is implicated in their continually shifting and elaborated organizational structures, as well as attempts to conceal this structure. Carter (1987: 168) notes the 'Many and changing corporate facades' of the Bhagwan Rajneesh movement:

> Businesses are incorporated in several countries with several profit and non-profit corporations (cooperatives, foundations and trusts) operating in the same locations and resources transferred routinely among these. Each corporation has a separate legal identity, somewhat distinct purpose and considerable interlock. As new challenges are encountered by the movement, new legal identities are created to receive resources, implement new policies, and obscure accountability (Carter, 1987: 151).

Bromley (1985), Grafstein (1984) and Moore (1980) offer somewhat similar observations with regard to the Unification Church and other NRMs which might be termed 'religious multinationals' (Beckford, 1981b). The manipulative volatility of some 'manufactured' social movements (Carter, 1987) may confuse attempts at analyses in terms of long-term institutionalization processes.

5

TYPOLOGICAL ANALYSES AND
EVALUATIONS OF NEW MOVEMENTS

The study of NRMs has been replete with various typologies of new movements (Bird, 1979; Robbins et al., 1978; Wallis, 1984) as well as attempts to extrapolate a concept of 'cult' and assimilate it to the tradition of church–sect theory (Stark and Bainbridge, 1985; Swatos, 1975; Wallis, 1974, 1975a,b). Scholars associated with the 'Anti-cult Movement' (ACM) have developed concepts of the 'extremist cult' (Enroth, 1977) or 'destructive cult' (Shapiro, 1977; Clark et al., 1981). Additional normative and critical typologists and models, also responding to the abuses and problems which have arisen in the context of contemporary spiritual innovations, have been advanced by theorists otherwise sympathetic to mystical and 'New Age' spiritual currents (Anthony and Ecker, 1987; Wilber, 1983, 1987).

The usefulness of these typologies is problematic. Some of the most interesting typologies have been formulated for future empirical employment which has been indefinitely deferred. Typologizing 'new movements' presupposes that the boundaries of the entity being typologized are known; however, 'NRMs' denotes a rather ambiguous phenomenon and the status of newer evangelical churches, older fundamentalist or Pentecostal groups presently experiencing surging growth, older mystical or occult groups (e.g. Vedanta, Rosicrucians) and older prophetic movements such as Mormons or Jehovah's Witnesses is unclear. How 'new' are current 'new religions' (Melton, 1987)? How does a typology of contemporary (largely Euro-American) movements relate to religious forms in other times and places?

The typologizing enterprise will optimally be linked to a specific theoretical or a normative objective e.g. to discriminate 'good' from 'bad' groups or to extrapolate a theory of the origins, evolution, processes, patterns, sources and consequences of different groups. Thus the typologizing work of Anthony and Robbins was initially linked to a theory of contemporary cultural dislocation involving a posited deepening climate of moral ambiguity stimulating the construction of new spiritual meanings in terms of 'dualistic' and 'monistic' responses to moral indeterminacy (Anthony, 1979–80; Robbins and Anthony, 1982b). The theoretico-normative grounding of a typology may partly obviate questions of universality and boundary definition, which are most pressing when the typology exists more or less for its own sake or is putatively preliminary to theory building. The more valuable or at least more interesting typological structures will probably be linked to theoretical constructions, which suggests a criterion for evaluating the effectiveness or 'success' of a typology:

> It must be recognized, however, that any given body of phenomena is susceptible to classification in terms of an infinite number of typological schemes. Thus, ultimately, the test of a typology lies not in its components, but rather in the uses to which it can be put, particularly that of identifying the significant characteristics of the phenomena in terms of a theory which turns out to be able to bear the heat of critical appraisal. It is at this point that the adequacy of the Robbins and Anthony schema falls most into question...(Wallis, 1984: 4).

New religious movements generally entail visions of a better world or a more perfected humanity; yet this 'utopian promise' has been said to have produced the 'infernal reality' of a noxious cultism (West, 1982). Some of the most interesting typological analyses of NRMs have understandably manifested an explicitly normative dimension.

Critical and Normative Schema: The Anthony Typology

A typology developed mainly by Dick Anthony is intended as the basis for a *critical sociology and psychology of religion*. There is an explicit normative focus involving the discrimination of 'authentic' from 'inauthentic' paths to transcendence, as well as a diagnosis of destructive social and psychological consequences arising in the context of contemporary spiritual innovation and resurgence. A subtext of the Anthony typology entails a vindication of contemporary spiritual seeking in the face of its acknowledged degraded and degenerate aspects. Formulated most recently in a lengthy essay by Anthony and Ecker (1987), the typology builds upon earlier and simpler versions developed by Anthony in collaboration with the present writer (Anthony, 1979–1980; Anthony and Robbins, 1982a,b; 1987; Robbins and Anthony, 1979, 1987; Robbins et al., 1978).

In Anthony and Ecker's view, contemporary movements reflect a fundamental cultural transformation in the West. 'Spiritual seeking in the new religions occurs in the context of this societal shift from paternalistic to autonomous authority, and in many groups the seeking is largely a search for that capacity to find meaning autonomously, within one's own experience, rather than having meaning conferred externally' (1987:9).

Given the enhanced search for authentic meaning, certain issues arise which are being addressed both by some New Age thinkers and by the Anti-Cult Movement. Anthony and Ecker discuss 'the spiritual seeker's dilemma':

> People need some way of relating to a source of knowing that goes beyond what they already possess, and they need to be open about that need. The issue then becomes how people can admit to having that healthy need and seek help without opening themselves up to manipulation and exploitation by those who are merely pretending to have achieved genuine autonomous authority...The seeker has to sail between the Scylla of groups in which the search for autonomous authority is believed futile and is therefore relinquished in favor of group identity and submission to paternalistic authoritarianism, and the Charybids of groups in which members are educated in the *simulation* of real autonomy, generating not autonomy but aloofness, atomistic individualism, and existential isolation (1987: 9–10).

Monistic vs. Dualistic Perspectives. The Anthony typology has three dimensions; the *metaphysical dimension* of monism–dualism: the technical –charismatic *mode of practice dimension*; and the dimension of unilevel–multilevel *interpretive sensibility*. The monism–dualism distinction is ethico-salvational and entails the contrast between absolutist conceptions of good vs. evil and the 'oneness' which is ultimately 'beyond good and evil'. Monism also relativizes the eschatological polarity of saved vs. damned. However, *ontological* dualism, which simply bifurcates mundane and transcendental realms, would characterize some worldviews which Anthony would designate as monistic.

Monism actually involves a complex of meanings (Anthony and Ecker, 1987; Anthony and Robbins, 1982a,b) which include illusoriness of the phenomenal world (*Maya*), *Karma* and reincarnation, and derivative notions of the ultimate relativity of mundane values, the ineffability of experience and the premium on intrapsychic exploration and inner mystical *gnosis*. Some groups, most notably Hare Krishna, accept key concepts such as *Maya* and *Karma*, but deny the monistic end-state of merging of the self with the Godhead or with all other selves in an impersonal absolute such as *Nirvana*. There are also quasi-monistic therapeutic movements which lack coherently worked out monistic systems but stress certain monistic derivations such as the primacy of inner consciousness. Monism is associated with Max Weber's concept of exemplary prophecy and with 'oriental' or Hindu–Buddhist traditions, while dualism is linked to ethical –emissary prophecy and with the dominant traditions of 'Abrahamic' religion (Hexham and Poewe, 1986). Monism conceives of salvation as a quasi-cognitive process, i.e. *enlightenment*, while dualism stresses *volition* and heightens the sense of eschatological *contingency*, 'of individual destinies dividing into two primary directions symbolized by the themes of heaven and hell' (Anthony and Ecker, 1987: 38).

The *technical–charismatic* practical dimension deals with whether 'techniques — any repetitive mental or physical processes that can be taught through explicit instruction — are the basis for seeking spiritual transformation' or whether spiritual attainment is sought mainly through a direct (and transformative) contact or relationship with a spiritual leader or master who is perceived 'as a direct link with, or embodiment of divine authority, knowledge, and love. . . ' (Anthony and Ecker, 1987: 39). Most unambiguously technical groups are monistic, for example, Scientology *qua* 'technological Buddhism' (Flinn, 1983).

Unilevel and Multilevel Religion. This is really the key critical dimension of the typology. Unilevel groups, according to Anthony and Ecker (1987), 'are overly literal and "definitive" in their appreciation of language and texts, with too little appreciation of symbolic and metaphoric levels of meaning' (p. 41); religious statements are interpreted univocally, 'as if they were scientific statements with decisive, unambiguous meanings' (p. 59); unilevel interpretations foster an idolatry of the self, often in subtle, unconscious, and covert ways' (p. 59). Unilevel interpretations of spiritual meanings manifest epistemological consequentialism or 'the attitude that the value as well as the proof of spiritual tranformation lies in predictable, observable consequences in the mundane sphere' (p. 41), e.g. enhanced personal efficacy, ecstatic trance states, a sense of cognitive closure, etc.; univocality and consequentialism 'are the defining features of the unilevel category' (p. 41).

Multilevel groups regard spiritual systems and teachings as encompassing various levels of meaning, 'There is nothing like a definitive understanding of spiritual teachings, except for the understanding that comes with ultimate or final enlightment' (Anthony and Ecker, 1987: 42). Multilevel groups distinguish between mundane and transcendental realms such that 'ultimate' truths are seen as pertaining to the latter and do not necessarily have direct mundane consequences, e.g. the indoctrinated devotee who 'knows' that the phenomenal world is illusory cannot therefore levitate or walk through walls, or immediately get rich or heal ulcers.

Some (unilevel) monistic groups such as TM (Bainbridge and Jackson, 1981) and Scientology (Bainbridge and Stark, 1980) do appear to promise devotees superhuman powers, while also stressing the latters' enhanced instrumental efficacy, a theme also promoted by some (putatively unilevel–dualist) Christian evangelical mystiques. Unilevel, monistic, technical groups tend to emphasize standardized techniques (e.g. meditation, chanting, 'auditing', seminar training) which enhance mundane personal well-being as well as produce higher spiritual enlightenment. Unilevel, dualistic, technical groups tend to stress healing plus the reaping of instrumental rewards through prayer and faith, and thus seem to imply the *synonymity of spiritual virtue and success*. Unilevel groups generally tend to *resolve spirituality into terms which evoke dominant cultural motifs* such as technical rationality, competitive individualism, etc.

This dynamic can also be seen in the relationship between unilevel monism and the hedonistic and permissive cultural style highlighted by American social critics in the 1970s. 'Since Eastern systems tend to see collective social reality as illusion... salvation therefore involves the transcendence of society's moral rules, the socially conditioned notions of good and evil' (Anthony and Ecker, 1987: 63) But this 'Eastern' idea tends to be interpreted from the standpoint of 'the American's utilitarian–individualist mentality'. Some unilevel monistic groups seem to have developed an ethos of 'Tantric Freudianism' which synthesizes the popular Freudian emphasis on attaining freedom through cathartic release of repressed impulses with a simplistic unilevel understanding of Tantra in terms of a prescription for acting out proscribed urges as a means of 'transcending one's socially conditioned limited identity, revealing good and evil in their true light as arbitrary cultural constructs' (Anthony and Ecker, 1987: 66). Tantric Freudianism has most conspicuously been manifested among the devotees of Shree Rajneesh (Hummel and Hardin, 1983; Palmer, 1988; Wallis and Bruce, 1986).

Radical antinomianism and deviant acting out are most likely in unilevel, monistic, charismatic groups such as the 'Manson Cult' in which the monistic theme of getting 'beyond good and evil' may have been taken too literally (Nielsen, 1984). Charismatic groups lack the disciplining and centering influence of rationalized spiritual techniques and may therefore encourage impulsivity and dramatic, disruptive acting-out.

Most charismatic monistic groups tend to be rather small and often unstable. They lack the appeal which derives from the appropriation of technical rationality in unilevel, monistic, technical movements such as Scientology, TM, est and Silva Mind Control which emphasize the attainment of enlightenment, mastery and autonomy through teachable procedures and knowledge. 'The techniques involve a considerable degree of disciplined attention to immediate, pragmatic, means–ends relationships which breaks the impulsivity and grandiosity which is associated with unilevel monism' (Anthony and Ecker, 1987: 69). However, the rewards obtained through monistic, technical, unilevel movements such as Scientology may be associated with other costs related to the systematic legitimation and extrapolation of utilitarian individualism in such groups, e.g. participants are arguably socialized in a mode of ruthlessness and ethical callousness. Unilevel monism is said to promote a style of personal mastery which entails a repudiation of binding commitments to others in favor of limited, specific contractual arrangements.

Less is said about unilevel dualism. 'As a rule, unilevel dualistic ideas carry to a rigid extreme the emphasis on a collective or group-oriented sense of identity that characterizes the dualistic traditions' (Anthony and Ecker, 1987: 60). Some unilevel dualist groups explicitly combine religious and political themes and thus represent 'civil religion sects' (Anthony and Robbins, 1981a, 1982b), which tend to develop absolutist quasi-theocratic ideologies and to form authoritarian communal enclaves intended to be exemplary models of a future perfect society.

Such sects may articulate a dualistic moral absolutism in which the group sees itself as totally uncorrupt in sharp contrast to a degraded milieu. This idealized in-group image may be associated psychologically with repression–projection processes and sociologically with intensified conflict with the surrounding society. These processes may be mitigated in dualistic technical groups, which include Pentecostal groups, faith-healing groups and Christian positive thinking groups, and 'gospel of health and wealth' systems. Unilevel dualistic groups which are also charismatic tend to be the most volatile.

Anthony and Ecker's discussion of *multilevel groups* is less interesting to the social scientist. The discussion of multilevel groups is somewhat idealized and tends to be proscriptive and less analytical in social scientific terms. However, the ideal of the 'authentic path' involving more subtle understandings of symbols and less egoistical or authoritarian extra-polations of spiritual identities is an essential baseline for delineating the analytical and critical concept of distorted unilevel spirituality as a complex of interrelated deviations, fallacies and epistemological errors which connect with mundane cultural motifs or with pathological psycho-dynamics to enhance varieties of malaise, psychopathology and destructive social tensions. Unilevel monistic mysticism ultimately amounts to 'another form of instrumental rationality' (Anthony and Ecker, 1987: 354) which reinforces rather than undercuts cultural controls over con-sciousness. Anthony thus partly supports the debunking views of Cox (1977), Lasch (1979) and Wilson (1976) to the effect that the dominant 'secular' complex of instrumental rationality and institutional controls can coexist with a 'spiritual supermarket' of irrationalist mystiques.

Problems and Criticisms. The Anthony typology is extrapolated from
the earlier typological work by Anthony and Robbins, which has been
widely commented on. As Anthony and Ecker (1987) acknowledge, there
are sometimes difficulties in applying the categories, e.g. what about
a monistic group led by a guru who is viewed as embodying higher
awakening (i.e. a charismatic leader) but who teaches *techniques*? Bird
(1979: 37) argues that the blanket description of various Eastern-originated
groups as monistic blurs the distinctions between Buddhist, Hindu and
Taoist traditions. Wallis (1984: 65) notes that while Anthony and Robbins
(1981a) tend to associate political aspirations with dualistic 'civil religion
sects' and see monism as quietistic–apolitical, they ignore the imperial
political aims of an expansionist 'monistic' movement such as Scientology. Wallis also notes the failure of Anthony and Robbins to present
empirical evidence in support of their argument (Anthony and Robbins,
1981a, 1982a,b) that monistic and dualistic movements are now arising
in response to a crisis of civil religion and a disorienting milieu of
moral ambiguity.

Beckford (1985a: 74) argues that the attention given by Anthony and
Robbins to monism obscures the fact that varieties of dualism are much
more prevalent in American spiritual culture. Beckford praises the
typology for being directed at theoretical issues regarding the evolution
of modern Western society and for highlighting the reciprocal relationship between the growth of NRMs 'and problems of societal order,
meaning, identity, legitimation, and integration. But the precise articula-
tion between the various subtypes of movements and the diverse facets
of these high-level problems has not been clarified.' It has not yet been
shown that the typology 'can be fruitfully applied in empirical investigations of NRMs' (Beckford, 1985a: 74).

Compared to the earlier Anthony–Robbins papers, the Anthony–Ecker
discussion is much richer in terms of the analysis of psychological
dynamics. The sociological dimension is less developed. It is unclear
whether the 'types' really pertain to *groups*, abstract *systems* of thought
and practice, or *individual orientations* and styles varying within the same
group or system. Anthony and Ecker do discuss how some groups alter
their central tendencies over time and thus shift the categorical location.

From a sociological standpoint the most provocative aspect of the
Anthony typology is the analysis of how NRMs, through their unilevel
or technical–charismatic properties, respond to and incorporate dominant
sociocultural motifs such as utilitarian and competitive individualism,
technical rationality, civil religion themes, etc. (see also Wuthnow, 1985).
In the process, unilevel religion also frequently supports the socioeconomic

status quo. Thus, unilevel monism may legitimate complacency about social inequality via Karmic explanations of poverty and suffering, which, from a multilevel standpoint, entail an 'epistemological sleight of hand' (Anthony and Ecker, 1987: 51). It would seem to be implied that it is largely unilevel distortions of authentic spiritual meanings which 'sell out' to mundane social values and class privilege. But may not the literalist and epistemologically empiricist quality of unilevel interpretations promote social radicalism, while more subtle multilevel formulations accommodate the status quo of social hierarchy?

Finally, the provocative unilevel–multilevel distinction is particularly difficult to operationalize. Concrete applications of the key critical concept are really somewhat akin to subtle clinical judgements and arguably lack 'reliability'!

Ken Wilber's Hierarchical Model. The present writer has argued (Robbins, 1983a, 1985, 1988) that the rise of controversial 'cults' as well as present tendencies in terms of the overt politicization of religion have undercut the value-neutral positivist 'scientific study of religion' and have given an impetus to normative and critical sociologies of religion. Ken Wilber's sociology of religion, developed in his volume *A Sociable God* (Wilber, 1983) and summarized in a more recent essay (Wilber, 1987) has attracted some attention among sociologists of religion and is significant in terms of typological analysis and evaluation of NRMs.

Wilber's 'developmental structuralist' perspective synthesizes structuralist cognitive psychology (e.g. Piaget) and classical and contemporary mystical literature. Wilber proposes an evolutionary hierarchy of stages or levels of spiritual development. *Pre-rational* or subconscious stages include 'archaic', 'magic' and 'mythic' levels of consciousness. *Rational self-consciousness* represents a kind of evolutionary midpoint which is also a foundation for future spiritual growth in terms of ascent to *transrational* or superconscious 'psychic', 'subtle' and 'causal' levels. This view thus annihilates the simple dichotomies of rationalist/irrationalist, secular/supernatural, or scientific/intuitive worldviews which embody the 'Pre–Trans Fallacy' (Wilber, 1980) which confuses pre-rational (e.g. infantile magic) orientations with advanced transrational perspectives. In different ways, Freud, Jung, Robert Bellah, secularists and evangelical revivalists are caught in this fallacy (Wilber, 1987).

Wilber discusses religious 'surface structures' and 'deep structures' as well as the key distinction between *authenticity* or the capacity of a religious institution to promote transformative spiritual growth, and *legitimacy* or the capacity of a religious institution to respond to problems of individual identity and sociocultural integration. 'Most orthodox sociologists, unfortunately, seem intent upon seeing the new religions as nothing but a search for a new legitimacy prompted by the breakdown of traditional or civil religion, and fail to consider that some of the new religions — the expressly transrational ones — are also in search of a higher authenticity. . .Some of the new religions are explicitly and structurally in search of that authentic, not merely legitimate dimension: for example, Zen, Vedanta, Raja yoga, Vajrayana' (Wilber, 1987: 256).

Finally, Wilber discusses the properties of *problematic groups* which engender 'bad' patterns with respect to dimensions of authenticity, legitimacy and authority. Thus, Jim Jones's People's Temple was paradigmatic of a problematic group. It was regressively pre-rational, stressing primitive mythic-belongingness and magico-sexual ritual, and was headed by a permanent rather than spiritually phase-specific leader. Moreover its legitimacy rested precariously 'upon a sole person, Jones' (Wilber, 1987: 251).

A short essay by the editors of *Spiritual Choices* (Anthony et al., 1987: 260–4) delineates possible correspondences between Wilber's 'assessment categories', the categories of the Anthony typology (e.g. transrational corresponds to multilevel) and the distinction between *disintegrative, integrative* and *transformative* movements developed in a paper by Robbins and Anthony (1978). However, the latter was primarily a sociologistic treatment which was not concerned with spiritual authenticity–transcendence. Thus, if a devotee of Reverend Moon were elected president of the United States and 'established' the cultural primacy of Unificationism, the latter would become a (socioculturally) 'transformative' religion, notwithstanding its regressive–mythic status in terms of Wilber's perspective.

The approaches of Anthony and Wilber imply that incisive judgements can be made as to the spiritual authenticity as well as the sociocultural significance and psychologically adaptive quality of particular groups. Yet such judgements are still deemed too problematic to be given the coercive force of law. Anthony sometimes seems to imply that some of these decisions can only be made by (a very few) advanced spiritual masters, although this view undercuts the social scientific utility of the typology.

Critical Types and the ACM

The sociological literature associated with the multiple meanings of 'cult' will be discussed later in this chapter. It is necessary here to briefly mention the evaluative and critical conceptions of 'cult' and its extrapolations associated with the ACM.

Destructive Cults. This is not the place to discuss at length the popular and ACM typifications of 'cult', which tend to center around conceptions of coercive indoctrination through 'mind control' and associated authoritarian regimentation and totalism (see Chs. 3 and 6). However, since the mid 1970s there has been some recognition that the ubiquitous conception of 'cult' is too broad and colloquial to serve as an effective critical or evaluational concept. Thus writers associated with the ACM have employed labels such as 'destructive cult' (Shapiro, 1977), 'extreme cult' (Enroth, 1977), or 'high-coercion cult' (Singer, 1979). The works by John Clark and Michael Langone (Clark et al., 1981; Langone, 1985) are probably the most systematic formulations along these lines. However, the criteria which mark off a destructive cult are still too broad and heterogeneous, as well as highly psychological. Any communal and closely knit movement might be labeled 'destructive' by virtue of alleged 'mind control', although there are tremendous variations among such groups with respect to violence, child abuse, involvement in other criminal activities, etc.

Anderson's 'Cultic System'. 'Identifying Coercion and Deception in Social Systems' is a significant article by psychologist Susan Anderson (1985). Noting the confusions abounding in social scientific, popular and critical notions of 'cult', Anderson states that 'no reliable means of defining and distinguishing religious and political "cults" from other powerful social organizations in society presently exists' (Anderson 1985: 12–13). Yet theoreticians and critics 'must first agree upon the target of the cult discussion before they can communicate effectively with each other about these systems and about the non-cultic social groups to which the targeted cultic systems might sensibly be compared' (Anderson, 1985: 18).

The normative and critical dimension of social groups is for Anderson a legitimate focus of theory and research:

> Although many researchers interested in the 'new religions' have discarded the term 'cult' because of its pejorative connotations and definitional ambiguities, no such moratorium on terminology in the social sciences is likely either to remove the term from public awareness or to ameliorate the phenomenon that powerful leaders, situations, and social influences can lead people to engage in behaviors that are not in their best interests. People in powerful social situations 'control the minds' of other individuals. And powerful or 'cultic' systems, while they may be benign or malignant at any given

time have the power to wield vast punishments and to manipulate constituents in a manner that may become psychologically damaging. Because it is by now a truism that 'power corrupts absolutely,' it is arguable that cultic influences are best defined as those which provide powerholders or systems with precisely this degree of power, whether a totalitarian system is large or small, right-wing or left-wing, political or religious, private or public, a tremendous potency for exploitation exists to identify this *potency* as cultic and to leave aside factors such as religious ideology, morality and group size...is to remove the cult concept from the present quagmire of ideological debate and place it within the domain of science...(Anderson, 1985: 20–1).

'Cultic systems', for Anderson, are defined in terms of the presence of 'high degrees of control over individual freedoms' (Anderson, 1985: 14). More specifically, Anderson discusses *psychological coercion* which has ten subdimensions (e.g. love and support contingent on expression of particular beliefs or commitments), plus six dimensions of *deception* (e.g. attempting to prevent converts at certain stages of initiation or indoctrination from becoming aware of the end results of the conversion–initiation process).

Anderson recognizes that these elements are not 'always "bad" or harmful'; rather, they create the potentiality for damaging and destructive outcomes. Anderson also acknowledges that the influences employed by cults may differ from those used by other groups largely by degree rather than kind. The task of identifying cultic systems is thus 'very complicated'.

Two criticisms might be advanced here. Firstly, the continued use of 'cult' (or 'cultic system') creates confusion in the context of numerous other social scientific, popular and media notions of cult, including a sociological tradition of denoting by the term *cult* a loosely organized, ambiguously bounded and 'epistemologically individualistic' group which is necessarily fairly tolerant and non-authoritarian. Secondly, it must be asked whether the scope of Anderson's conception is too broad? Can a dyad, a neighborhood gang, Scientology and the CIA really be analyzed in terms of a single model? If so, is anything, beyond topical labeling, gained by employing the 'cultic system' model in place of existing social psychological and sociological models of social influence, social exchange and organizational dynamics?

Sociological Typologies of Contemporary NRMs

Several writers (Beckford, 1985a; Bird, 1979; Wallis, 1984) have formulated typologies which are not overtly normative and are said to pertain specifically to today's 'new religions' and religiotherapy groups (see Beckford, 1985a: 70–93 and Wallis, 1984: 1–40, 64–9, for summaries and evaluations of some of these models).

Bird's Moral Accountability Types. The theoretical context of Frederick Bird's (1979) schema is partly convergent with the earlier formulations of the Anthony typology (Anthony and Robbins, 1982a; Robbins et al., 1978) in which dualistic and monistic responses to a posited deepening cultural climate of moral ambiguity were delineated. Bird sees contemporary NRMs operating to mitigate moral accountability among members, whose feelings of moral sensitivity, anxiety, guilt and confusion have been heightened by the emergence of a cultural milieu permeated by 'multiple, relativistic and comparatively permissive moral expectations' (Bird, 1979: 344). Moral conflicts arise between this relativist–subjectivist moral culture and persisting traditional objectivist foundations of moral commitment. Confused young individuals are disposed to 'pursue innocence' through spiritual–ideological mystiques which reduce feelings of moral accountability. Each type in Bird's threefold typology of devotee, discipleship and apprenticeship movements provides a distinctive mode of mitigating moral accountability related to a distinctive relationship of followers to revered leaders or to posited sources of sacred power.

According to Bird (1979) participants in contemporary NRMs tend to become (1) *devotees* surrendering themselves to a sacred master or truth putatively embodying higher powers or consciousness, (2) *disciples* seeking to achieve a state of enlightenment through mastery of spiritual/psychic/physical disciplines, or (3) *apprentices* who 'seek to master particular psychic, shamanic and therapeutic skills in order to tap and realize sacred powers within themselves' (Bird, 1979: 336). Each type embodies a distinctive participant role which relates to each movement's fundamental relationship to sacred power, mode of authority and moral model.

Devotee groups, which would include Hare Krishna, the Divine Light Mission, Meher Baba and neo-Pentecostals, suggest the attainment of moral 'innocence' through a relativization of received moral expectations which is related to members' identification of their 'real' selves with sacred alter egos or identity symbols. Disciples seek to sustain a state of compassionate detachment from the distraction of various involvements and desire and envision life as a harmonious whole to which (putatively arbitrary and imposed) standards are irrelevant. Various Yoga and Zen groups fall into this category. Apprenticeship groups such as est, Silva Mind Control, Scientology or Transcendental Meditation inculcate in members a sense of personal autonomy whereby each individual is deemed the primary evaluator of his or her moral status. Apprenticeship groups appear to correspond somewhat to Anthony's unilevel monistic technical groups, i.e. they convert spiritual awakening into a search for the mastery of techniques which will enhance apprentices' personal efficacy and enable them to maximize rewards free of guilt in instrumental and interpersonal realms. Bird and Reimer (1982) note the greater prevalence of apprenticeship groups relative to the other types, and thus infer the primacy of the instrumental motif in the present growth of NRMs. The latter are often perceived as sources of power and keys to material well-being in a period of slower economic growth and blocked mobility.

Beckford (1985a: 71–3) praises the Bird typology for its concreteness; it attends to moral and metaphysical doctrines in such a way that *practical ethics* are highlighted. 'The usefulness of typologies based on such sweeping criteria as oriental/Western origins or monistic or dualistic philosophies is thereby called in question' (Beckford, 1985a: 73).

While interrelating doctrine and practical ethos, Bird's schema also links the distinctive types to an analysis of moral conflict and change in modern Western culture. 'NRMs are thereby shown to exist in an important relationship with major societal trends and forces' (Beckford, 1985a: 73). But Roy Wallis comments critically that the circumscribing of moral accountability 'may be true for some converts and especially true for certain movements'; nevertheless, 'the theory overgeneralizes a limited and particular feature into a universal explanation' (Wallis, 1984: 69).

> The rigorous moral lives of Unification Church member or ISKON devotees scarcely seem designed to reduce a sense of moral accountability. Indeed, 'Moonies' are particularly prone to associate a sense of intense moral responsibility, not only with their own sins and behavior, but that of the whole world. I find no obvious way in which life is less morally accountable for the 'Moonie' or the disciple of Brother Evangelist. . . after, as compared with before, his conversion. Nor do I find the evidence compelling that such considerations predominate among those which lead individuals to join the new religions (Wallis, 1984: 69).

Anthony and Bird appear to share with each other and also with Steven Tipton (1982a,b; see Ch. 2) a concern with the implicit moral ideologies of NRMs and how they are related to metaphysical doctrine, practical social action and shifting values in the cultural milieu. Tipton's celebrated comparison of a Zen group, est and a charismatic Jesus group is proto-typological in the sense that it delineates three distinctive patterns whereby three different groups assist members in coping with moral dilemmas arising from the conflict of utilitarian individualist, consciousness–expressive and biblical absolutist values in 'post-countercultural' society.

Roy Wallis's Types: Orientations to the World. Roy Wallis (1984: 9–39) has recently developed a rather general schema which delineates 'three types of new religion', and which is linked to a Wilsonian (Wilson, 1976, 1981) view of NRMs responding to the stresses deriving from rationalization. However, persons in particular social circumstances will be more disposed to join one or another of the three basic types. The typology is grounded in a trichotomy of 'orientations to the world': affirmation, rejection and accommodation.

For Wallis groups such as the Children of God, the People's Temple, the Unification Church and Hare Krishna exemplify *world-rejecting* movements, which are hostile to the prevailing social order which is defined as demonic and/or irrevocably corrupt. Such groups often tend to form authoritarian communal enclaves in which 'the ego or the former self must be completely repudiated' (Wallis, 1984: 18). In contrast, groups such as Silva Mind Control, Transcendental Meditation, Nichiren Shoshu or est exemplify the *world-affirming* type of movement which claims to provide the means whereby participants may actualize their physical, spiritual or moral potential without separating from or opposing 'the world'. World-affirming groups seem to be somewhat similar to Anthony's unilevel dualist groups and to Bird's apprenticeship type. Wallis' distinction between world-rejecting and world-affirming groups, (the latter said to lack many features traditionally associated with 'religion') may also be viewed as a reprise of the Malinowskian distinction between religion and magic (Shinn, 1985b).

World-affirming and world-rejecting types seem to represent opposing poles of a continuum. But, Wallis's schema also includes a third type, the *world-accommodating* movement. This label is applied to many neo-Pentecostal or charismatic renewal groups, which stress the enrichment of the spiritual life of the followers as individuals. These groups differ from world-accepting groups in placing less emphasis on 'worldly' benefits linked to spiritual gnosis, as well as more emphasis on collective worship and ritual. But there is less 'world-rejecting' emphasis on the movement as a new and purified society. World-accommodating movements appear similar to movements more traditionally designated as 'quietist'.

Wallis really says rather little about accommodationist groups, and his synthesizing volume, *The Elementary Forms of the New Religious Life* (Wallis 1984) is dominated by the dualism of world-accepting/rejecting movements. Thus, 'Wallis is not at all convincing in his argument that there are three basic types of NRMs, but instead seems to confirm that there are two basic types, one of which is predominantly religious and points to some kind of supernatural power ("God") and one which points to some kind of pervasive power which humans themselves can control' (Shinn, 1985b: 330). But Mol (1985) sees Wallis's tripartite schema as rather conventionally Troeltschian and Wallis's three orientational types are said to resemble some of the types in H. R. Niebuhr's *Christ and Culture* (1950). Wallis's preoccupation with orientations toward 'the world' links his typological analysis with some of the traditional preoccupations of church–sect theory.

The value of Wallis's schema 'lies in the sweeping economy with which it promises to handle empirical detail' (Beckford, 1985a: 71). World-rejecting groups tend to recruit socially isolated and marginal youth who are often deeply alienated, while world-affirming movements are joined by mainline young persons frustrated by a perceived blockage of goal attainment in vocational and interpersonal realms. Wallis 'offers clarification of the affinities between members' experience of life in rationalized societies and the message of typical NRMs (Beckford, 1985a: 71).

The typical evolutionary trajectories of world-rejecting and world-accepting movements diverge. The institutionalization of the former is undercut by the problem of the 'precariousness of charisma' (Wallis, 1985: 105–18) whereby the charisma of the authoritarian guru/prophet/founder of the movement may be difficult to sustain during the founder's lifetime (see Ch. 4). World-accepting movements sometimes have less of a problem with charisma but are more likely to be beset by the 'precariousness of the market', which inheres in the shifting fads and competitiveness of the spiritual and therapeutic scene. Yet today's world-rejecting groups also face a market problem in terms of the decline of available 'alienated' recruits after the decline of the 'counterculture' of the late 1960s and early 1970s.

'The basic question of whether many of the NRMs *are*, in fact, "new religions" lurks behind any careful reading of Wallis's types' (Shinn, 1985b: 330). One would think that the trichotomy or at least the world-accepting/rejecting duality would be employable in *other* historical periods. But Hans Mol writes of Wallis's categories:

The 'world' in his rejecting and affirming categories is very much a modern world in which individualism or the personality system has remarkable prominence, as compared with collectivism or the social or group system. But this was not always so, nor it is true for other cultures. Consequently a 'theory' which takes this particular and peculiar world as given suffers rather badly from inapplicability to other times and places. A good theory adopts a cross-cultural and diachronic perspective (Mol, 1985: 95).

Finally, it should be noted that Wallis's schema is really intended to delineate *ideal types* to which actual groups will only approximate. A Pentecostal group whose participants report improved health or vocational success after receiving the Holy Spirit might be interpreted as perching precariously on the boundary between world-affirming and world-accommodating groups. Indeed what may really be involved is a triangle in theoretical space (Wallis, 1984: 6) formed by three continua: rejection–affirmation, rejection–accommodation, accommodation–affirmation, with some groups (e.g. Meher Baba, Divine Light Mission) being at a considerable distance from any extreme pole. Most groups thus incorporate elements of all three types. Change and evolution in a movement, as well as splits and schisms are generally a response to strains related to the unstable combination of tendencies in a given group, e.g. the emergence of the accommodating Foundation from the more occult Process (Bainbridge, 1978). Change can also generally be 'mapped' in terms of the triangular schema. Thus, Jim Jones's People's Temple became more distinctly world-rejecting over time (Hall, 1981, 1987), although the more frequent pattern entails a gradual shift toward greater accommodation. Although the subtleties of Wallis's schema may operate as permissive 'hedges', they also could provide a theoretical basis for a dynamic analysis of conflict and change in particular movements.

'Corporate' Types. Given the focus of earlier typologies on 'orientations to the world', moral accountability and responses to moral ambiguity, there now seems to be a movement to focus more restrictively and precisely on the *organizational and communal features* of religious movements. Prominent in this thrust is the delineation by Lofland and Richardson (1984; Lofland, 1985; see also, Beckford, 1985a: 75–6) of the distinctive *religious movement organization* (RMO). This concept, intended as an ideal type, is broader than the preceding NRM typologies in that it is explicitly made applicable to religious movement organizations in general; but it is also narrower in that it focuses only on one particular property of NRMs: their 'corporateness'.

Lofland and Richardson identify five ideal types or 'elemental forms' representing the differential degrees of 'corporateness' of an RMO, i.e. the degrees to which a set of persons are actively promoting and participating in a shared and valued collective life: *clinic, congregations, collectives, corps* and *colonies*. This typology is intended to provide a basis for identifying and analyzing the organizational dynamics of the RMO as a specific mode of religious collectivity and for analytical comparisons with other social movement organizations (SMOs) such as political movement organizations (PMOs).

Lofland and Richardson (1984) suggest that the traditional terms, 'sect' and 'cult' are not sociologically useful because they are general and imprecise, ultimately multidimensional and encumbered with historical particularities, and therefore do not really facilitate comparative analysis of SMOs. Somewhat similar points have been raised by Beckford (1975b, 1977, 1984, 1985c). In Beckford's view, 'the multifunctionality of these time-honoured terms allows culture-specific complications to cloud considerations of the purely organizational aspects of NRMs'. Yet, 'these considerations do not exhaust the wide range of problematics associated with church–sect theorizing' (Beckford, 1985a: 76). We turn shortly to non-normative conceptions of 'cult' developed to assimilate today's NRMs to church–sect theory.

Chapter 6 in this report discusses Beckford's (1985a: 76–94) quasi-typological 'framework' for analyzing the differential susceptibility of particular NRMs to controversies with environmental forces. A profile of a particular movement and its susceptibility to different kinds of conflict and controversy can be drawn by considering its 'internal' relations with devotees, adepts, clients, patrons and apostates, as well as its 'external' 'mode of insertion' into society involving alternative modes of retreat, revitalization and release. Beckford's 'framework' appears to combine the 'external' orientational focus of Wallis's types with the 'internal' relational or follower–authority focus of Bird's types.

Recent Sociological Conceptions of 'Cult'

'The appearance of many new religious movements in the late 1960s and early 1970s has spurred a renewed interest in the concept of 'cult' in the sociology of religion. To a considerable degree this has also involved an attempt to reintegrate or at least relate "cult" to the church–sect framework' (Swatos, 1981: 17). The 'cult' had formerly appeared to be somewhat of a residual category in socioreligious typologizing (Campbell, 1972; Swatos, 1981).

Cults as Dangerous, Authoritarian Groups. The popular-media–ACM conceptions of cult/destructive cult/cultic system (see above) present certain difficulties from a sociological standpoint (Anthony and Robbins, 1981b; Robbins and Anthony 1982b: 58–9). Some of the popular as well

as the psychological, psychiatric and critical writing on NRMs seems
to impute an illusory homogeneity to 'cults' or 'destructive cults', which
have been widely typified as authoritarian, centralized, communal and
'totalistic' movements which are destructive of the biological families
of devotees, e.g. the Unification Church, Hare Krishna, Jonestown.
But there are significant organizational variations among even fairly
authoritarian and communal groups, e.g. between the People's Temple
at Jonestown and other authoritarian groups (Richardson, 1980, 1982b).
A study of the once controversial Divine Light Mission (DLM) of Guru
Maharaj-ji, which was highly stigmatized in the 1970s as a destructive cult,
revealed that the DLM was significantly less communally insulated and
internally regimented than Hare Krishna; moreover, a large proportion
of DLM members reported continuity with respect to pre-involvement
ties with friends and relatives (Pilarzyk, 1978a; see also Downton, 1979).
Many groups seem to manifest a *concentric ring structure* entailing 'core'
participants who may be wholly or partly encapsulated and outer layers
of 'lay' members or 'clients' with 'limited liability' involvements (Bird
and Reimer, 1976). 'The properties of the movement and its devotees
will look differently to an observer depending upon which layer is taken
to demarcate the group "boundary"' (Robbins and Anthony, 1982b: 58).

The concept of *destructive cult* and allied concepts (Clark et al., 1981;
Enroth, 1977) have emerged to distinguish particularly sinister and
authoritarian groups from less objectionable 'cults'. However, there
appears to be a substantial variation among putatively 'destructive'
groups. Lifton (1979) and others see volatile charismatic leadership as a
hallmark of dangerous cults (see also Rudin and Rudin, 1980). Anderson
(1985) arbitrarily defines 'cultic systems' as coercive and deceptive in
terms of their internal and outreach processes. Confusion is bound to
arise due to very different sociological concepts of 'cult', as well as a
popular usage connoting merely an exotic or unfamiliar religious movement. Many of the authoritarian groups which are labeled 'cults' or
'destructive cults' might actually fit the more traditional sociological
conceptions of sects (Anthony and Robbins, 1981a; McGuire, 1986).

In terms of recent attempts to assimilate the concept of cult to the
sociological tradition of church–sect theory, *two basic conceptions of
'cult' appear to have emerged*: (1) cults as organizationally loose, fluid
and 'individualistic' movements with amorphous boundaries; and (2) cults
as highly esoteric and innovative groups which make a radical break with
the dominant religious culture or are imported from a foreign culture.
These two conceptions are interrelated in that they both see cults as
deviant spiritual groups, and in that the properties which each conception

treats as definitive tend to be featured in the alternative conception as secondary or correlated tendencies of cults. Each of the concepts of cult juxtaposes cults to sects, which are conceived of as either deviant groups which are more authoritarian, centralized and clearly bounded than cults, or as deviant groups which originate from schisms and conflicts within a dominant cultural and spiritual tradition and are orientationally backward-looking or restorative rather than innovative.

Cults as Culturally Innovative or Trans-Cultural Groups. Glock and Stark (1965: 245) define cults as 'religious movements which draw their inspiration from other than the primary religion of the culture, and which are not schismatic movements in the same sense as sects whose concern is with preserving a purer form of the traditional faith' (see also Nelson, 1969a). Nelson (1968a,b) makes a similar distinction between cults and sects, but he adds that cults are also groups based on mystical, psychic or ecstatic experiences, are concerned primarily with the problems of individuals and represent a *fundamental break with religious traditions*. In contrast, sects reject the social order and are theologically and doctrinally grounded within the prevailing religious tradition.

A similar distinction between (schismatic, restorative) sects and (alien or innovative) cults has been made by Stark and Bainbridge (1979, 1980b, 1983, 1985). Sects 'have a *prior tie with another religious organization*. To be a sect, a religious movement must have been founded by persons who left another religious body *for the purpose* of founding the sect. The term *sect*, therefore, applies only to schismatic movements' (Stark and Bainbridge, 1983: 11). Cults thus embody 'an independent religious tradition in a society' (Stark and Bainbridge, 1983: 12). However, cults, like sects or non-deviant churches, are also subject to internal fission. 'A theory of sect formation can then be applied to cults to explain their schismatic tendencies. But it is vital to see that a theory of sect formation *will not serve as a theory of cult formation*. The genesis of the two is very different (Stark and Bainbridge, 1983: 12). Not all cults, according to Stark and Bainbridge, develop into full-fledged religious movements. Stark and Bainbridge present a valuable subtypology of cults, which we will review later.

Some eminent sociologists of religion have criticized the basing of a distinction between cults and sects on novelty and esotericism. Cults, according to Nelson (1968a,b, 1969a) make a fundamental break with religious traditions. 'How *fundamental*, after all, is ''fundamental''?' asks Roy Wallis. 'What makes Jesus' break with Jewish tradition of messianism any more fundamental than Charles Taze Russell's with

Christianity? Yet, Nelson would have us classify one as a cult, the other as a sect' (Wallis, 1975b: 39). Do the 'Moonies' represent a thoroughly novel cult or a Christian sect? The sect–cult distinctions advanced by Glock and Stark, Nelson, and Stark and Bainbridge would appear to have a problem of boundary or cutting point indeterminacy. This is a significant problem, because so many groups such as Mormons, Moonies and Jehovah's Witnesses lie along the ambiguous boundary. Difficulties may also be presented by the necessary reference point of a given 'host' society, e.g. the Hare Krishna movement is perhaps both an American cult and a Hindu sect!

In David Martin's view, Stark and Bainbridge's focus on the *foreignness* of cults as a distinguishing element 'obscures the very different character of varied importations and removes the continuity of social character which so often survives the crossing of frontiers' (Martin, 1983: 39). Martin also criticizes the notion of a continuum of *tension* with the wider society which Stark and Bainbridge (1983), following Johnson (1963), see as distinguishing both cults and sects from more institutionalized groups. But, 'the kinds of tension are, in fact, so varied that it is difficult to see how they can be placed along a continuum of *degrees* of tension' (Martin, 1983: 41). It does not follow that because the Roman Catholic Church and the Jehovah's Witnesses are both in tension with a given wider (e.g. communist) society or polity 'that they have a common sociological character' (Martin, 1983: 40).

Finally, Martin attacks the polarity of schismatic/innovative origins as the grounding for the sect/cult dichotomy. The notion that schismatic origins are necessarily associated with a backward-looking or restorative focus is problematic:

> Of course, the dynamics of schism within an existing body emerges *de novo*. But it does not follow that this difference can immediately be linked to restoration of the old in the one case, and innovation in the other. Schism is notoriously innovative, as the case of the Old Believers illustrates, and religious orders, which are a sort of schism without an explicit break restore and innovate simultaneously...After all, restorations work by *creatively imagining* the past, not by reproducing it (Martin, 1983: 41).

Swatos (1981) argues that a typology which distinguishes between sects and cults in terms of schismatic vs. spontaneous–foreign origins is 'theoretically unconnected to a wider corpus and becomes theoretically inefficient when it is put to any use beyond that of origins' (Swatos, 1981: 18–19). Stark and Bainbridge err 'in alleging that church–sect theory is a theory of origins. Even in Niebuhr [see Niebuhr, 1929],

church–sect theory is a theory of changes in religious organization
as a part of a larger socio-cultural context, not a theory of origins'
(Swatos, 1981: 19). Swatos endorses the complaint of Wallis (1975c:
90) that if 'cults are to be identified in terms of their alien "inspiration",
and sects in terms of their concern to preserve the purity of the "traditional faith" and their schismatic origins, cult and sect are types of
ideological collectivity which bear no developmental relationship to
each other. We cannot predicate of a cult its possible transformation
into a sect.'

Cults as Loosely Structured Proto-Religions. Looseness and diffuseness
of organization and an absence of clear group boundaries have been
identified as the key property of cults, as opposed to more authoritarian,
cohesive and clearly bounded sects. In this model cults are viewed as
bereft of centralized leadership, clear organizational boundaries and
standardized and clearly defined doctrine (Campbell, 1977; Eister, 1972,
1974; Richardson, 1979; Swatos, 1981; Wallis, 1974, 1975a,b). Defined
in this manner, cults are often presumed to be ephemeral, e.g. a college
'Ouija board cult' (Quarantelli and Wenger, 1973), although they may
persist, e.g. Meher Baba (Anthony and Robbins, 1974), or they may
evolve into more cohesive and centralized sects (Richardson, 1979;
Wallis, 1975b,c). Several sociologists have identified the cult type as
bearing a relationship to Troeltsch's category of 'mystic religiosity'
(Campbell, 1977, 1978; Jackson and Jobling, 1968) which Troeltsch saw
as coexisting throughout European history with churches and sects as
a third and distinctly individualistic mode of Christianity.

A pioneering study by Wallis (1975c, 1977) analyzed the transformation
of Scientology from a loosely bounded cult of *Dianetics* to an authoritarian
sect. Following Campbell (1972, 1977), Wallis sees cults emerging from
a diffuse *cultic milieu* and persisting only if they surmount problems of
doctrinal precariousness, authority and member commitment (Wallis,
1974; see Ch. 4). Richardson (1979) has extrapolated Wallis's cult-to-sect
evolutionary process and applied it to groups within the diffuse 'Jesus
Movement' of the early 1970s. Pilarzyk (1978b) has applied Wallis's
analysis to the Divine Light Mission of Guru Maharaj-ji, which he labels
a 'centralized cult', an intermediate type possessing a partly centralized
authority structure but not (yet) a standardized doctrine. Pilarzyk (1978b)
compares the DLM to Hare Krishna, which Pilarzyk considers to fit
Wallis's sect type with a centralized, authoritarian leadership, standardized
dogma or interpretive framework and a clearly delineated boundary
differentiating insiders from outsiders.

Wallis (1975a) has sought to assimilate his cult/sect analysis to a broader typology of contemporary (Western) religious groups deriving from church–sect theory. *Churches* and *denominations* are non-deviant or respectable groups; however, the church is 'uniquely legitimate' or intolerant (i.e. defines itself as the exclusive route to truth or salvation), while the denomination is tolerant or 'pluralistically legitimate'. The sect and the cult are distinctly deviant groups; however, the former is uniquely legitimate while the latter is pluralistically legitimate. A neat 2 × 2 table is thus produced (for similar schemes, see McGuire, 1986: 118–21; Swatos, 1975, 1981). Many controversial groups currently stigmatized as cults are identifiable in terms of this schema as sects, e.g. the Unification Church, the Children of God, the Alamo Foundation, Hare Krishna and Scientology. Some of these sects clearly emerged from earlier cultic phases, such as the Unification Church (Lofland, 1977) or Scientology (Wallis, 1977). Groups such as the Unification Church and Scientology, which Wallis's schema identifies as centralized authoritarian sects, would probably be classified as cults by Stark and Bainbridge (1983, 1985) owing to their striking esotericism, symbolic innovations and non-schismatic origins. Contemporary groups which would appear to be cults from the standpoint of Wallis's and similar schemas would include many spiritualist groups (Nelson, 1969a) as well as Human Potential and New Age groups (Wallis and Bruce, 1986) and numerous other groups including, 'Vedanta, astrology, flying saucer groups, Silva Mind Control, 3HO, Rosicrucianism, and American Zen' (McGuire, 1986: 121).

Inasmuch as Wallis's fourfold schema relies on *deviance* as a key property (marking off sects and cults from churches and denominations), it is open to the criticism that 'What is deviant or conventional depends largely on where one sits, and involves a heavy dose of value judgement' (Swatos, 1981: 19). Swatos (1981) seems to accept Wallis's developmental distinction between cult and sect, but rejects bringing the cult type into a broader church–sect schema as *cults are not religious organizations*. Cults are 'collectivities centering around either a real or legendary figure whose followers believe that their lives are made better through their participation in activities which honor or are prescribed by the leader' (see also Campbell, 1977). Cults need not be religious; there have been cults of 'the Beatles and Elvis Presley as well as of faith healers and gurus' (Swatos, 1981: 20; see Quarantelli and Wenger, 1973). Unlike sects, the membership of cults is not clearly bounded or exclusive, hence a person may belong simultaneously to more than one cult. 'When a cult does begin to make formal religious claims . . . it begins to move into the category of formal religious organizations and can then be treated in a church–sect framework' (Swatos, 1981: 20).

Richardson's (1978b) 'oppositional' conception of cult, which emphasizes the contrast between cultist ideology and beliefs in a broader culture or subculture, combines elements of the two cult vs. sect conceptions which we have been contrasting. Oppositional cults may evolve into more clearly structured sects (Richardson, 1979).

Stark and Bainbridge's Subtypology of Cults. Stark and Bainbridge (1979, 1983, 1985) differentiate cults in terms of a three-point ordinal scale of increasing formal organization. The most diffuse and least organized kind of cult is an *audience cult*. Membership in such collectivities is a consumer activity which manifests 'virtually no aspects of formal organization' (Stark and Bainbridge, 1983: 13–14), although some members may occasionally gather to hear a lecture, witness a demonstration, etc. Attempts to extrapolate more cohesive movements from existing audience cults are frequently made but generally fail due to scarcity of serious commitment in the 'audience'.

According to Stark and Bainbridge, the bulk of cult activity in the United States is not linked to organized cult movements and generally resembles 'a very loose lecture circuit' (audience cult), or it is organized in terms of *client cults*, in which the relationship between promulgators and partakers of cult doctrine closely resembles the relationship between therapists and patients, or consultants and clients. 'Considerable organization may be found among those *offering* the cult service, but clients, remain little organized' (Stark and Bainbridge, 1983: 15). These groups are not usually intense, full social movements, 'Indeed, client involvement is so partial that clients often retain an active commitment to another religious movement or institution' (Stark and Bainbridge, 1983: 15). Yet client cults mobilize participants more rigorously than do 'audience' cults. Clients are linked to other members and central offices and leaders through social networks and through transactions involving valued goods and services. Participants who work for the organization (e.g. the Church of Scientology) may actually become encapsulated in a totalistic involvement and subject to rigorous social control (Straus, 1986; Wallis, 1976). 'Most participants remain clients, not members. Some of them participate in two or more cults simultaneously' (Stark and Bainbridge, 1985: 15) and may still remain involved with a conventional religious organization.

Some client cults become large-scale businesses as well as service and therapy occupations:

In the past the primary services sold were medical miracles, forecasts of the future, or contact with the dead. Since Freud, however, cults increasingly have specialized in personal adjustment. Thus, today one can 'get it' at *est*, get 'cleared' through Scientology, store up orgone and seek the monumental orgasm through the Reich Foundation, get rolfed, actualized, sensitized, or psychoanalyzed (Stark and Bainbridge, 1983: 15).

Finally, there are *cult movements*, which 'are fully fledged religious organizations which attempt to satisfy all the religious needs of converts. Dual membership with any other faith is out. Attempts to cause social change, by converting others to membership, become central to the group agenda' (Stark and Bainbridge, 1983: 16). But cult movements vary substantially in the degree to which they energetically mobilize or stringently regiment members. Some are 'essentially study groups' whose adherents may gather regularly to receive or discuss new revelations or spirit messages from a guru or prophet (or his disciples). Little may be expected of members except modest financial support, attendance at occasional functions and general assent to certain doctrines or at least concern with certain questions, e.g. the Meher Baba community (Robbins, 1969; Robbins and Anthony, 1972). In a weak cult movement, group boundaries are unclear, i.e. 'Unless an outsider gets into a religious discussion with members, no indication of their religious deviance is likely to be evident' (Stark and Bainbridge 1983: 17).

But 'some cult movements function much like conventional sects' (Stark and Bainbridge, 1983: 17) with high levels of commitment and fervor. Participation may be partial, with members leading conventional 'secular' lives, or may amount to a 'total way of life' such that converts become 'deployable agents', and may become mendicants soliciting funds on the street, or may work full time in cult-linked economic enterprises. This description is clearly applicable to groups such as the Unification Church or Hare Krishna, which figure in Wallis's schema as *sects*.

The continuum of audience–client–movement cults corresponds, according to Stark and Bainbridge, to continua of generality, clarity and intensity of the 'compensators' (promissory postulations of rewards) offered by the cult. Audience cults promise very vague and weak rewards such as a mild thrill or entertainment. The compensators offered by client cults are likely to be more highly valued and fairly specific, e.g. a higher IQ, more social efficacy, or more interpersonal or instrumental power, though they are less likely to promise eternal life. 'Cult movements present a much larger package of compensators, including the most *general* compensator offered by full-fledged sects and churches' (Stark and Bainbridge, 1983: 18). They constitute *genuine religions* which offer very general and intense compensators evoking the ultimate meaning and nature of eternity. 'Client cults are *magical* rather than *religious*', and their 'compensators are relatively specific and not embodied in a total system of ultimate meaning' (Stark and Bainbridge, 1983: 18).

Magical client cults can evolve into religious cult movements, key instances being Scientology (Bainbridge and Stark, 1980) and 'The Power' (Bainbridge, 1978). As client cults become transformed into full cult movements 'their environment heats up', i.e. they elicit increased opposition and hostility, and 'the more total the movement, the more total the opposition to it' (Stark and Bainbridge, 1983: 21).

Swatos (1981) rejects Stark and Bainbridge's genetic (in the terms of origins) distinction between cults and sects. But he seems to see value in the subtypology of cults, with the proviso that 'cult movements' are actually sects; 'As soon as cults become *religious organizations*, they may be treated as sects' (Swatos, 1981: 19). Client and audience cults are true 'cults' and really lack the organizational coherence and religious specificity to be included in the church–sect framework. 'Christian Science and Scientology began as cults and have now come to an organizational state that fits them into church–sect modeling. Many other types of faith healing or ''divine science'' have never become ''cult movements'' and thus are inappropriately treated in a church–sect framework' (Swatos 1981: 21). Wallis, of course, would also treat 'cult movements' as sects and would treat 'client cults' and 'audience cults' as cults; however, cults are integral to Wallis's reformulation of the church–sect schema in terms of the four-cell typology discussed earlier.

For Swatos, cults are not the only exclusive religious entity excluded from the church–sect schema. The *religious order* operates 'within the established framework of a church' (Swatos 1981: 21). But cults and orders also diverge in terms of Weber's concepts of *asceticism and mysticism*: 'cults are collective mystic responses to both the world and the central problem of meaning, whereas orders are ascetic responses to these same categories of experience' (Swatos 1981: 22). The recent rise of cults has been 'accompanied by a corresponding decline in religious orders' (Swatos, 1981: 24). Swatos would reformulate church–sect theory in Weberian (as opposed to received Troeltschian) terms.

Conclusion

Were it not for the recent publication of *The Future of Religion* (Stark and Bainbridge, 1985), conceptual refinements of the cult type to distinguish it from the sect and to fit it into church–sect theory would appear to be passé. Wallis's recent synthesizing monograph on NRMs (Wallis, 1984) ignores his earlier cult-to-sect developmental theory and focuses on his trichotomy of world-accepting, world-rejecting and world-affirming movements. Wallis's developmental focus seems useful to this writer, but what other purposes have led so many writers to extrapolate church–sect theory to assimilate NRMs qua cults? Perhaps the hoary corpus of church–sect theory was simply *there*, and so it had to be applied somehow to new movements.

As indicated earlier in this chapter, typologies which have been deliberately constructed with reference to contemporary NRMs will encounter a boundary problem (what is a 'new religion' and how *new* are NRMs?) as well as a problem of generalizability to other groups at other times and places. Church–sect theory, however, may be parochial in the sense that it may pertain primarily to recurrent patterns in the history of Christianity (Johnson, 1963, 1971).

One of the critics, Beckford (1975b, 1977, 1985c) has argued that fidelity to church–sect theory has created an artificial separation between general sociological organizational theory and a hermetically sealed enclave of socioreligious organizational theory. Beckford (1985c: 133) notes 'a declining sense of the distinctiveness of religious organizations as social phenomena. They are treated little differently from other kinds of organizations; and they are expected to perform like other organizations.' He also notes that the 'notion of religious organization has come to lose much of its rootedness in distinctive problems' (Beckford, 1985c: 126).

Should specifically religious typologies such as cult or sect give way to broader social movement concepts, i.e. 'movement organizations' and their theory (Beckford, 1977; Harper, 1982)? The typological work of Lofland and Richardson (1984) both follows through on their line of reasoning and tries to cautiously delineate possible differences between 'religious movement organizations', political movement organizations, etc. On the other hand, Wallis's world affirming/rejecting/accepting types, as well as the Anthony typology, suggest that what might be called value-oriented movements have special characteristics and problems and require particular conceptual frameworks for their analyses.

At present it does not appear that a single framework for the analysis of either all religious collectivities, new religious collectivities, or contemporaray NRMs exists. Particular typologies are vindicated by their theoretical purposes, e.g. Wallis's cult/sect theorizing is important because of its contribution to the analysis of the institutionalization and evolution of new movements. Bird's typology of devotee, discipleship and apprenticeship groups is itself a theory of the function and appeal of contemporary NRMs which is comparable to Tipton's better known comparative and prototypological analysis (Tipton, 1982a) of the role of NRMs in resolving conflicts of moral ideologies. On the other hand, the recent typological works of Anthony and Ecker (1987), Wilber (1983) and Stark and Bainbridge (1985) are partly normative (Anthony and Wilber) but are also tied to broader ventures of reconstructing and reintegrating the scientific study of religion.

6

SOCIAL CONFLICTS OVER
NEW RELIGIOUS MOVEMENTS

This chapter deals with the conflicts and controversies which are raging over new religious movements. Much of the earlier sociological work on conflicts over 'cults' has focused on the activities of a distinct 'anti-cult movement' (Shupe and Bromley, 1980a; Bromley and Shupe, 1981). While this work is valuable, it is arguable that the hostility impinging upon NRMs transcends the activities of the 'ACM'. A movement such as the Bhagwan movement of Shree Rajneesh (Carter, 1987; Palmer, 1988), which purchased vast acres of land in Oregon, took over a town and attempted to build and legally incorporate a city (and thereby claim a share of the state liquor and gasoline taxes), inevitably elicited strong opposition and hot controversy, and would probably have done so even if there had been no prior general climate of suspicion directed toward 'cults'.

This chapter attempts to encompass a substantial body of research and theory dealing sociologically with the controversiality of NRMs and to assimilate it to a theoretical framework presented elsewhere by the author (Robbins, 1985a,d) and partly compatible with the analysis of the pioneering volumes of Beckford (1985a) and Shupe and Bromley (1980a) which we will briefly discuss.

Parenthetically it must be noted that the involvement of sociologists in cult controversies has been particularly significant for the sociology of religion (Robbins, 1987). Through their partisanship and sometimes collaborative sympathy with NRMs sociologists have *become part of their own data*, as Barker (1986) and Robertson (1985b) note. Although a few sociologists have become 'anti-cult' partisans, a larger number of sociologists and religious studies scholars have explicitly or implicitly evinced sympathy with embattled cults through their analyses, through testimony as 'expert witnesses' in courts and legislative chambers and through their participation in conferences sponsored by religious movements (e.g. Wilson, 1981; Fichter, 1983; Stark, 1985a). Criticism of these activities has been substantial, both within the sociological community (Beckford, 1983b; Horowitz, 1978, 1983a) and elsewhere (Keiser and Keiser, 1987; West, 1982). Sociologists have sought to define and explain their roles in these controversial settings (Barker, 1983a; Bromley et al., 1987; Robbins, 1988; Robertson, 1985b; Shupe and Bromley, 1980b; Wallis, 1983,) and a special issue of *Sociological*

Analysis (Volume 44, No. 3, 1983) was devoted to these issues. The impact of NRM research and cult controversies *on the sociology of religion* will be discussed further in the concluding chapter of this report.

Patterns of Conflict

The range and scope of social conflicts revolving around NRMs are striking. Although 'anti-cult' mobilization began in the early and middle 1970s (Delgado, 1977; Sage, 1976; Shupe and Bromley, 1980a), popular antipathy and critical media scrutiny escalated substantially after the horrendous mass suicide/murder at Jonestown in Guyana (Beckford and Cole, 1987; Hall, 1987; Robbins and Anthony, 1982a; Shupe and Bromley, 1980a; Van Driel and Richardson, 1988). After Jonestown, notes Eileen Barker:

> Constant attempts were made to pass legislation controlling practices of movements and/or giving the courts the right to grant parents custody of their adult children...Although the clamor for legislation that would allow parents to obtain 'conservatorship orders' and/or to hospitalize their adult children has died down, it certainly has not died away. Many other legal issues have arisen: The new religions have fought for custody of their infant children, immigration rights, tax relief, definition as a religion, charitable status, and redress against deprogramming. They have defended themselves against charges of brainwashing, fraudulent practices, breaking-up of families, violations of by-laws, obstruction, tax evasion and so on...Some of these disputes reach right to the heart of complicated constitutional principles; they explore the limits of the rights of groups whose actions (possibly as a direct consequence of their beliefs) are at variance with the perceived interests of the rest of society. Here we find the new religions testing boundaries of permissible behavior, the balance between relief and action, and, for the United States, the interpretation of the First Amendment (Barker, 1986: 331).

Recent trends regarding 'cult controversies' are described by Beckford:

> In the early 1980s the cult controversy was sustained by long-running legal battles involving a small number of NRM's. In conjunction with contemporary concerns about the legality of the practices of some other religious groups, the controversy began to feed into debates about church–state relations in the USA. It retained a degree of distinctiveness, however, because of continuing agitation about the allegedly deceptive and exploitative recruitment methods employed by some movements, but it has to some extent been subsumed under a broader heading concerning the powers of the state to oversee *any* religious group. This was partly because the proliferation of NRM's had slowed down and partly because the rate of membership growth had also declined in the most controversial movements (Beckford, 1985a:1).

In terms of broader sociological theory, Euro-American cult controversies may sometimes appear anomalous or trivial. Beckford (1985a) notes that, unlike religious movements in many countries 'NRMs in the West cannot be interpreted as an expression of social class or caste divisions. They do not follow the contours of any major social divisions except perhaps that of age groups' (Beckford, 1985a: 11). NRMs are thus *not likely to consolidate existing social divisions or to create the basis for new divisions*. Nevertheless, a number of sociologists have argued that cult conflicts have raised issues which are significant in terms of the moral boundaries of modern society:

> The central most general problem has to do with regard to changing conceptions of the relationship between individuals and society, and between extra-societal agencies and society itself. In view of the nonconformity of many of these movements to the Weberian principle of 'consistency,' it is interesting to note that in part because of their 'inconsistency' (that is inconsistency between claims concerning collectively claimed autonomy and denial of individual autonomy), they apparently create the necessity for those who claim to act on behalf of *society* to formulate principles of *consistent societal participation* (Robertson, 1979: 379).

NRMs, according to Beckford, 'represent an extreme situation which, precisely because it is extreme, throws into sharp relief many of the assumptions hidden behind legal, cultural, and social structures. The operation of many NRMs has, as it were, forced society to show its hand and to declare itself ' (Beckford, 1985a: 11). 'The issues raised by the controversy are probably more significant for the future of western societies than are the NRMs themselves' (Beckford, 1985a: 11).

Most sociological analyses of NRM controversies have implicitly or explicitly drawn upon either versions of *conflict theory* (Kilbourne and Richardson, 1984a; Robbins, 1985d; Shupe and Bromley, 1980a) or variations of *labeling theory* such as medicalization theory (Kilbourne and Richardson, 1984a; Robbins and Anthony, 1982a), the deviance amplification model (Hampshire and Beckford, 1983; Robbins, 1986a; Wallis, 1986) and social constructionism (Bromley et al., 1983; Harper, 1986; Robbins, 1984; Wolf-Petrusky, 1979). *Social movement models* such as resource mobilization and related movement organization theory have been employed (Bromley and Shupe, 1979a; Harper, 1982; Shupe and Bromley, 1979, 1980a). Hampshire and Beckford (1983) critically evaluate deviance-amplification and church–sect theory approaches, and Beckford (1985a, 1987) critiques various other analyses.

Below we update an analysis drawing from the more recent work of the present writer (Robbins, 1981, 1985a,d) which combines elements of conflict theory and structural functionalism, and which has recently been extrapolated and critically evaluated by Beckford (1986a).

Dominant Early Mode of Discourse. In our view (Robbins, 1979–80, 1981, 1985a,d,e, 1987) controversies over today's 'cults' reflect *an emerging general crisis of church and state relations* (Robbins, 1985 a,e, 1987; Robbins and Robertson, 1987). The relationship between cult controversies and the broader sociocultural context has been somewhat obscured by the way in which controversial discourse over cults has been patterned in the 1970s and very early 1980s:

> Primary attention has been directed toward the question of *how people become converts*, and, in particular, whether they are victims of 'forced conversions' accomplished and sustained through 'mind control.' The most vigorous critics of cults attempted to define the issues and conflicts surrounding cults as constituting primarily a *mental health problem*. Defenders of cults have argued that, in actuality, esoteric beliefs and rituals have been arbitrarily transvalued as 'coercive' and as pathological mind control (Robbins, 1985d: 7).

Although in tactical terms this mode of discourse 'articulates an "appropriate" attack on disfavored religions which disavows the intent to control beliefs' (Robbins, 1985d: 8), a number of sociologists feel that this approach may obscure the underlying sources of conflict and the challenges which authoritarian or collectivistic movements present to existing groups, institutions and norms (Beckford, 1979, 1982a, 1985a; Kilbourne and Richardson, 1984a; Robbins, 1984, 1985b,d).

Church, State and Cult

In our view the deepening American tension over church–state relations is partly a product of the increasingly comprehensive governmental regulation of society and organizations within the society. Public authority increasingly regulates almost every type of organization in the United States, both businesses and non-profit groups. But in the United States religious organizations and specifically 'churches' enjoy special regulatory exemptions. They are set apart from the increasingly regulated society as *privileged enclaves*. As the state becomes increasingly dominant over society, the privileges and exemptions of churches become highly visible and more controversial. A variety of operators and entrepreneurs are therefore motivated to label their operations 'religious' to take advantage of the privileges accorded to churches (Ofshe, 1980a, 1986). A number of movements such as Synanon or Scientology would probably not have defined themselves as churches or as 'religious' movements were it not for the legal protections the Constitution affords such groups.

The omnicompetence of the state now extends to matters which were formerly of mainly private concern and which pertain to the subjective 'life-world' (Beckford, 1986a). The state's 'increasing reach into so many domains of life raises a number of religion-related matters' (Robertson, 1981: 201) and enhances church–state conflict. But certified 'religious' operations claim special protections from regulatory intrusions on the part of public authority.

A regulatory gap might thus be said to exist between 'secular' and 'religious' organizations. But it is not the regulatory gap by itself which underlies today's escalating tensions. *The more the activities and functions of churches broaden and begin to resemble those of secular organizations, the more provocative are the privileges and exemptions of churches and the more opposition they elicit.* Conversely, the more restricted is the scope of religious authority and activity — the more specialized and 'privatized' religion becomes — the less likely it is that the potential for conflict inherent in the regulatory gap will be actualized.

One aspect of 'secularization' in the twentieth century has been a reduction in the scope of activities and societal 'functions' performed by churches. But there are currently some indications of a reversal of 'modern' tendencies toward religious 'privatization'. For example, a number of factors including the decline of public education, resistance to racial integration and the desire to ensure that the right values are being transmitted to one's children has produced the present proliferation of new 'Christian Schools' (Peshkin, 1986; Skerry, 1980) in the United States. Religious movements appeared in the 1970s to become more important in the United States as meditating structures filling the gap left by the decline of other institutions such as extended families, homogeneous 'folksy' neighborhoods, personalistic work settings, etc. (Robbins, 1981; see Ch. 2). As two anthropologists noted, in the United States religion is now 'the only place where social experimentation is possible'. Today's proliferation of diversified religious movements is said to represent 'a folk answer to a system that is over-diplomaed, over-certified, too specialized and too conscious of where one receives certification. It is the last voice for decentralization and the free enterprise system' (Zaretsky and Leone, 1974b: xxxv).

Given the 'regulatory gap' we have identified, expansion of the authority and diversification of the activities of religious organizations will likely lead to an increase in church–state tension and resentment against religious organizations. Groups such as the Unification Church or the Church of Scientology are situated at the cutting edge of church–state tension and the proliferation of disputes over 'church autonomy' (Robbins, 1985a,d,e) in part because they represent extremely diversified and multifunctional entities with their fingers in many pies. Although this certainly holds for many other religious organizations, e.g. surging evangelical movements (Hunter, 1983), certain groups stigmatized as 'cults' appear to present somewhat extreme examples. It might appear that today's diversified cults are moving toward the 'Japanese model' of a broadly omnicompetent sectarian organization embodying diffuse and paternalistic socioreligious authority (White, 1970).

In short, cults are particularly controversial in part because they tend to constitute highly *diversified and multifunctional enclaves lying outside of the web of governmental supervision which increasingly enmeshes 'secular' organizations and enterprises*. It may also be significant that, unlike diversified evangelical groups, 'cults' are unfamiliar and lack grass-roots support and are thus particularly vulnerable to stigmatization and punitive social control.

Nevertheless, a number of movements have arguably consolidated 'protected empires' consisting of myriad activities and enterprises which would be subject to substantially greater governmental scrutiny and regulation were they not carried out under 'religious' auspices (Ofshe, 1982). They are involved in numerous commercial and financial enterprises (e.g. Sun Myung Moon's fishing fleet), education, residential structures, child care arrangements, nursing homes, political lobbying, healing, psychotherapy and other quasi-medical processes (Richardson, 1988c; Robbins, 1988b). Some movements can be said to have developed vast commercial and financial empires which are alleged to be underregulated (Grafstein, 1984; Moore, 1980; Robbins, 1985a). Some groups have such an extensive web of operations and enterprises that Beckford (1981b) has termed movements such as Scientology, Hare Krishna and the Unification Movement as 'religious multinationals'.

The diversification and alleged underregulation of certain 'cults' creates resentment against unorthodox religious groups. Boundary disputes over 'church autonomy' involving NRMs are multiplying (Robbins, 1985a,e). An example of this kind of conflict involves proliferating religiotherapeutic movements, which are accused of harmful and fraudulent practices, and of labeling therapy practices 'religion' to evade licensure and to exploit the exemption vouchsafed to pastoral counselling (Ofshe, 1980a). Religiotherapeutic movements are accused of 'practicing therapy without a license' and inflicting harm on clients (Richardson, 1986). Advocacy groups have now emerged to pursue the goal of gaining protection for the 'religious consumer' through public authority. A crackdown is demanded on alleged deception, fraud, coercion and the infliction of psychological damage by authoritarian or psychiatrically incompetent gurus and spiritual healers (Beckford, 1986a; Richardson, 1986; Robbins, 1986).

The state may be quite amenable to facilitating the aims of anti-cult groups on behalf of religious and therapeutic 'consumers' because the demands of the advocacy groups fit 'into the pattern of attempts by present-day states to derive some legitimacy from their consumer-protection work' (Beckford, 1986a: 10). The state's vaunted 'watchdog' role is highlighted, 'and it conveniently combines the notion of citizens as individual consumers with that of the state as the neutral regulator of various markets' (Beckford, 1986a: 10). State intervention is justified in terms of defending individual autonomy and correcting 'abuses' in a normally harmonious spiritual realm (Beckford, 1985a; 1986; Robbins, 1985a).

The claims of the state and the advocates of enhanced consumer protection in the religiotherapeutic realm are countered by affirmations on the part of religionists that 'religious liberty' must have priority such that there is a strong constitutional barrier to government intervention in this area (Richardson, 1986). Religiotherapy is said to have an irreducible charismatic–inspirational element and cannot be treated as simply a rational business or professional activity (Robbins, 1985a). Nevertheless, the use of a consumer protection model by opponents of cults points to the underlying conflict between the expansion of religious entrepreneurship under the shield of the First Amendment and the trend toward broader regulation of organizational behavior and enhanced professional liability for harmful or fraudulent practices (Robbins, 1985a,d, 1987).

Normative Factors. The diversification of NRMs also elicits a feeling that the more authoritarian and 'totalistic' of today's new religions fail utterly to 'know their place' and acknowledge the stringent separation of secular and religious realms which is normative in our 'secular' culture (Anthony et al., 1983; Robbins, 1984). On the individual level, a person who is encapsulated in a communal movement may appear to lack the *personal autonomy* and dignity which is expected of adult citizens in a modern, highly differentiated society, i.e. he may appear to lack a 'self' which transcends multiple segmental roles and group ties (Beckford, 1979, 1982b, 1985a). The encapsulated convert is thus perceived as being less than a 'legitimate person' capable of competent decision-making and self-directed social action — hence the interpretation of cultists as unhumanly 'programmed'. Ironically, it is precisely the presumptive personal autonomy of individuals which, in the view of some civil libertarians, coercive therapeutic intervention and 'deprogramming' violates (Robbins, 1979).

Culturally conditioned conceptions of 'legitimate persons' and typifications of dehumanization through organizational 'programming' pertain to the normative or valuative dimension of cult controversies (Anthony et al., 1983; Anthony and Robbins, 1981b; Beckford, 1979, 1985a; Bromley and Shupe, 1981; Richardson and Kilbourne, 1983a; Richardson et al., 1986). An additional normative dimension entails the status of some of the more authoritarian groups as 'uncivil religions' which contravene the American civil religion qua 'religion of civility' or American 'intolerance of intolerance' (Hammond and McCutcheon, 1981; Robbins, 1986c). Such groups see themselves as exclusive beacons of spirituality in a degraded or demonic world. Persons assimilated into such a close-knit exclusivist subculture may thus appear to have dropped out of the broader culture of civility (Robbins, 1986c). An additional normative conflict entails the *contractual* normative ethos of modern Western society and the *covenantal* ethos of close-knit sects (Busching and Bromley, in press). Is the sectarian convert really making an *investment* for which he should be compensated if promised rewards (e.g. enhanced personal efficacy, insight and tranquility) do not ensue?

Exploitation. Because many NRMs are multifunctional, they address multiple needs and encourage a strong *dependency*. There are implications for the exploitation of dependent participants; de facto *slavery* has even been alleged (Delgado, 1979–80; Grafstein, 1984). Certainly there is often a substantial imbalance of power between the authoritarian leadership of some movements and the individual participants (Ofshe, 1980b; Robbins, 1981). The latter may surrender substantial resources to a communal movement in exchange for an implicit (but non-enforceable) understanding that the devotee will be cared for in perpetuity by the group (Ofshe, 1982). The helplessness and dependency of devotees, as well as their difficulty in breaking with a diffusely functional and exploitative organization may thus be largely structural rather than psychiatric (Robbins, 1985d; Skonovd, 1981).

Cults and Competitors

In performing communal, therapeutic and other 'mediating' functions in an innovative and relatively unregulated manner, religious movements come into conflict with more conventional mediating institutions and groups, e.g. families, conventional clergy, the certified therapists and healers, which ordinarily enjoy a monopoly of mediating and therapeutic functions.

Cults and Families. Modern society is characterized by a high degree of structural differentiation which underlies the increasing isolation of the nuclear family and which is exacerbated by the concurrent decline in recent decades of traditional supportive mediating structures such as extended family systems, folksy neighborhoods and conventional churches (see Ch. 2). NRMs have arguably exploited the problems of modern familism.

Religious movements vary significantly in their overt attitude toward conventional American familism (see Ch. 2). The traditional family concept has been alien to Hare Krishna practices, but the Unification Church confers a sacred significance on the institution of the family, defined as a 'God-centered family' (Bromley et al., 1982) centred on 'Father' Moon, who, together with his wife, have been referred to by devotees as 'Our True Parents'. Although the Unification community can under certain conditions, provide a supportive context for family stability among devotees (Fichter, 1979, 1985), it is also a *surrogate family* for devotees and it is therefore often involved in a sharp conflict with their putatively non-God-centered' (i.e. non-Moon-centered) original families. Converts frequently sever relationships with parents and spouses when they join the movement. Bitter child custody disputes explode when only one partner in a marriage joins or leaves a communal movement such as the Unification Church.

Bromley et al. (1982) report that the Moon movment 'involved a fictive kinship system' in which the Reverend and Mrs Moon 'were designated as the devotees's true parents' (as opposed to biological parents). The general supercession of the biological family by the 'true family' of the spiritual community represented one basic source of tension between devotees, relatives and the church. A second source involved converts' rejection of lifestyles, values and career/domestic aspirations which they had hitherto shared with their parents. Two therapists, who work with families who have 'lost' a member to a close-knit diversified religious movement such as the Unification Church, report that the families feel as if they have been superseded 'by a bigger, richer, more powerful alternative family' (Schwartz and Kaslow, 1979).

A study by Beckford (1982a) of Unificationists and their families in Great Britain reveals diverse family responses to the involvements of progeny, which the researcher reduces 'for the purposes of exposition' to three basic types of response: *incomprehension, anger* and *ambivalence*. The anger response, however, 'has virtually monopolized the accounts given in the mass-media of reactions to new religious movements' (Beckford, 1982a: 45). Sullivan (1984b) reports predominantly hostile parent responses from his sample, whose members were largely convinced that their children had been mind-controlled. Parents making an 'angry' response do sometimes hold factually erroneous beliefs such as the paucity of disengagements not mediated by deprogramming (Hershell and Hershell, 1982).

The relations and tensions between NRMs and converts' families of origin have elicited a considerable sociological literature (Anthony and Robbins, 1981b; Beckford, 1982a; Harper, 1982; Kaslow and Sussman, 1982; Marciano, 1982; Kilbourne and Richardson, 1982; Schwartz, 1985; Wright, 1986; Zerin, 1985). There are some indications that the spread of fundamentalist and charismatic orientations beyond rural, southern and lower-class settings has created a potential for spreading alarm among educated parents whose children become involved in putatively regressive and anti-modern groups. Some parents tend to apply to born-again groups the 'mind control' mystiques applied earlier to the classical 'destructive cults' such as Hare Krishna or the UC (Robbins, 1986c).

It must be noted that there is increasing concern over *child abuse* in NRMs (Rudin, 1984), which is sometimes associated with biblical sanction for corporal punishment or with faith-healing and rejection of modern medicine in born-again groups.

Cults and Clinicians. Therapeutic and 'helping' professionals such as psychiatrists, psychologists and social workers may be predisposed to be hostile to NRMs. Mental health professionals are naturally concerned with the negative consequences for mental health which have surely developed in connection with some persons' participation in new religions. Although the frequency and intensity of mental injuries associated with 'destructive cultism' may be debatable (Kilbourne and Richardson, 1982, 1984a), the reality of divided and traumatized families is palpable. Mental health professionals often tend to define their clientele as *families* as well as individuals. They are therefore naturally predisposed to view conflicts between cults and families from the standpoint of the concerned relatives and to perceive engagements with cults as similar to drug use and other 'deviant behaviors' which undermine familial relationships, career prospects and general social adjustment. Middle-class families feel increasingly dependent upon health professionals for assistance and support, and they are therefore attracted to quasi-medical and social scientific metaphors such as mind control to account for the apparent desertion of their children. Families have implicitly surrendered much of their authority to clinical and social welfare professionals, although they are nevertheless still held 'responsible' for their children's development (Keniston, 1977). By accepting a medical–psychiatric mode of explanation they hope to mobilize the support of those professionals on whom they feel dependent and to whom they have ceded their authority (Anthony and Robbins, 1981b).

The conflict between health professionals and cult leaders is heightened by the hegemonic desires on the part of both groups. NRMs and licensed therapists are 'competitors in the therapeutic and experiential marketplace' (Kilbourne and Richardson, 1984a). Competing with conventional psychotherapists, gurus may benefit from the inadequacies of the standard medical model in coping with the routinization of psychotherapy as a conventional life experience for 'normal' persons (Anthony et al., 1978). It is in this competitive context that established psychiatry must oppose 'cults, quacks and non-professional psychotherapists' (Singer and West, 1980).

It is notable that the intense agitation over 'destructive cultism' creates the basis for the elaboration of an *opportunity structure* whereby certified professional helpers can develop new and prestigious roles as counselors and rehabilitators of 'cult victims' (Kilbourne and Richardson, 1984a; Robbins and Anthony, 1982b; Shupe, 1985). Therapy and counseling have been urged for cultists, ex-cultists and families traumatized by the involvement of a family member with a cult (Galper, 1982; Schwartz and Kaslow, 1982). Some clinicians have been activist crusaders in this area (Bromley, 1988b; Richardson, 1987).

Different kinds of therapists and mental health workers may, however, have different orientations towards cults and the prospects of therapeutic intervention. In a widely cited, but perhaps overly simplistic article, Robbins and Anthony (1982a) appeared to equate several items: the medical model (discussed below), allegations of cultist 'brainwashing', the practice of deprogramming and the interests and predispositions of clinicians. A reader could easily conclude that clinicians tend generally to view cults as pathological (i.e. to impose a medical model), as well as supporting brainwashing theories of conversions to NRMs. This analysis may downplay the role of therapists who are either sympathetic to NRMs (Coleman, 1985a,b) or otherwise at variance in their analyses from anti-cult demonology (Kuner, 1983; Gordon, 1988; Ungerleider and Wellisch, 1979).

Upon closer inspection there appear to be *two* distinct medical models of cultist pathology. The familiar controversial model affirms the operation of mind control processes and suggests that cultist indoctrination and rituals *create psychopathological conditions in converts* (Conway and Siegelman, 1978; Clark, 1979; Shapiro, 1977; Singer, 1979; Singer and West, 1980; see Ch. 3). Clinicians who are associated with this approach have often been supportive of coercive deprogramming (Shapiro, 1977; Singer, 1979). Yet some articles appearing in prominent psychiatric journals seem to represent a distinctively different version of the medical model of cults which emphasizes the tendency for cults to become 'refuges' for persons who are already disturbed or maladjusted, i.e. *involvements in cults are created by existing psychopathological conditions in converts* (Maleson, 1981; Spero, 1982). Exemplars of this approach consider cults to represent an essentially pathological phenomenon susceptible to (non-coercive) therapeutic intervention, but they are skeptical of brainwashing theories, which are said to function as rationalizations for ex-devotees. This variant of the medical model may appeal to therapists with backgrounds in personality theory and family therapy, who may sense that the brainwashing model, as an extreme *situation-centered* approach, implicitly devalues their own clinical expertise in family problems, personality disorders and developmental psychology. Clinicians may also sense competition from marginal and specialized anti-cult 'exit counselors' (Sullivan, 1984a). On NRMs and mental health, see also Kilbourne and Richardson (1984a,b), Richardson (1980) and Rochford et al. (1988).

Cults and Churches. Certain church leaders have been active in attacks on cults. Other church spokesmen have been active in the defense of the rights of cults. The competitive relationship between conventional churches and unorthodox religious movements is obvious. Some dynamic NRMs have succeeded in eliciting from devotees an intense and diffuse commitment which most conventional non-evangelical church organizations have not been able to match. Among evangelical and fundamentalist groups there is a long tradition of fulmination against cults, which are often designated as satanic. *The Kingdom of the Cults* (Martin, 1968) is a classic but moderate example of this genre which castigates the 'cults' of the 1960s — Baha'i, the Nation of Islam, Jehovah's Witnesses, Christian Science, etc. Contemporary televangelical presentations frequently feature attacks on cults, particularly 'New Age' movements and witchcraft–satanist groups. But some church leaders are sensitive to civil liberties issues and are quick to perceive threats to the 'free exercise of religion' and 'church autonomy' (Robbins, 1985e) from any governmental intervention. Cases such as the successful prosecution of Reverend Sun Myung Moon for tax fraud and the receivership imposed on the Worldwide Church of God in California in 1979 have been perceived by many church leaders as *boundary-defining engagements* which will determine the rules and interpretations to be applied to more conventional churches (Robbins, 1985a). Some anti-cult critiques do indeed pinpoint the financial privileges and non-accountability of churches as a key permissive context facilitating cultist deviance (Wooden, 1981). The diversification of some reputable groups renders them dependent upon broad interpretations of religious liberty. A recent 'clergy malpractice' civil suit focused on the psychological effects of evangelical counselling.

It is worth noting that for a while Jewish leaders appeared to be highly conspicuous among anti-cult activists. Jewish youth have been alleged to be disproportionately represented among cult recruits, although this may represent merely a preponderance of urban intelligentsia or persons from nominally Jewish secularist backgrounds (Stark, 1981). Judaism does not generally proselytize and therefore Jewish leaders may be more likely to perceive interfaith conversion as intrinsically pernicious. On Jewish participation in NRMs, see Richardson (1988b).

'The family that prays together stays together' reflects the practice of many churches and synagogues in organizing themselves in terms of family rather than merely individual involvement. The onset of a religious flux in which individuals join religious groups as individuals arguably strikes at the base of American denominationalism. Thus, clerics may share the grief of parents over the 'defection' of a youthful cult convert. In contrast, professional students of religion are often supportive of NRMs, whose surge seems to enhance the importance of religion and provides interesting research opportunities (Robbins, 1983a, 1985c, 1988a).

We have discussed above the relationships and tensions between NRMs and families, clinicians and clerics. There is a great deal of literature in these subareas, but a paucity of studies in the broader area of cults and communities, i.e. NRMs relating problematically to their immediate social environments. Social movement monographs such as Wallis's account of Scientology (1977) contain relevant material, as do works on the ACM (Shupe and Bromley, 1980a) or on cult tensions in general (Bromley and Shupe, 1981; Beckford, 1985a). With regard to a specific focus on tensions in particular religious or secular communities, Harper's (1982) comparative analysis of three groups in Omaha is a pioneering work. Fitzgerald's (1986) account of the Rajneesh settlement in Oregon is an excellent journalistic study (see also Carter, 1987; Palmer, 1988).

Strategy of Medicalization. Key allegations against contemporary NRMs entail notions of 'mind control' and allied constructs which implicitly identify involvement in a cult as entailing *mental pathology* induced through trauma and conditioning, i.e. the pathological syndrome of 'destructive cultism' (Shapiro, 1977; see Ch. 3). Persistent involvement in a cult is thus viewed as essentially *involuntary* — a kind of disease process from which helpless 'cult slaves' must be rescued and healed (Ottinger, 1980). On this basis arguments have been made for enhancing the regulatory authority of mental health professionals (and of the state via *parens patriae*) over religious movments (Robbins and Anthony, 1982a).

Although controversies over cults rage in countries other than the United States, particularly in Western Europe (Beckford, 1985a) the situation in the United States is unique with respect to the degree and frequency with which the charges against such movements are formulated in medical and psychiatric terms. This may reflect in part the greater influence of psychiatry in the United States as well as the weaker norms of tolerance in France and Germany, where there is no rigorous civil libertarian tradition which has to be circumvented through highlighting medical and mental health issues. In Europe it is easier to attack cults directly as both anti-social and subversive of dominant social values (Beckford, 1981b).

In the United States, however, in the context of the constitutionally grounded guarantee of the 'free exercise of religion', it is difficult for those who feel disturbed or threatened by cults to proceed effectively against them directly for being totalistic, authoritarian or too diversified, or for competing with other institutions. The focus of the attack accordingly shifts to the allegation that the processes of indoctrination in cults in effect 'brainwash' converts so that the latter's involvement *does not entail a truly 'free' exercise of religion* (Delgado, 1984).

The application of an 'involuntarist' medical model also serves the needs and interests of various groups which are antagonistic to cults: *mental health professionals*, whose role in the rehabilitation of 'cult victims' is highlighted; *parents*, whose opposition to cults is legitimated; *ex-devotees*, who find it meaningful to reinterpret their prior involvement with highly stigmatized groups as basically passive and unmotivated; and *clerics*, who oppose cults but are concerned to avoid appearing to persecute competitors.

The employment of a medical model thus highlights those controversies over cults which relate primarily to the psychological process through which individuals enter, become committed to and exit from new religious movements. These sensational issues initially overshadowed more mundane issues concerning the tax privileges of diversified religious movements or the regulation of their commercial, political, financial, social service and employment policies, although legal outcomes pertaining to these latter areas may ultimately be more crucial to the continued viability of new movements (Moore, 1980; Robbins, 1985a, 1988b).

The medical model of cultist brainwashing has been associated with the practice of *deprogramming* (Robbins and Anthony, 1982a). There have been numerous studies of deprogramming by social scientists (Barker, 1983b; Kim, 1979; Langone, 1984; Shupe and Bromley, 1980a; Shupe et al., 1978; Skonovd, 1981; Solomon, 1981; see Ch 3). Although the legal situation with respect to coercive deprogramming is still ambiguous (Bromley, 1983; Robbins, 1985f, 1986c), the practice waned in the middle 1980s in part due to the decline or cessation of growth of the notorious 'destructive cults' of the 1970s such as the Unification Church, Children of God, Hare Krishna, etc. On the other hand, the range or variety of groups targeted may have increased in the 1980s with the increasing concern about eccentric born-again groups (Robbins, 1985f).

The sensational medical model of cults — the model which pinpoints 'destructive cults' as a dynamic pathogenic force disrupting the lives of 'cult victims' and producing disease states — has gained particular prominence in the popular media (Beckford and Cole, 1987; Van Driel and Richardson, 1988) and has moreover recently been enshrined in the current *Diagnostic and Statistical Manual* (DSMIII) of the American Psychiatric Association (see Kilbourne and Richardson, 1984b for a vigorous critique of the relevant DSM formulations).

The ACM. Shupe and Bromley's *The New Vigilantes: Deprogrammers, Anti-Cultists and The New Religions* (1980a) is a pioneering volume on the 'Anti-Cult Movement'. Because coercive deprogramming, a major focus of *The New Vigilantes*, is presently becoming more peripheral to ACM activities and advocacy (Shupe, 1985) the volume is now dated, yet it represents a ground-breaking study of a significant American movement and pattern of social and religious conflict. In subsequent papers the authors have continued to report on the evolution of the ACM (Bromley and Shupe, 1987; Shupe and Bromley, 1985a; Shupe, 1985), and have also compiled a documentary history' of the ACM (Shupe and Bromley, 1985b; Shupe et al., 1984).

The New Vigilantes was intended as a companion volume to the authors' earlier analysis of the American Unification Church from a resource mobilization standpoint (Bromley and Shupe, 1979a). In the late 1970s the UC was specifically pinpointed by the ACM as the archetypal pernicious cult. Counter-mobilization and agitation against the UC by the ACM 'could serve as a precedent for attacking other marginal religions' (Shupe and Bromley, 1980a: 31). Movement and countermovement thus formed an organic dyad and needed to be studied in conjunction (Shupe and Bromley, 1979, 1980b).

The New Vigilantes combines the resource mobilization approach employed in the earlier monograph with conflict theory and social constructionist analysis of the production of 'typifications of evil' and 'atrocity stories' (see also Bromley and Shupe, 1981; Shupe and Bromley, 1981a,b; Shupe et al., 1978). Shupe and Bromley attempted a detached even-handedness which seemed to entail bracketing the meanings and claims of both movement and countermovement (UC and ACM) as arbitrary constructions of reality which require demystification. Movement participants are seen as more or less imprisoned in typifications which facilitate mobilization, but which somewhat distort their perception. This mode of 'objectivity' implicitly places the concerned citizens, parents, clinicians and clerics composing the ACM on the same epistemological level as cultist zealots, thereby predictably infuriating the latter. Initially the authors had envisioned themselves 'walking a tightrope' (Shupe and Bromley, 1980b), dealing with 'both sides' and trying to mediate the fierce strife (Bromley and Shupe, 1981). But it is not hard to understand why the 'anti-cult' partisans appear to have strongly resented the analysis of Shupe and Bromley, which they have not perceived as objective.

Shupe and Bromley identify two distinctive 'ideological models' in the ACM 'brainwashing' discourse: a *religious* model involving allegations of satanic influence and a *secular–rational* model involving claims about psychological manipulation and traumatically induced mental pathology. Each model manifests two alternative metaphors of levels of differential dehumanization: a radical *possession* metaphor (see also Shupe et al., 1978), implying direct control over converts attained by an overwhelming, irresistible, antisocial force, and a moderate *deception* metaphor depicting 'a less coercive, indirect control that is gained by taking advantage of human weakness (Shupe and Bromley, 1980a: 60) This distinction is similar to Eileen Barker's (1984) distinction between *mind control* and *suggestibility* propositions (see Ch. 3).

Shupe and Bromley see the 'brainwashing ideology' as *honorably* explaining ex-devotees' past deviant episodes without implying either innate individual derangement or prior social pathology such as deep family conflicts. In the context of the possession metaphor, deprogramming is seen as an essential if sometimes traumatic remedy which reverses the brainwashing process and restores the individual to personal autonomy and normal functioning (see Conway and Siegelman, 1978). However, the term *deprogramming*, to ACM participants, refers to a 'wide array of behaviors, some of which deserved the notoriety accorded them and others which were relatively innocuous and infringed on no one's civil liberties and moral sensibilities' (Shupe and Bromley, 1980a: 122). Shupe and Bromley describe a traumatic, confrontational model of deprogramming which frequently succeeds in eliciting a sudden and dramatic rejection of the NRM on the part of the devotee (see Ch. 3). The apparent metamorphosis of the deprogramee is facilitated by the latent doubts and ambivalence which lurk beneath sectarian discipline and communal solidarity.

According to Shupe and Bromley, the ACM, which emerged in the early and middle 1970s as various spontaneous citizens' groups began to coalesce and develop a network, was in decline by the late 1970s. It was revitalized by the national shock of Jonestown, when 'the nation literally paused to consider "the cults" in precisely the terms which the ACM had for so long hoped' (Stark and Bainbridge, 1980a: 230). Legislative hearings transpired — symbolic degradation rituals — at which cults were denounced and deprogramming was sometimes praised. The immediate tangible upshot of these verbal exorcisms and the subsequent media hegemony of the ACM (Van Driel and Richardson, 1988; Beckford and Cole, 1987) seemed ambiguous, although the climate for NRMs became more hostile.

The passage of time has revealed some drawbacks in Shupe and Bromley's pioneering study, not the least of which is the lurid title, which implicitly belies the subsequent professionalization of the ACM and the institutionalization of cult conflicts (Bromley and Shupe, 1987; Shupe, 1985). The theoretical framework of *The New Vigilantes* makes the organized ACM and its mind control demonology central to the evolution of cult conflicts. This framework may not be optimal either for looking at cult conflicts in Europe and cross-culturally (Beckford, 1981b) or analyzing the broader range of disputes and controversies involving NRMs in the United States, e.g. the multiple conflicts and tensions which destroyed the Rajneesh settlement in Oregon (Fitzgerald, 1986) seemed to emerge and escalate without much noticeable input from the ACM. Finally, while hardly a 'whitewash' of militant cults, *The New Vigilantes* may still downplay somewhat the irrational, provocative and self-destructive behavior manifested by some NRMs which contributes to the escalation of conflicts, e.g. the use of vehement hostility to outsiders as a boundary-maintaining device to sustain internal cohesion (Fitzgerald, 1986; Galanter, 1985; Hall, 1981, 1987). 'Normalizing' of cults is more notable in the authors' subsequent volume, *Strange Gods* (Bromley and Shupe, 1981), the dominant theme of which is the demystification of the extreme stereotypes which are seen as contributing to an exaggerated 'cult scare'.

'Cult Controversies' and the Modern State. A somewhat different perspective is presented by English sociologist James Beckford (1985a). For Beckford, cult 'controversies' can be distinguished from mere *conflicts*; the term *controversy* points to the 'continuing *extension* of the debate...The initial issue has become overlain with so many different issues that the sense of a simple conflict of interests has been lost. More importantly, it has become clear that some of the isues have serious implications for major institutions such as the law, law enforcement, medicine, and the family' (Beckford, 1985a: 10):

> Even if the movements were suddenly to disappear, the consequences of some of their practices would still be felt for years to come. In particular, they have inadvertently or indirectly helped to reinforce (a) major cultural and social boundaries between images of the normal and abnormal person, (b) legal definitions of the limits of defensible action to be taken against an individual's wishes but allegedly in his own or her own best interests as determined by agents of the state or close relatives, and (c) new ideas about the extent to which the economic base of religious groups can benefit from protection by the law on charities. In these, and other respects the cult controversy is a barometer of changes taking place in a number of different societies (Beckford, 1985a: 11).

Beckford notes that contemporary Western society has institutionalized the expectation that 'individuals' be involved in a myriad of limited and cross-cutting commitments to functionally specific organizations. The 'person' is expected to manifest an autonomous 'self' which will be detached from his or her multiple limited commitments and will thus embody his supra-organizational 'humanity'. Organizations which aspire to comprehensive direction of their participants' activities may be stigmatized for depersonalizing their 'victims'; moreover, they will necessarily become entangled with myriad regulations through which individuals' relationships to putatively specialized employment, health, social service and financial entities are mediated. Controversial movements thus become enmeshed in litigation, especially as they learn to take advantage of their 'religious' status to use the courts against their adversaries. They win some and lose some, but there is a sense in which even their victories are partly self-defeating and subvert the absolutism of some movements, i.e. 'the legitimacy of deciding issues of religious authenticity in courts of law is thereby enhanced' (Beckford 1985a: 290).

Of course, it is indeed the institutionalized fragmentation of personal identities in modern societies which increases the appeal of movements which provide holistic mystiques and total identities for participants. In a recent article, Beckford has analyzed the *holistic* themes which so many NRMs seem to share (Beckford, 1984; see also Westley, 1983). Holistic movements need not to be communally totalistic, but they are likely to relativize established institutional boundaries, e.g. between religion and psychiatry.

Beckford sees each movement as being characterized by a 'moral and political economy'. This has an 'internal' dimension involving a distinctive ensemble of roles and relationships which bond the members to each other and to the group. There is also an 'external' dimension which involves the movement's primary 'mode of insertion' into society. Devotee, adept, client, patron and apostate are the primary internal roles within movements, and retreat, revitalization and release constitute the three basic external modalities. Beckford's framework does not generate neat 'types', but it does establish the basis for constructing a 'profile' of each movement's characteristic relational and insertive patterns 'which can help to explain how and why it is involved in controversies' (Beckford, 1985a: 91).

Although Beckford devotes much of his volume to delineating patterns involving recruitment and disengagement, his framework nevertheless has the distinct advantage of providing a basis for *broadening the analysis of cult conflicts beyond entry–exit issues*. Unlike many other social scientists working in this same area, Beckford's work seems relentlessly dispassionate and devoid of special pleading for either NRMs or 'cult victims'. Beckford has also broadened the cultural horizon of the analysis of cult conflicts by examining issues involving NRMs in Europe and Japan (Beckford, 1981a, 1985a, 1987).

Ultimately, Beckford sees the patterns of cult controversies in the USA and Europe as reflecting the nature and problems of social control in the liberal capitalist state. The control of NRMs in the USA and Europe is typically 'indirect, piecemeal and *ad hoc*' (Beckford, 1985a: 288) as controllers disavow interference in religious matters by claiming to be exclusively concerned with exceptional abuses (e.g. of recruitment). 'Wider issues of ethics and policy are ignored' (Beckford, 1985a: 286). Religion is implicitly compartmentalized as a private realm only incidentally related to other social patterns. 'Legislators shrink from the task of confronting the spiritual and moral challenges presented by NRMs... They hide behind the excuse that only piecemeal sanctions are required to prevent harm to people' (Beckford, 1985a: 287). Nevertheless, the proliferation of legal conflicts involving NRMs 'illustrates the increasing statutory surveillance by agencies of the modern western state of *all* social (and therefore religious) activities. It follows that, the more comprehensively a group tries to provide services for its members, the more subject will it be to state control' (Beckford 1985a: 284).

The liberal state endeavors to constrain the absolutism of religious movements and subordinate it to civil religion, but in a manner which seeks to conceal the fact that it is really *religion* which is the problem. Not only is 'religious liberty' a sacred 'individual right', but religious groups which in the past have been deemed compatible with the ideology of liberal utilitarianism and which have 'served as the foremost defenders of the dominant culture and agents of moral socialization' (Beckford, 1985a: 289) have been customarily granted privileges. The NRMs' conflicts with the state thus tend 'to widen out into more general conflicts centering on the definition of "authentic" religion' (Beckford 1985a: 289). 'Courts of law, administrative tribunals, and individual law enforcement agents therefore find themselves obliged to decide what is to count as "religion" for legal purposes' (Beckford 1985a: 289–90).

The Comparison of Cult Control in the United States and Great Britain. James Beckford has written prolifically on the patterns of social control of NRMs and on cult–anti-cult conflicts in the United States and Europe (Beckford, 1981, 1985a, 1986a). Eileen Barker (1987c) has published an important paper probing the effects in terms of religious discrimination of the divergent establishmentarian and separationist traditions in Great Britain and the United States. However, perhaps the most provocative comparative analysis of NRM controversies in the United States and Britain has been developed by Roy Wallis (1986b, 1988). Wallis presents a key paradox:

> The United States embodies freedom of religion in its Constitution, yet nowhere in the English speaking world, as far as I can see, is there a more active and vociferous anti-cult movement, nor a more elaborated development of 'deprogramming' as an enterprise, both of which appear determined to abridge toleration and freedom in respect to certain kinds of religious believer. Moreover, nowhere have the confrontations which have occurred between new religious movements...and the state been sharper...I shall argue that while the United States has institutionalized greater freedom of religion than the United Kingdom, it is precisely that high level of institutionalized freedom which permits — paradoxically — the greater abuse of freedom and toleration which occurs there (Wallis, 1988).

Wallis contrasts the 'institutionalized freedom' vouchsafed to religious groups in the United States with the pervasive 'low level regulation' which constrains the expansion and diversification of NRMs in England. In Great Britain 'the activities of all citizens are highly regulated by a cohesive and centralized political system which has extensive powers to monitor and intervene in their affairs, and which permits few concessions to religious organizations' (Wallis, 1988). A small and densely populated nation, Britain affords few opportunities for religious movements to buy up large tracts of land and develop large settlements distant from population centers in which they can cultivate a distinctive and deviant lifestyle facilitated by low visibility and local political hegemony. A web of not always formal regulations impose upon NRMs in Britain 'restrictions upon their freedom to develop as they might choose'. But:

> In America, however, such routine low level regulation is relatively ineffective, and readily deflected by a determined NRM. In the absence of an effective formal low level social control apparatus, concerned parents and others have been obliged to take a more active role themselves, forming anti-cult groups, lobbying and propagandizing. There has also been a market for more entrepreneurially organized anti-cult specialists offering their services in the capture and deconversion of young people when the formal agencies have proven incapable of securing their return (Wallis, 1988; see also Wallis, 1986b).

Existing professionals such as lawyers, social workers and clinicians adapt their services to the new market, and thus a powerful 'anti-cult movement' arises, achieves a degree of professional legitimation and strongly influences popular and media images of 'cults'. However, the latter, buoyed by their initial 'institutionalized freedom' and insulation from routinized controls, stridently affirm their 'rights', which are interpreted as granting to 'churches' freedom from all interference.

Conflicts and controversies over NRMs thereby become intensified in the USA, and anti-cult mobilization is encouraged. When regulatory intervention and control is belatedly brought to bear on cults, it is likely to be highly conspicuous and often cataclysmic, e.g. Reverend Moon jailed for tax fraud; Bhagwan Rajneesh convicted of immigration fraud and deported; Synanon's Chuck Dederich convicted of conspiracy to commit murder; Hare Krishna officials investigated for murder and drug sales; and Scientology appealing multimillion dollar civil court awards to ex-members, etc.

Wallis's thesis is consistent with other analyses of how opportunity structures provided by the United States tax system and the privileges of churches encourage cultist deviance (Ofshe, 1980a, 1986; Wooden, 1981). But the analysis may be partly time-bound, i.e. once the stigma on 'cults' crystallized in the United States, new movments were not granted the preliminary immunity enjoyed by American NRMs in the early 1970s. Beckford and Cole (1987) criticize Wallis's model for neglect of cultural and other factors.

The Jonestown Tragedy

'In our culture we have not done well in coming to grips with the cultural legacy of Jonestown' writes John Hall in his recent monograph, *Gone From the Promised Land: Jonestown in American Cultural History* (Hall, 1987: 303). Indeed it is a little shocking to reflect on how little sociological work was done on the People's Temple and its cataclysmic denouement in the initial half-decade after the terrible event. Prior to 1986 there was one slim monograph (Weightman, 1983), a reader (Levi, 1982) and a mere handful of articles available to the student.

John Hall's article on Jonestown (Hall, 1981) develops an analysis which is amplified and supplemented in his monograph (1987). The late Shiva Naipaul has contributed a meritable journalistic account which looks at Jones and his movement in the context of American culture and various mystical and apocalyptic countercultures which explosively interacted in California (Naipaul, 1981). Robbins (1986a) has applied Hall's analysis of the special volatility of Jim Jones' movement (Hall, 1981) to the self-immolation mass suicides of the Russian Old Believers in the late seventeenth century. Lindt (1981–2) has published a masterly analysis of early media, popular and intellectual interpretations of Jonestown (see also Jorgensen, 1980). Coser and Coser (1979) apply to the totalistic People's Temple their earlier theory of 'Greedy Organizations'.

As Barker notes, 'prior to 1978, the People's Temple was not found featured in the anti-cult literature' (Barker, 1984: 1). After the end of 1978, the holocaust became a prime object lesson discussed prominently and continuously in hortatory literature (Yanoff, 1984). Wooden (1981) exposes the exploitation and treatment of children by the People's Temple and concludes his monograph with an attack on cultist brainwashing and on the regulatory exemptions of churches, whose lack of financial accountability is alleged to make possible the development of abusive cultist empires. However, Richardson (1980, 1982b) pinpoints key differences between the People's Temple and other stigmatized 'destructive cults' of the late 1970s (see also Ahlberg, 1986). He delineates eight areas of contrast, including characteristics of members, organizational structure, social control patterns, resocialization methods, theology/ideology and ritual behaviors. Richardson highlights Jones' emulation of Father Divine and the relevance of the black church/sect tradition. Weightman (1983) argues that the People's Temple operated simultaneously as a middle class 'new religion' and a lower class 'cult'. An elite who were 'typical of the members of a new religion' tended to 'join for idealistic reasons of social healing', while 'rank and file members' typified the adherents of a marginal religion or 'cult' and were concerned with personal and physical healing (Weightman, 1983: 106). A recent paper by Hall (1987) discusses the People's Temple as a 'Poor People's Movement'.

Particularly notable among the initial wave of Jonestown scholarship is D. P. Johnson's (1979) analysis of the working out of 'Dilemmas of Charisma' in the later history of the People's Temple. Jones' strategic responses to various threats to his charismatic authority created new problems and threats such that the movement become locked into a process of intensifying authoritarian control and paranoid boundary-maintenance. Lifton (1979) analyzes the mutual destabilizing which occurs in the inter-action between the adulated prophet/guru and the worshipful followers (see also Johnson, 1987b; Lifton, 1985). The volatility of some NRMs is related to the precariousness of prophetic charisma (Wallis, 1984; Wilson, 1987) and to the contemporary stigmatization of messianic prophets (Mickler, 1987).

The short monograph by Weightman (1983) contains trenchant critiques of various ideas thought to illuminate the tragedy, including models of thought reform by Lifton (1961) and others and Naipaul's (1981) cultural analysis. Lincoln and Mamiya (1980) analyze the People's Temple as a 'political religion'. Political factors are also highlighted by Hall (1981, 1987) and Robbins (1986a), but are somewhat muted in the general theory of religious suicide developed initially in an unpublished conference paper by Chidester (1983), who draws on both Jonestown and the earlier Old Believer immolations to develop a theory grounded in quasi-theological and phenomenological categories, highlighting collec-tive responses to subhuman and superhuman statuses imputed to members of the collectivity.

'Second Wave' Works on Jonestown. The papers by Richardson and Hall cited above appear in a reader by Levi (1982) which also includes papers by Shupe and Bromley (on the public response to Jonestown); Robbins and Anthony (the issue of brainwashing); Edgar Mills ('cult extremism'); Louis Zurcher (religious violence and self-concept); Redlinger and Armour (social phenomenological analysis of resocialization); and several theologians and one Jonestown survivor (later murdered!). The papers in the Levi reader plus most of the other papers cited above might be

said to constitute the 'first wave' of Jonestown scholarship, which seemed to subside in 1983–5. There now appears to be a 'second wave' breaking, which features monographs by Hall (1987) and Chidester (1988) as well as the projected volume by Gillian Lindt.

John Hall: Jonestown, Sect and Society. This monograph presents a provocative sociological analysis. Part One deals with the origins and early history of the People's Temple. Part Two deals with the movement's ideology and organization: its reality as a diversified corporate conglomerate, its vision of a 'collectivist reformation', and its involvement in politics and use of public relations. Under the rubric of 'collectivist reformation' Hall also provides a detailed treatment of the authoritarian social control and socialization patterns within the movement. In Part Three the author depicts the final years of the movement: the settlement in California, the move to Guyana, the intensifying struggle with the 'Concerned Relatives', and the opposing and mutually reinforcing typifications emerging on either side. The final chapters of Section Three analyze the actual 'Apocalypse at Jonestown' and formulate afterthoughts ('After Jonestown').

In the final chapter Hall restates and extends the analysis of his earlier article (1981) according to which the key to understanding the tragedy 'lies in the dynamics of conflict between a religious community and an external political order'. The embattled sect has demonized the external order; the escalation of external pressure thus 'forces a choice between the sacred and evil', which becomes 'a question of honor, and it is the seedbed of martyrdom' (Hall, 1987: 296).

The People's Temple was caught between a collective identity as an other-worldly sanctuary 'on the other side of the apocalypse' and that of a 'warring sect' engaged in an inescapable conflict with an overpowering and malevolent order. The inescapability of the conflict and the omnipotence and relentlessness of the anti-Temple conspiracy was increasingly stressed by Jones and his close associates. Although functional in terms of internal solidarity and control, this emphasis undercut the insulated sanctuary conception which other world-rejecting sects construct, thus condemning the environing society while evolving a de facto accommodation. Jones 'vacillated between an ethic of confrontation and an ethos of sanctuary' (Hall 1987: 298). Mass suicide ultimately united 'the divergent public threads of meaningful existence at Jonestown — those of political revolution and religious salvation' (Hall 1987: 300).

Like Naipaul (1981), Hall sees the Concerned Relatives and other opponents of the Temple contributing to the descent into horror. The gradual escalation of their campaign to intervene against the Guyana settlement was perceived by Jones and his followers as a powerful threat to the mission, which they saw as a 'conspiracy' embodying the inevitable retaliation of a racist–fascist society against a group which presented an alternative model of social cooperation which could not be allowed to survive. The visitation of Congressman Ryan appeared to be the initial touch of an inevitable crushing embrace. The spectacle of hundreds of dedicated followers voluntarily laying down their lives was supposed to be a symbolic vindication which would repudiate the Concerned Relatives' depiction of the Temple as a prison and keep the flame of social justice burning.

The author also explores the historical 'sociology of martyrdom'. He reminds us that there is a Christian tradition of millennarian suicide in which dying devotees (e.g. the Russian Old Believers, see Robbins, 1986a) perish in the conviction that their deaths will spark or hasten the imminent world apocalypse. Yet, in some respects Jonestown did not continue this tradition but really harked back to the earlier militant Jewish suicidal tradition in which collective suicide is envisioned as a rebuke to the larger society and a vindication of the group *but not as itself a redemptive demiurge*. 'The leaders of Jonestown styled their act in the traditions of pre-Christian Jewish martyrdom and ancient Greek heroism, mediated through the Black Power concept of ''Revolutionary Suicide''' (Hall, 1987: 303) Hall also notes that at Jonestown 'attitudes and behavior that would be necessary to martyrdom' were shaped by practices of social control and indoctrination strikingly similar to practices which facilitated early Christian martyrdom (Hall, 1987; Riddle, 1931). Jones's vision:

> . . .fused the central dilemmas of modern Christianity — personal salvation versus the social gospel, with the philosophical antithesis of Christianity — a 'godless' yet prophetic vision of communism. These ideological themes found their concrete expression in a movement of *déclassé* true believers — black, white, poor, working class and professional — who renounced their professional lives for a cause. In life they adopted the legacy of black suffering as the vehicle that carried forward their quest for redemption. In death, they relinquished the burden of history to those of us who remain (Hall, 1987: 303).

David Chidester: Phenomenology of Reactions to Jonestown. John Hall also discusses the reactions to Jonestown and the popular and media typifications of the episode, which was widely interpreted as being intrinsic to the nature of a demonic 'cult' and thus *alien to the American way of life*. The mass suicide could not thus 'be understood as a more complex product of the struggles between the People's Temple and its opponents'. Using Durkheimian concepts, Hall posits the socially com-pulsive establishment of a mythic antithesis of the 'positive cult' or idealized conception of American society and the 'negative cult' or 'cancerous evil of the People's Temple — a group that cut itself off by migration, murder, and mass suicide' (Hall, 1987: 310).

David Chidester, a religious studies scholar, presents a somewhat more intricate analysis of the phenomenology of the cultural exorcism of Jonestown. Chidester explores *cognitive distancing* whereby the absolute 'otherness' of Jonestown to ourselves, our orientations and affiliations, society and culture is insisted upon. Through *psychological distancing* the People's Temple participants are dehumanized through the applications of psycho-medical and popular conceptions of mental illness, brain-washing, 'cult madness', etc. The actions and destinies of these putatively non-free agents may now appear 'less threatening to the larger human community' (Chidester, 1988). On the other hand, political distancing was used by State Department bureaucrats, Guyanese authorities, political extremists, American leftists and liberal San Francisco politicians who were once allied with Jim Jones to disclaim any responsibility for the events leading to the holocaust, or for the growth of the Temple, or for any possible similarity of Jones' movement to their operations.

Finally, *religious distancing* allowed the Disciples of Christ (who had originally ordained and backed Jones), other Christian churches, other evangelists, black churches and even stigmatized authoritarian NRMs such as the Unification Church to disavow any *fundamental* connection or convergence with the reality of the excoriated Temple. 'The cumulative effect of such Christian interpretations was a religious distancing which disavowed any connection between the People's Temple and what these authors regarded as legitimate Christianity' (Chidester, 1988). The imagery of cognitive distancing reinforces 'the sheer *otherness*, of the event; Jonestown. . .emerged as an impossible event within the familiar world of America' (Chidester, 1988). The People's Temple was not normal, sane, voluntary, American, black, Christian, Socialist, human, etc. It was other!

On an epistemological level, the various distancing strategies reveal the 'inherent limits in explanation itself'. To confront the otherness of Jonestown may require

> not an *explanation* which would reduce a complex life-world to a set of causal factors, but an *interpretation* that would work to clarify the conditions of possibility under which the People's Temple emerged as a meaningful human enterprise in human terms. The

systematic history of religions may provide a frame of reference within which such an interpretation of *otherness* might be carried out' (Chidester, 1988).

The bulk of Chidester's monograph thus deals with the People's Temple in terms of history-of-religions categories: cosmic/historical/body *time*; cosmic/geographical/body *space*; and human/subhuman/superhuman *classifications of persons*. The suicidal denouement of the People's Temple enacted a 'symbolic inversion' of the perceived subhuman categorization of devotees (Chidester, 1983). With explicit reference to the exchange theory of religion formulated by Stark and Bainbridge (1980b), Chidester attacks the reductive 'explanatory' focus of social scientists who treat religion as a mode of false consciousness or epiphenomenal product of desires, 'rather than interpreting desires in terms of the very human activity within which they derive their meaning' (Chidester, 1988).

Violence and NRMs

One proposition which crops up repeatedly in extensive accounts of conflicts between NRMs and their social environments, such as Hall's account of the destruction of the People's Temple (Hall, 1981, 1987) and Fitzgerald's depiction of the end of Rajneeshpuram (Fitzgerald, 1986), is the likelihood that hostility to outsiders was *deliberately cultivated by leaders for the purpose of enhancing solidarity and social control*. External hostility to NRMs may also generate or intensify such 'Durkheimian' processes such that internal cohesion and boundary clarity become pegged to conflict with outsiders (Barker, 1984; Harper, 1982). The projection of hostility and aggression outwards enhances the potential for violence. A recent formulation of a 'system model' for charismatic groups (Galanter, 1985) seeks to interrelate 'aggressive paranoia' with other patterns observed in 'cults' and with underlying system dynamics, which can replace explanations in terms of individual psychopathology:

> The importance of maintaining the group's homeostasis, for example, helps to explain why attention may be invested in recruitment practices and in rituals which define the group's distinct character. Certain areas are also highlighted in which a large group may demonstrate unexpected behaviors. For example, aggressive paranoia may emerge as a function of boundary control, when the group is threatened from without; seemingly impractical or *grandiose plans* may be undertaken when internal monitoring functions define a need for stabilizing feedback; and surprisingly *zealous commitments* can be produced in initially uncommitted recruits as part of the group's transformation function (Galanter, 1985: 76).

The dominant cultural interpretation of violence related to NRMs has been in terms of individual pathology arising from pathogenic mental conditioning. Cultist indoctrination 'results in increased suggestibility, dependency, and a willingness to obey orders without reflection' (Appel, 1983: 169). Such analyses, according to Richardson and Kilbourne (1983b), ignore the *relational* or interactive quality of violence associated with NRMs which inheres in the situated relationship between new religions and their antagonists and should not be viewed as a simple property of the movement. The actual enacting of violence 'often depends on the mutual dependency of each social actor or social group in relation to the other' (Richardson and Kilbourne, (1983b: 3).

The relational dynamic is stressed in Hall's analysis of Jonestown (1981, 1987, see discussion above). As the intervention of the Concerned Parents and allies escalated, Jones' 'paranoia' and the stringency of internal controls intensified. However, the horrendous violence of the People's Temple, like that of the Russian Old Believers (Robbins, 1986a), was *situated* and not simply immanent in the movement or in 'cults' in general (Richardson and Kilbourne, 1983b).

A somewhat similar position is taken by Melton (1985) who looks at violence against cults, cult against cult violence and intragroup violence. Cult-related violence is linked to the youthfulness of much NRM leadership and to dualistic belief systems which dehumanize outsiders or critics as 'satanic', 'enemy', or 'fairgame', etc. (see also Anthony and Ecker, 1987).

Finally, *charismatic leadership* enhances the likelihood that a movement will be volatile and violent (FitzGerald, 1986; Huber and Gruson, 1987; D. P. Johnson, 1980; B. Johnson, 1987b; Wallis, 1984: 86–102; Wallis and Bruce, 1986: 115–28; see Ch. 4). The volatility of charismatic leadership interacts with internal factionalism and conflicts with the social environment and the youth and inexperience of the leaders.

Conclusion

There now seem to be emerging several different models of the relationship between regulatory or other external pressures on NRMs and deviant behavior by NRMs.

One model is epitomized by James Richardson's (1985b) argument that the initial organizational patterns of NRMs tend to be 'deformed' by the interaction of internal pressures of various kinds and external pressure often related to environmental hostility and regulatory contingencies. The abusive or exploitative patterns of NRMs are often associated with the subsequent 'deformed' structure. This perspective contrasts with the emphasis of Ofshe (1980b, 1986) and Wallis (1988) on the initial privileges and immunities of NRMs which supposedly encourage deviance and which may ultimately elicit intense hostility and devastating retaliation.

Occupying the middle ground between these perspectives is the feed-back model of *deviance amplification* (Hampshire and Beckford, 1983; Robbins, 1986a; Wallis, 1977) which delineates a spiraling process of mutually interdependent and escalating recriminations on the part of an increasingly alienated and extremist deviant group and an increasingly hostile and persecutory environmental structure. The strength of this approach is its focus on the interactive *process* quality of certain escalating conflicts such that it is seen to be *misleading to focus on the extreme behavior arising late in the process in isolation from the process itself and the dynamic interaction of antecedents*. The weakness of the model (Hampshire and Beckford, 1983) is related to its very ubiquity and flexibility, i.e. it is too easy to apply and is actually compatible with both Richardson's (1985b) approach and Wallis's recent analysis (1988). The amplification model itself does not specify the conditions for 'de-amplification', which must be postulated ad hoc (e.g. Shupe, 1985) or provide any systematic formulation of the impact of exogenous variables.

Finally, mention should be made of provocative quasi-historical analy-ses which have compared contemporary cult controversies with prior episodes involving Mormons, American Catholics, Freemasons, Christian Scientists and Johovah's Witnesses (Bromley and Shupe, 1981: 1–20; Hampshire and Beckford, 1983; Cox, 1978; Moore, 1985; Robbins and Anthony, 1979a; Shupe, 1981) as well as English Puritans (Kent, 1987) and Russian Old Believers (Chidester, 1983; Robbins, 1986a).

7

NEW RELIGIONS AND THE
SOCIOLOGY OF RELIGION

The sociology of religion in North America and Europe has, according to Bryan Turner, been characterized by a 'narrow empirical focus on Western forms of religion' (Turner, 1983: 5). Once 'largely the sociology of Christianity', this tradition has been increasingly supplemented by studies of cults and sects in America and Britain. 'The trend toward the sociology of cults has now gone so far that mainstream Christianity has to some extent been neglected' (Turner, 1983: 5). Perhaps Dr Turner's last statement is a bit exaggerated, nevertheless the corpus of sociological literature on 'new religious movements' is certainly becoming vast. A 27-page review essay by Robbins et al. (1978) cited over 200 works. Beckford and Richardson's more recent (1983) bibliography listed over 350 works. Most issues of three American journals — the *Journal for the Scientific Study of Religion, Sociological Analysis* and the *Review of Religious Research* — now contain one to three papers on new movements, and there are many additional articles in European journals (e.g. *Social Compass*), general sociology journals, religious studies journals, anthropology journals and specialized journals dealing with ethnography, qualitative methodology, deviance, lifestyles, etc. 'At the present time', noted Long and Hadden in 1980, 'the literature on new religions constitutes perhaps the single largest corpus of scholarship in the sociology of religion' (Long and Hadden, 1980: 280). This may still be the case (Robbins, 1988a), notwithstanding the greater popular and media (and substantial scholarly) interest in the topics of evangelical revival and evangelical politics.

The study of contemporary 'cults' is arguably *helping to transform the sociology of religion* (Robbins, 1988a). The revitalizing effect has perhaps been somewhat similar to the effect which the discovery of 300 new species of lizard — including a few maneaters — might have on an association of herpetologists! Greater numbers of scholars and more younger scholars and graduate students appear to have been drawn to the field in recent years by the availability of colorful and dynamic movements to investigate and by the controversies surrounding some of the stranger groups. The effect of the new religions was particularly notable in the early and mid 1970s, prior to the heightened concern and controversies over politicized evangelism, Islamic militance and religious terrorism. The growth of NRMs instigated the trend, since reinforced by other developments, toward rendering the sociology of religion more 'relevant' and a bit less marginal in general sociology. The proliferation of new movements has also at least slightly weakened the ties of the sociology of religion to the needs and interests of conventional churches and has also helped to emancipate the sociology of religion from received theoretical traditions such as 'church–sect theory' (Robertson, 1979).

The study of new religious movements is now a prominent subarea within both sociology of religion and religious studies. It remains a prominent area despite the present overshadowing of its topicality by the politicized evangelical revival. Substantial research opportunities (particularly for comparative analyses) have been afforded. Indeed, the proliferation of unconventional 'cults' may be said to have somewhat 'anthropologized' the sociology of religion in the sense that a young doctoral candidate will now go out and study a 'cult' somewhat in the manner in which an aspiring anthropologist of yesteryear might embark on the study of a primitive tribe. We refer here to the proliferation of research settings and to the methodological and epistemological consequences of confronting esoteric 'cultures'. 'Cult is culture writ small' (Bainbridge, 1978: 14) and cults direct us to the 'generic processes of culture creation' (Long, 1979: 423). Notwithstanding the above, there has arguably been, considering the vast body of substantive research, at least a *relative* paucity of methodological and epistemological reflections pertaining to the distinctive hermeneutic problems of studying groups which seem bizarre, are highly controversial, and can be rigidly absolutist and intolerant plus highly manipulative and reactive to being studied. Some salient papers have, however, appeared (Balch, 1985a; Barker, 1983a; Beckford, 1978a; Bromley et al., 1987; Gordon, 1987; Heirich, 1977; Horowitz, 1983a; Lewis, 1987; Long, 1979, Lynch, 1977; Peshkin, 1984; Richardson et al., 1978; Richardson, 1985a; Robbins et al., 1973; Robbins, 1983b, 1985b,c; Shupe and Bromley, 1980b; Stone, 1978a; Wallis, 1983; Wallis and Bruce, 1986: 11–80; Wallis, 1984: 132–44; Wilson, 1983).

It is worth noting at this point that a number of recent commentaries have bewailed the malaise of the (allegedly moribund, marginal, trivialized, parochial and conceptually isolationist) contemporary sociology of religion (Beckford, 1985b; Marshall, 1987; Robertson, 1985c; Turner, 1983). Some writers feel that the current surge of NRM research has enhanced the relevance and centrality of the subdiscipline (Hadden, 1987b; Richardson, 1985c; Robbins, 1988), while others assert that the sociology of religion's concern with 'fringe religion' really *epitomizes* its cul de sac, e.g. 'Periodically the "if it's Tuesday it must be the Moonies" tendency threatens to trivialize the sociology of religion' (Marshall, 1987: 380; see also Turner, 1983). Some other writers appear to believe that the study of NRMs *could* render the sociology of religion the linchpin of sociology, but only *if* its theoretical approach to NRMs is reoriented away from functionalism (Batiuk, 1987), or towards a comparison of NRMs with 'new social movements' such as feminism, environmentalism, etc. (Hannigan, 1987).

New Religions and Theory in the Sociology of Religion

The study of new movements has given an impetus to the use of 'anthropological' methods such as participant observation and related perspectives such as phenomenology (Pilarzyk and Bharadnaj, 1979) and sociolinguistics. The study of new religious movements has influenced both the development and importation into the sociology of religion of new theoretical frameworks and perspectives such as symbolic realism (Bellah, 1970; Robbins et al., 1973), Mary Douglas's neo-Durkheimian structuralism (Westley, 1978a, 1983), resource mobilization theory (Bromley and Shupe, 1979a), related movement organization theory (Beckford, 1977; Harper, 1982; Gordon, 1984a; Lofland and Richardson, 1984) and Touraine's (1977, 1981) perspective (Bourg, 1983; Hannigan, 1987). Even neo-Marxian world systems theory has been introduced into the sociology of religion through the analysis of new religious movements (Wuthnow, 1982).

An outstanding example of theoretical innovation in the sociology of religion (as well as the introduction into the sociology of religion of general sociological theory) is afforded by the comprehensive Homansian exchange theory of religion developed by Stark and Bainbridge (1985), which has drawn largely on the authors' research and on new movements. The earliest critics of the Stark–Bainbridge theory have also been researchers in this area (Wallis, 1984: 59–64; Wallis and Bruce, 1986; Wuthnow, 1981a).

The work of Stark and Bainbridge is also illustrative of the critical re-evaluation of 'secularization theory' which has been stimulated by the rise of cults and subsequently by the evangelical resurgence. 'Secularization, even in the age of science, is a self-limiting process' (Stark and Bainbridge, 1985: 454). Some researchers have cited their own and other research as evidence of the superficiality of secularization (Anthony et al., 1983;

Fichter, 1981; Greeley, 1972; Hadden, 1987b; Richardson, 1985c). In effect the rise of NRMs followed by the surge of politicized evangelism stimulated a sort of anti-secularization *triumphalism in the sociology of religion*. Yet some other students of new religions have argued that secularization as a sociocultural thrust actually tends to enhance religious diversity such that the growth of cults can be seen as a *product of secularization* (Wilson, 1976; Wallis, 1984; see Ch. 2).

'May the Force Be With You'

The sociological appropriation of new religious movements has extra-polated linkages between the sociology of religion and other subareas of sociology such as social psychology (see Ch. 3) and the sociology of social movements (Lofland and Richardson, 1984; Snow, 1979; Snow et al., 1986). The modern sociology of religion has heretofore tended to be simultaneously highly 'theoretical' in the sense of being closely attuned to Durkheim, Weber and classical theory and hermetically sealed from other areas of contemporary sociology as well as broader intellectual discourse (Beckford, 1985b; Turner, 1983).

A significant emergent linkage may be the growing interface of the sociology of religion with *medical sociology* via the study of '*alternative healing systems*' (Beckford, 1985d; Foltz, 1987; McGuire, 1982, 1983a,b, 1985; Neitz, 1987; Wallis and Morely, 1976). There is now an 'increasing prominence of healing in new religious movements' as well as a concomitant proliferation of alternative therapies which are 'in effect, new religions on the American scene. They do appear to function as religions for many adherents — providing cosmologies, rituals, a language for the interpretation of believers' worlds, a social context for belief and practice, and a group of fellow believers' (McGuire, 1985: 275). Medical practices are embedded in 'healing systems' which often function as religions, while religions, particularly non-institutionalized movements, tend to operate as healing systems. New research and theory in this area are challenging the secularized view of religion and healing as separate spheres (McGuire, 1985), as well as helping to direct renewed attention to conceptions and evocations of *power* in religion.

The sociology of *organizations* is one area in which linkages with the sociology of religion are underdeveloped. 'Church–sect theory' appropriated the classical Weberian substratum of modern organization theory, but also blocked further linkages by hermetically sealing off socio-religious organization theory from the modern sociology of organizations

(Beckford, 1977). The present interest in cult–community conflicts (Beckford, 1985a; Harper, 1982) and the problematic survival of new religions in the 1980s (Bromley and Hammond, 1987) might suggest an introduction into the sociology of religion of *organization–environment perspectives* (e.g. Aldrich and Pfeffer, 1976).

Much of the research on NRMs now involves the controversies in which cults are entangled (Beckford, 1985a). These controversies often revolve around allegations that potent psychotechnologies of 'mind control' are entailed in cultist indoctrination practices, or around the allegedly exploitative and underregulated economic empires which some movements consolidate behind the shield of constitutional protections (Robbins, 1985a). These conflictful and 'political' aspects of religious movements, as well as the provocative *potency* of dynamic movement processes in healing, identity transformation, social control and mobilization, have contributed to an increasing theoretical focus on *power* in the sociology of religion (Beckford, 1983a; Robbins and Robertson, 1987). A recent cogent formulation of this new focus is by James Beckford, who proposes 'that empirical attention should, as a matter of priority, be focused on the reported experiences and the perceived manifestations of power and power-struggles in religion' (Beckford, 1983a: 30). Professor Beckford has been a notable student of contemporary religious movements, which has influenced his developing theoretical approach:

> This new and basically political approach to the sociology of religion represents a shift away from the kind of work which emphasized the largely subjective importance of religion as a set of precarious cognitions sustained by social interaction and conversation with significant others. The emphasis is now veering towards the practical processes whereby religion is actually lived out at both the individual and collective levels in a struggle for power. The struggle is over the power to define situations, to effect the course of events, and above all to gain a hearing for religious testimony, declarations, and directions. I have been trying for some time to describe the cross-national ways in which this struggle is currently being acted out in the controversy surrounding cultism and anti-cultism (Beckford, 1983a: 23).

Students of religious movements are also directing their attention to the sense of *empowerment* as a linchpin of religious experience (Jacobs, 1986). The linkage between religion and power is increasingly made in the media and popular culture, which may partly reflect the absorption by the latter of themes from the science fiction subculture from which Scientology and its offshoots as well as UFO cults have emerged (Bainbridge, 1987; Morth, 1987; Wallis, 1977). Meredith McGuire writes:

What are we talking about when we speak of personal experiences of power? A few years ago, when *Star Wars* gave us the phrase, 'May the Force be with you', sociologists of religion were able to smile knowingly and perhaps tuck this example into a lecture on Durkheim's theory of religious 'force'. What I found extremely interesting was the readiness of the media to accept the imagery and plausibility of this blatantly religious conception, which bypassed conventional religious terms, yet could be easily translated into them. 'The Force' was not an utterly remote power; rather, a human being in tune with it could tap it for enormous personal powers — with material effects and consequences for life and death. The notion of 'The Force' in popular imagery bears remarkable resemblance to conceptions of power articulated by respondents in my own researches (McGuire, 1983a: 3).

McGuire's respondents in various healing groups recounted their personal experiences of spiritual power to the researchers (McGuire, 1983a,b; see also Jacobs, 1987; Walker, 1983; Wilson and Clow, 1981). 'Although the groups we have studied vary tremendously in their conceptions of that power — its locations and sources and how they symbolize it — their members are remarkably similar in describing *an experience of a great power which they believe they can now tap for personal empowerment*' (McGuire, 1983a: 3). Religious movements, notes James Beckford, 'are seen by prospective and actual members as sources of various kinds of power. Their expectation is that membership empowers them to cultivate and to achieve a number of things more easily than through other means, e.g. empowerment of women in spiritualist groups (Haywood, 1983; Jacobs, 1986). The chance to cultivate various spiritual qualities, personal goals, or social arrangements is the attraction' (Beckford, 1983a: 26). This analysis of religious movements implies an altered conception of religion and perhaps a new perspective on the sociology of religion. Beckford comments:

> What I have proposed is that, in focusing on the capacity or function of religion to supply meaning, integration, and identity, the theoretical cart has been put before the empirical horse. The sociologists' interpretations of religious phenomena have been mistaken for their subjects' motives and intentions. In short, I agree that meaning and identity are important aspects of religion; but at the same time I dispute whether actors act out of consideration for them directly. Rather, I believe that actors respond to perceived sources of power, and their responses may or may not supply the meaning and identity of which we have heard so much (Beckford, 1983a: 29).

Interestingly, as religiopolitical protest movements such as The Moral Majority, Liberation Theology and militant Shiism have gained prominence, religion has been 'rediscovered' by intellectuals and scholars concerned with social protest and revolution. *Religion is seen as having power*!

The Shifting Problematic

Partly convergent with Beckford's perspective is an important paper by
Roland Robertson (1979). 'Religious Movements and Modern Societies:
Toward a Progressive Problemshift'. Beckford's paper on 'The Restoration of "Power" to the Sociology of Religion' was published in 1983.
Robertson's analysis of the impact of the study of new religions on
sociological theory reveals that the *initial* effect on the sociology of
religion of the expansion in the 1970s of new religions studies was hardly
to enhance a preoccupation with power. Rather, a sort of 'new movements
movement' emerged within the sociology of religion which manifested
a 'symbolic realist' orientation in the sense of a tendency 'to operate
with something like a religious *a priori*, to pay considerable attention
to the interiority of religious ideation, and to wonder what religious
movements say about the portent for the interpretation of the modern
human condition' (Robertson, 1979: 297). Examples of this approach
are afforded by a number of papers written (if not published) during the
early or middle 1970s (Anthony et al., 1978; Anthony and Robbins,
1982a,b; Bellah, 1976a; Glock, 1976; Greeley, 1972). Gradually sociological study of NRMs, responding in part to the developments of the
late 1970s and the concerns raised by the horror of the People's Temple
explosion at Jonestown, 'has edged toward the establishment of a new
problem-base' (Robertson, 1979: 297).

The new problem-base raises 'again the conceptual status and problem
referents of the church–sect mode of analysis' (Robertson, 1979: 297).
'Church–sect theory' as Robertson notes, has been a *conceptual casualty*
of the rise of the new religions. Beckford (1975b, 1977) has criticized
the received church–sect model as parochial and quasi-theological and
as thereby inhibiting the desired integration of the analysis of religious
movements with the rapidly developing movement–organization theory.
More fundamentally, church–sect theory has receded into the background
because the emergence of new religions in the late 1960s and early 1970s
initially shifted the theoretical focus of the sociology of religion. 'The
post-Niebuhrian church–sect focus met its Waterloo at the hands of those
trying to make sociological (as well as theological) sense of "the new
religious consciousness". . . .' (Robertson, 1979: 298).

The study of marginal religious movements, formerly typified as 'sects',
has been a salient dimension of the sociology of religion throughout its
existence. In Robertson's view the sociological study of religious
movements has developed through *three phases*, although a fourth phase
may presently be emerging. The initial phase largely responded to the

classic Troeltschian analyses of H. R. Niebuhr (1929) and was concerned with the correlates and determinants of different types of movements and to the internal and external factors influencing the evolution of movements. A second phase was ushered in by Milton Yinger (1946) and entailed a greater interest in the societal (particularly eufunctional vs. dysfunctional) *significance* of different types of movements (e.g. Johnson, 1961). Some of the earliest studies of the movements of the past two decades, which focused on the latent integrative consequences of these movements (Robbins, 1969; see Ch. 2), were rooted in the concerns of this phase. However, both the first and the second phase were 'dominated conceptually by the church–sect mode of analysis derived from the work and teaching of Troeltsch. . . [and] centered upon the issue of the kind of *compromise* which religious movements had to make' (Robertson, 1979: 303).

The third phase commenced in the early 1970s and responded to the esotericism and diversity of the new groups while focusing 'attention on the overall phenomenon rather than. . . locating particular movements within the "ferment"' (Robertson, 1979: 304). The 'meaning' of the new religiosity or 'New Religious Consciousness' (Glock and Bellah, 1976) was the vital object of inquiry.

The earlier phases of sociological analysis of religious movements were marked 'by a strong impact of sociological organizational theory', such that 'the cultural element of religious organization and actions was frequently *bracketed*'. As the new religiosity emerged in the late 1960s, however, 'sociologists of religion attended less to the purely social aspects of religion and more to religious ideas' (Robertson, 1979: 304). Scholars such as Robert Bellah, Dick Anthony, Robert Wuthnow and Steven Tipton examined the relationship between the content of religious meanings and shifts in the operation of modern societies (e.g. Anthony et al., 1978; Anthony and Robbins, 1978, 1981–2, 1982a,b; Tipton, 1982a,b; Wuthnow, 1976b, 1978):

> However, since the mid-70's, increasing extra-sociological interest in the alleged 'mind control' practices of 'the cults' has led to a specialized interest in the psycho-social dynamics of marginal religious and politico-religious movements. Like the purely organizational focus evident among some analysts of the 1960's the contemporary concern with the dynamics of conversion to and control within cults and sects frequently brackets the distinctively ideational components of these religious movements (Robertson, 1979: 304).

A *fourth period* of the study of religious movements has now emerged and has been strongly influenced by controversies over the authoritarian nature and 'coercive' practices of new movements and their 'destructive' consequences. 'The sociological study of such movements appears to have gradually been led back to the older concern with the societal *consequences* of different types of religious activity' (Robertson, 1979: 306). 'Symbolic consequentialism', the target of the empathetic 'symbolic realist' approach (Bellah, 1970), has made an 'inexorable reappearance' which 'can in large part be attributed to the extra-sociological, public — indeed political — interest in the private and public implications of the newer movements (particularly since the Jonestown tragedy)' (Robertson, 1979: 306). The current interest in *power* (e.g. Beckford, 1983a) also seems to reflect some of the older 'church–sect' theme of compromise vs. exclusivity which has been explicitly applied to NRM controversies (Hammond and Gordon-McCutcheon, 1981; Robbins, 1986c).

For Robertson, 'the most important aspect of the study of religious movements is not the question of whether they constitute a new, viable form of transformative religiosity, let alone the question of what gives rise to them. The central, most general problem has to do with their general significance with regard to changing conceptions of the relationship between individual and society, and between extra-societal agencies and society itself' (Robertson, 1979: 306):

> . . . for in coming to terms legally and politically — as well as socially and psychologically — with the new cultism, "society" is, willy nilly, involved in the issue of what constitutes its own boundaries, and in a sense its own foundations (Fenn, 1978). The fascinating legal issues which surround the debate about the new movements — particularly since the eruption of the controversy surrounding the People's Temple — should not be allowed to obscure the wider *sociological* problem. Or, better, the legal and constitutional issues should be seen as embodying crucial sociological issues (Robertson, 1979: 308).

Robertson's agenda has been extapolated in Beckford's *Cult Controversies* (1985a), which has been discussed in a previous chapter. 'The operation of NRMs has . . . forced society to show its hand and declare itself' (Beckford, 1985a: 11).

As Robertson notes, the conflicts and controversies over cults ultimately direct attention to the present heightening of *church–state tensions* in the United States. Robertson's seminal essay anticipated the increasing preoccupation of sociologists of religion with church–state issues and particularly on the part of sociologists who have been previously involved in the study of NRMs (Bromley, 1983; Richardson, 1985b; Robbins, 1985a). As Fenn (1978) notes, these issues frequently involve questions of *religious authenticity*. 'The question of authentic religion', Fenn commends, 'is a problem not only for the theologians and sociologists, but for officials concerned with social policy' (Fenn, 1978: 58; see also Straus, forthcoming). For Fenn, Robertson, Beckford and others a major sociological concern in the present period must be the analysis of 'the way in which religion as a social category is produced, reproduced and transformed' (Robertson, 1979: 308ff; see also Robbins, 1988a). A key aspect of the new problem-base must be a recognition of the ongoing 'religionization of the State' which increasingly deals with quasi-religious issues such as when 'life' commences and terminates (Robertson, 1981, 1985a). To a degree 'the State itself becomes a "church"....' (Robertson, 1979: 311).

Sympathy and Objectivity

Sociologists of religion and religious studies scholars who study new religious movements have been frequently accused of being unduly sympathetic to manipulative and 'destructive' cults (Beckford, 1983b; Horowitz, 1983a; Keiser and Keiser, 1987; West, 1982). They are beginning to make responses to these criticisms (Barker, 1983b; Bromley et al., 1987; Robbins, 1983a; Wallis, 1983; and Wilson, 1983):

> A particularly evident feature of the third phase has been the greater empathy, indeed sympathy, exhibited on the part of the analyst, compared to previous attitudes towards religious movements. It is no accident that in the American context a 'pro-religious' orientation on the part of some prominent sociological practitioners developed generally in the same period as the 'new religious movements' motif crystallized. For some scholars, at least *some* of the new religious movements have constituted welcome harbingers of the new modes of individual existence. They were on occasion seen as the bearers of potentially effective critiques of the wider society. Since Jonestown, this orientation has been considerably refined — so that now the 'symbolic realists' have become much more selective in their expressions of religious sympathy. The main emergent criterion in this regard seems to be that of the degree of authoritarianism (or totalitarianism) of the new movements (Robertson, 1979: 305).

Even in Robertson's emerging post-Jonestown 'fourth phase', with its focus on church–state issues and debates over 'mind control' and the consequences of organizational totalism, scholarly sympathy for embattled movements is evident. The analyses of sociologists writing on controversies over cults often seem to be geared to a debunking of the insistent claims, negative stereotypes, 'atrocity tales' and strident conclusions purveyed by the more vehement critics of cults (Bromley and Shupe, 1981; Kilbourne and Richardson, 1984a,b; Robbins and Anthony, 1980, 1982a; Robbins, 1984; Shupe and Bromley, 1981a,b). Thus, 'Sociologists ...generally reject "brainwashing" altogether as a scientific concept;

even as a metaphor it appears to cloud more than it reveals' (Bromley et al., 1987: 216). The sociological perspective is seen as 'presenting a distinct threat to anti-cult sponsored ideology' (Bromley et al., 1987: 216).

It is due in part to these orientations that some controversial movements are quite *eager to be studied*, perhaps because they anticipate getting more favorable treatment from students of religion than from journalists or from psychiatrists on the lookout for psychopathology. Nevertheless, 'there may be pitfalls in too close a collabortion of scholars with manipulative authoritarian sects, which want to use the researcher to project a favorable image' (Robbins, 1983b: 233). But 'collaboration' between cults and scholars in this area sometimes seems to get rather close:

> For example, in addition to attending conferences (at which they have comprised an audience and have been presenters), individual behavioral scientists have authored articles in books published by movement controlled presses, served as consultants to movements on various issues, served as expert witnesses in trials involving new religious groups or their members, and acted as lobbyists regarding pending legislation designed to regulate new religious groups (Bromley et al., 1987: 213).

These activities have been strongly criticized (Horowitz, 1978, 1983a) and vigorously defended (Bromley et al., 1987; Wallis, 1983; Wilson, 1983). Bromley et al. (1987) argue that social scientists must 'get close' to rapidly changing and internally differentiated movements to really understand them. Moreover, some scholars are really less close to stigmatized movements than they appear to be: 'they are monitoring and studying the conflict in which new religious groups are involved' (Bromley et al., 1987: 213). But Beckford (1983b) questions whether attending conferences or becoming a consultant or advocate really provides a good angle to study movements (e.g. how 'typical' are the well-scrubbed devotees who attend conferences?). 'Monitoring the conflict' by studying movement and countermovement simultaneously is a very difficult enterprise and one which Shupe and Bromley (1980b) have analyzed perceptively; however, their work has been excoriated in anti-cult circles, although they seem to have initially considered themselves to be detached observers mediating between 'both sides'. The strident rejection of their work by one 'side' has undercut their contacts and field research opportunities with regard to the ACM (Shupe, 1987), thus possibly enhancing empathy with the 'other side'.

Finally, it is arguable that it is precisely because sociological perspectives and findings are likely to undercut the more extreme 'Invasion-of-the-Bodysnatchers' stereotypes of cults that it is essential for sociologists to avoid appearing to be too closely connected to cults. The issue here is the extrinsic one of *credibility*. Sociologists might be well advised to avoid any appearance of being 'in the pocket' of those who sometimes benefit from (and eagerly trumpet and exploit) their findings.

One writer has argued that studying a controversial group such as the Unification Church has now become somewhat of a *political act* and the quality of scholarship has thereby suffered. Hargrove (1982) compares recent politicized work on the Moonies with the more objective early work of John Lofland (see Lofland, 1977).

> While popular opinion does much to create the climate of research, pressures from scholars like Horowitz have made it most difficult to treat the Unification Church or other new religion in the balanced way that Lofland achieved in the early years of the movement. Most articles on the subject in the late 1970's tended to be less studies on the group as a religion than on the civil liberties of their members, whether in terms of loss of freedom to an authoritarian leader or of rights to free choice of religion thwarted by deprogrammers. Unification theology and practice do unite themes of religion, politics and economics, as well as that of the family, so that choosing one of these issues is not without some justification. But such a concentration on politics, for example, in isolation from other factors, does not do justice to the nature of unification doctrine and practice (Hargrove, 1982: 212).

In effect, the politicized climate of controversiality has a *reductive* impact, e.g. the Unification Church is 'reduced' to its 'coercive' indoctrination processes or to its right-wingedness or even to its 'persecuted' status.

In Robertson's emerging fourth phase, sociologists studying religious movements receive their problem-focus from extra-sociological moral entrepreneurs and the popular media (Robertson, 1979). 'Cults', and, indeed, religion in general are viewed increasingly as a *social problem* (Long and Hadden, 1980; Robbins 1985c). This development is implicitly welcomed by Irving Horowitz (1983b) who hopes for an infusion of 'neutral' (i.e. not proceeding from religious groups) funds to support objective research in this area. A critical social problems/deviance orientation toward the analysis of religious movements is evident in a recent essay by a criminologist, 'Cult Members as Victims and Victimizers' (Kramer, 1983), in a volume of *Annual Reviews of Studies of Deviance* (other papers in the volume deal with alcoholics, addicts, prostitutes and homosexuals). A more sympathetic treatment influenced by antinomian or anti-control perspectives on deviance such as labeling theory and social constructionism has appeared in the journal *Social Problems* (Robbins and Anthony, 1982a). In this connection the application of the concept of

deviance amplification by Roy Wallis (1975d, 1976: 205–24) to conflicts
involving the Scientology movement in the British Commonwealth has
been particularly influential (Hampshire and Beckford, 1983; Robbins,
1986a).

Sources of Sympathy

Sociologists studying controversies over cults have generally debunked
the brainwashing argument regarding commitments to cults (Bromley and
Shupe, 1981; Kilbourne and Richardson, 1984b; Robbins and Anthony,
1980, 1982a; Robbins, 1984; Snow and Machalek, 1984). An eminent
psychiatrist and 'brainwashing expert' has criticized social scientists who
'serve in the ranks of the apologists [for cults]. . .Some of the apologists
appear to be romantics, projecting into the cults some of their own hopes
for religious reform, spiritual rebirth, a rejection of materialism. . .'
(West, 1982: 11).

There clearly *are* reasons why sociologists of religion and religous
studies scholars tend to sympathize with new religious movements
and/or reject analyses of conversion in terms of brainwashing and
psychopathology:

(1) Biases against 'psychological reductionism' are deeply embedded
in sociology. Opposition to the medical model is deeply embedded in the
sociology of deviance and social problems, as is a somewhat antinomian
orientation towards relatively powerless and arguably persecuted 'devi-
ants' such as mental patients or addicts (Bromley et al., 1987; Robbins
and Anthony, 1982a).

(2) The sociology of religion is not subsidized by government and foundations to the degree that other sociological subareas such as criminology
or gerontology are. This is largely due to the American 'separation of
church and state' and the resulting absence of government or corporate
'programs' in the area of religion. The traditional 'patron' of the sociology
of religion, at least in the United States, has been the *churches*, which
have sponsored sociological research pertinent to their interests and
objectives. The effects of the dominant role of churches in directing the
problematic of research and inquiry in the sociology of religion have
only occasionally been deplored (Berger and Luchmann, 1963). The
liaisons between scholars and movements, which Bromley et al. (1987)
have defended, can be viewed as 'merely a continuation of the pattern
of church–social science cooperation which has characterized the modern
sociology of religion' (Robbins, 1985c: 174).

(3) Critics of cults have expressed to the author the view that sociologists or other scholars who seem sympathetic to new movements are really 'in love with religion'. Arguably there is a general 'pro-religion' bias in the sociology of religion. When the vital cultural significance of religion or at least Christianity was taken for granted, intellectuals such as Marx, Feuerbach, Freud or Nietzsche who lacked sympathy for religion or Christianity nevertheless felt compelled to study it. Today, however, the context of secularization renders the sociocultural salience of religion problematic, with the consequence that (prior to recent ferment and conflicts) religion has been partly downgraded to the status of *cultural esoterica*. Those who bother to collect rare stamps or Victorian pornography tend to be fond of the object of their inquiries. Similarly scholars who study religion have tended to be either personally religious (many sociologists of religion are ordained) or favorable to religion. The religious involvements of scholars are not always traditional: 'a growing trickle of scholars in the area of religion have commitments to groups such as Zen Buddhism, Scientology, est, Gurdjieff or Meher Baba' (Robbins, 1983a: 210).

(4) The effects of any 'pro-religion' bias in the sociology is possibly reinforced by the particular 'esprit de corps' of the sociology of religion and solidarity of its practitioners. Since the sociology of religion has been marginal within general sociology, sociologists of religion have assiduously developed their own reference groups and their own systems of status-conferral, i.e. conferences and journals. These 'frog ponds' tend to involve both sociologists and religious studies and divinity scholars, the latter being even more likely than sociologists of religion to be ordained and pro-religion. Many sociologists of religion have thus been tied more closely to interdisciplinary reference groups (e.g. The Society for the Scientific Study of Religion) with substantial religious studies and religionist contingents than to sociological associations (Beckford, 1985b).

(5) Students of religion are aware that exotic new religious movements afford interesting research opportunities; moreover, the rise and growth of such groups pleasingly testify to the importance of religion and the study of religion in an allegedly 'secular' age.

(6) Some movements seem to have mounted a sophisticated effort to co-opt academics as fellow travelers, sympathizers and defenders (Beckford, 1983b; Robertson, 1985b), although the same might conceivably be said about movements and orientations such as liberation theology (Robertson, 1985b). They have eagerly sought to recruit scholars to study them. They have organized conferences in which sociologists have participated and

conference volumes in which sociologists have published. The Unification Church, which has adopted a 'philomandarin' pose, is somewhat unique in the frequency and quantity of expenditure on academic conferences, publications, etc., which it undertakes (Robertson, 1985b). The UC thus constitutes 'the most recent controversial manifestation of the process whereby an object of the analytic orientation of the sociology of religion has become inserted into the discipline itself' (Robertson, 1985b: 180). Beckford (1983b) has expressed anxiety lest the UC corner the market on opportunities for scholarly publication on new movements, especially as 'legitimate' publishers forsake the area to chase newer fashions. The anxieties of Beckford and of Horowitz (1978) helped stimulate a symposium on 'Scholarship and Sponsorship' in the sociology of religion (Symposium, 1983). At any rate, the collaboration of sociologists with some movements is partly due to the active 'courtship' of scholars by the latter, wearing their 'philomandarin' robes and quite cognizant of the unfavorable predispositions of other professionals such as mental health clinicians or social workers (see Ch. 6).

(7) Finally, compared to clinicians and social workers, sociologists of religion are more likely to view the allegations against 'destructive cults' in historical and comparative terms. Todays's movements and controversies do not appear to sociologists of religion as unique; they are often seen as comparable to former irruptions involving excoriated 'sects' (Niebuhr, 1929) and to American groups such as Mormons, Freemasons, American Catholics, Jehovah's Witnesses and Christian Scientists (Bromley and Shupe, 1981; Hampshire and Beckford, 1983; Robbins and Anthony, 1979a). Controversies and 'atrocity stories' relating to cults are thus implicitly *relativized*, e.g. students of religion realize that the alienation of converts qua 'spiritual brethren' from their 'mere fleshly kindred' is an old sectarian story (Kanter, 1972). They are predisposed to doubt that 'coercive' processes in cults represent a novel, esoteric and omnipotent psychotechnology of brainwashing.

There are thus a number of factors pertaining to traditions in general sociology, the sociology of deviance and social problems and the sociology of religion which tend to render scholars either distinctly sympathetic to struggling new movements or negatively disposed towards both enhanced social control of NRMs and psychologistic and medicalistic interpretations of individual commitments to new religions. Nevertheless, it is also likely that sociologists analyzing religious movements have sometimes been unfairly stigmatized and have been misperceived as apologists for cults when in fact they have arguably been conforming to strict norms of value neutrality.

Toward a New Sociology of Religion

Much of American religious history has been turbulent and contentious. Nevertheless, the period from the advent of World War II to the 1970s seems to have constituted a deviant period of relative religious peace and consensus. This writer has argued elsewhere (Robbins, 1983a, 1985c, 1988) that the dissipation of this period of 'religious detente' began with the rise of cults and the controversies swirling around them, and has been subsequently reinforced by controversies relating to the Evangelical Right, Liberation Theology, religious terrorism, etc. However, the post-Second World War milieu of relative religious peace and consensus has arguably been the formative social context for the emergence of a putatively value-neutral and 'scientific' study of religion. The modern sociology of religion, in this view, has been made possible by the post-war 'detente' between social science and religion/theology (Friedrichs, 1974; Johnson, 1977), which in turn was facilitated by the relative non-controversiality of 'Eisenhowerian' religion (Robbins, 1983a, 1988a). The present erosion of this detente, partly under the impact of heightened religious conflict arguably imperils the sociology of religion as we have known it.

By the advent of the Second World War the major religious communities in the United States — Catholicism, (liberal mainland) Protestantism and Judaism had become assimilated to the American 'religion of civility' (Cuddihy, 1978) and had implicitly surrendered much of their intolerance, apocalyptic expectation and claims to an exclusive monopoly of religious truth. The 'cold war' between these groups and between each of them and American civil religion had given way 'to a thirty-year period of religious ecumenism and theological detente' (Cuddihy, 1978: 28). After the Second World War, according to Will Herberg's well-known analysis, the three major American religious traditions appeared to shed their distinctive doctrinal perspectives and to converge on a consensual worship of the American way of life (Herberg, 1960). The resulting religion of *Americanism* was seen 'as a kind of secularized Puritanism, a Puritanism without transcendence, without a sense of sin or judgement' (Herberg, 1960: 81).

During this period, President Eisenhower, in a probably misquoted and misinterpreted statement, supposedly observed that the American government is necessarily 'founded in a deeply felt religious faith, and I don't care what it is' (quoted in Turner, 1983: 58). In other words, religion is certainly a good thing, but *particular religions are interchangeable* — any religion will do. This attitude has not remained external to the American sociology of religion. Functionalist sociology of religion has implied that religion is good in the sense of being functionally imperative, while simultaneously insisting that the 'truth' of religion is beyond the purview of value-neutral science (Johnson, 1977). This really amounted to a somewhat reductive and secularist *endorsement* of religion which, moreover, implicitly de-emphasized the cognitive content of religion and in this sense implied the interchangeability of particular faiths.

The 'Eisenhowerian' premise of the interchangeability of particular faiths depended for its plausibility on the *relative limitation of American religious conflict in the post-war period of 1945–70*, when 'religion seemed tamer and less controversial than in preceding periods or in the present period' (Robbins, 1985c: 172). Although there were some controversies (Father Divine, Bishop Pike, Senator McCarthy's attack on Protestant clergymen), religious conflict was not tumultuous as in previous 'Great Awakenings'. There were wild ecstatic sects, but they tended to inhabit the margins of society and, moreover, they could often be seen as really 'socializing in dominant values' (Johnson, 1961). However, the current milieu is very different. Roland Robertson writes:

> The modern sociology of religion was,...established in the U.S.A. largely in terms of the cultural maxim that religion is a good thing, regardless of its actual content. Since the rise of the modern 'cults' and even more particularly since Jonestown, it has become impossible for a president or any other major political leader to say, as Eisenhower did, that the particular nature of a religious orientation is societally unimportant (so long as the populace at large manifests religious sentiments). The noncontroversial nature of religion was thus a major factor in the crystallization of the sociology of religion — at least in the U.S.A. Insofar as religion was found to be problematic, it was widely assumed to be "safely" marginal. In the present circumstance, however, the problematic is no longer marginal (Robertson, 1985b: 183).

The shattering of the postwar religious consensus and the rise of 'bad religions', e.g. 'cults', politicized charismatics and fundamentalists (spreading beyond their traditional rural–southern confines), liberationists and other religious opponents of American foreign policy, have undercut not only the interchangeability premise and the putative ultimate beneficence of religion, but also the scholarly premise of value-neutrality. As many Americans look to a religious revival as the hope of humankind, many others devoutly wish to see the last guru strangled with the entrails of the last TV evangelist! In this context both the possibility and desirability of a value-neutral sociology of religion have come to seem doubtful. The heightened religious conflict and ferment encourages both affirmations of the desirability of a *religious* social science (Paloma, 1984) and critical investigations into the implicit religious assumptions embodied in putatively value-neutral sociological theory (Cavanaugh, 1984). 'But as it becomes clear that no social science is value-free and that sociology does have implications for religious truth, separation is harder to maintain' (Johnson, 1977: 375). Marxists, Christians and others who have evinced (or have been perceived to evince) an antipathy to 'positivistic' social science and the doctrine of value-neutrality, and who have not really been welcome in the modern 'scientific' study of religion, will now be granted a hearing. The range and saliency of theoretical discourse in the sociology of religion should increase.

There are other likely consequences of the accentuation of religious controversy. The 'clericalist' quality of the modern American sociology of religion (Robbins, 1983a, 1985c), which refers to the patronage and sponsorship of the sociology of religion by churches which have partly directed the focus of disciplinary inquiry, is likely to be increasingly challenged. This tendency has only occasionally been criticized (Berger and Luckmann, 1963), but the enhanced controversiality of American and world religion could lead to more criticism of church–social science liaisons. 'Just as anger over the tax privileges and financial–commercial finagling of cults will eventually raise questions about the tax privileges and financial diversification of "respectable" churches, the concern over sympathy for cults in the sociology of religion cannot but ramify into a broader concern with the precariousness of objectivity in the sociology of religion. The "detente" between religion and social science is waning' (Robbins, 1983a: 211). On the other hand, the clericalist pattern is arguably continued in 'cultist' patronage of our subdiscipline!

Finally, the controversies over cults, together with controversies over other contemporary religious tendencies will continue to enhance the perceived 'relevance' of religion and its scholarly study. The prestige of the sociology of religion is rising, notwithstanding inadequacies in its empirical investigations of new movements. The repute of religion as a *social force* is rising. Perhaps one day religion shall attain the epitome of 'relevance' indicated in Edward Gibbon's *Decline and Fall of the Roman Empire* which depicted fourth-century Constantinople in the grip of intense Christological controversy (quoted by Gibbon from an 'intelligent observer' source):

If you desire a man to change a piece of silver, he informs you wherein the Son differs from the Father; if you ask the price of a loaf, you are told, by way of reply, that the Son is inferior to the Father; and if you inquire whether the bath is ready, the answer is, that the Son was made out of nothing (Gibbon, 1932: 9).

Bibliography

AARGAARD, J. and L. W. DUDDY (1984) 'Denmark vis-à-vis new religious movements', *Update* 8(2): 37–42.

ABRAHAM, G. (1983) 'The Protestant ethic and the spirit of utilitarianism: the case of est', *Theory and Society* 12: 739–73.

ADAMS, Robert L. and Robert J. FOX (1972) 'Mainlining Jesus: The new trip', *Society* 9(4): 50–6.

AHLBERG, Sture (1986) *Messianic Movements: A Comparative Analysis of the Sabbatians, The People's Temple, and the Unification Church.* Stockholm: Almquist and Wiksell.

AIDALA, Angela A. (1984) 'Worldviews, ideologies and social experimentation', *Journal for the Scientific Study of Religion* 23(1): 44–59.

AIDALA, Angela A. (1985) 'Social change, gender roles, and new religious movements', *Sociological Analysis* 46(3): 287–314.

ALDRICH, Howard and Jeffrey PFEFFER (1976) 'Environments of organizations', *Annual Review of Sociology* (2): 79–107.

AMBROSIO, G. (1984) 'I nuovi movimenti religiosi in Italia', *Teologia* 9(2): 141–65.

American Studies (1985) Special issue on 'sects and cults', 26(2), Fall.

ANDERSON, Susan (1985) 'Identifying coercion and deception in social systems', pp. 12–23 in B. K. Kilbourne (ed.)

ANTHONY, Dick (1979–80) 'The fact pattern behind the deprogramming controversy: An analysis and an alternative', *New York University Review of Law and Social Change* 9(1): 33–50.

ANTHONY, Dick and Bruce ECKER (1987) 'The Anthony typology: a framework for assessing spiritual and consciousness groups', pp. 35–106 in Dick Anthony, B. Ecker and K. Wilber (eds).

ANTHONY, Dick, Bruce ECKER and Ken WILBER (1987) *Spiritual Choices: The Problem of Recognizing Authentic Paths to Inner Transformation.* New York: Paragon.

ANTHONY, Dick and Thomas ROBBINS (1974) 'The Meher Baba movement', pp. 479–501 in I. Zaretsky and M. Leone (eds).

ANTHONY, Dick and Thomas ROBBINS (1978) 'The effect of detente on the growth of new religions: Reverend Moon and the Unification Church', pp. 80–100 in J. Needleman and G. Baker (eds).

ANTHONY, Dick and Thomas ROBBINS (1981a) 'Cultural crisis and contemporary religion', pp. 9–31 in T. Robbins and D. Anthony (eds).

ANTHONY, Dick and Thomas ROBBINS (1981b) 'New religions, families and "brainwashing"', pp. 263–74 in T. Robbins and D. Anthony (eds).

ANTHONY, Dick and Thomas ROBBINS (1982a) 'Contemporary religious ferment and moral ambiguity', pp. 243–63 in E. Barker (ed.).

ANTHONY, Dick and Thomas ROBBINS (1982b) 'Spiritual innovation and the crisis of American civil religion', pp. 229–48 in M. Douglas and S. Tipton (eds).

ANTHONY, Dick and Thomas ROBBINS (1987) 'Contemporary religious movements and cults — the United States', in M. Eliade et al. (eds), *Encyclopedia of Religion*. New York: Free Press.

ANTHONY, Dick, Thomas ROBBINS, Madeline DOUCAS and Thomas CURTIS (1978) 'Patients and pilgrims: changing attitudes toward psychotherapy of converts to eastern mysticism', in James Richardson (ed.) (1978a), pp. 43–64.

ANTHONY, Dick, Thomas ROBBINS and Paul SCHWARTZ (1983) 'Contemporary religious movements and the secularization premise', in J. Coleman and G. Baum (eds) (1983).

APPEL, Willa (1980) 'Satanism in politics', *New York Times* Op-ed (January 15), A19.

APPEL, Willa (1983) *Cults in America*. New York: Holt, Rinehart and Winston.

AUSTIN, Roy L. (1977) 'Empirical adequacy of Lofland's conversion model', *Review of Religious Research* 18(3): 282–7.

BABBIE, Earl (1987) 'Methodological challenges of studies of New Age phenomena', presented to the Midwest Sociological Society, Chicago, April.

BAECHLER, Jean (1979) 'Mourir à Jonestown', *Archives européennes de sociologie* 20: 173–210.

BAER, Hans (1978) 'A field perspective of religious conversion: the Levites of Utah', *Review of Religious Research* 19: 279–94.

BAFFOY, Thierry (1978) 'Les sectes totalitaires', *Esprit* January: 53–9.

BAINBRIDGE, William S. (1978) *Satan's Power: Ethnography of a Deviant Psychotherapy Cult*. Berkeley: University of California.

BAINBRIDGE, William S. (1985) 'Cultural genetics', in R. Stark (ed.) (1985a), pp. 115–29.

BAINBRIDGE, William S. (1987) 'Science and religion: the case of Scientology', in D. G. Bromley and P. H. Hammond (eds) (1987), pp. 59–79.

BAINBRIDGE, William S. and Daniel H. JACKSON (1981) 'The rise and decline of transcendental meditation', in B. Wilson (ed.) (1981), pp. 135–58.

BAINBRIDGE, William S. and Rodney STARK (1979) 'Cult formation: three compatible models', *Sociological Analysis* 40(4): 285–93.

BAINBRIDGE, William S. and Rodney STARK (1980) 'Scientology: to be perfectly clear', *Sociological Analysis* 4(2): 128–36.

BAINBRIDGE, William S. and Rodney STARK (1981) 'The "consciousness reformation" reconsidered', *Journal for the Scientific Study of Religion* 20(1): 1–16.

BALCH, Robert W. (1980) 'Looking behind the scenes in a religious cult', *Sociological Analysis* 41(2): 137–43.

BALCH, Robert W. (1982) 'Bo and Peep: a case study of the origins of messianic leadership', in R. Wallis (ed.) (1982a), *Millennialism and Charisma*, pp. 13–22. Belfast: The Queen's University.

BALCH, Robert W. (1985a) 'What's wrong with the study of new religions and what we can do about it', in B. K. Kilbourne (ed.) (1985), pp. 24–39.

BALCH, Robert W. (1985b) ' "When the light goes out, darkness comes": a study of defection from a totalistic cult', in R. Stark (ed.) (1985a), pp. 11–64.

BALCH, Robert W. and David TAYLOR (1976) 'Salvation in a UFO', *Psychology Today* 10: 56–66, 106.

BALCH, Robert W. and David TAYLOR (1978) 'Seekers and saucers: the role of the cultic milieu in joining a UFO cult', in J. Richardson (ed.) (1978a), pp. 43–64.

BALCH, Robert W. and Joann COHIG (1985) 'The love family: disintegration of a utopia', presented to The Society for the Scientific Study of Religion, Savannah, October.

BALCH, Robert W., Gwenn FARNSWORTH and Sue WILKINS (1983) 'Reactions to disconfirmed prophecy in a millennial sect', *Sociological Perspectives* 26(2): 137–58.

BALSWICK, Jack D. (1974) 'The Jesus People movement: a generational interpretation', *Journal of Social Issues* 30(3): 23–42.

BANKSTON, W. B., C. J. FORSYTH and H. H. FLOYD (1981) 'Toward a general model of radical conversion', *Qualitative Sociology* 4: 279–97.

BARKER, Eileen (1979) 'Whose service is perfect freedom: the concept of spiritual well-being in relation to the Reverend Sun Myung Moon's Unification Church', in D. Moberg (ed.), *Spiritual Well-being*, pp. 153–71. Washington, DC: University Press of America.

BARKER, Eileen (1981) 'Who'd be a Moonie?', in B. Wilson (ed.) (1981), pp. 59–96.

BARKER, Eileen (ed.) (1982a) *New Religious Movements: A Perspective for Understanding Society*. New York: Edwin Mellen.

BARKER, Eileen (1982b) 'From sects to society: a methodological programme', in E. Barker (ed.) pp. 3–15.

BARKER, Eileen (ed.) (1983a) *Of Gods and Men: New Religious Movements in the West*. Macon, GA: Mercer University Press.

BARKER, Eileen (1983b) 'Supping with the Devil: how long a spoon?', *Sociological Analysis* 44(3): 197–205.

BARKER, Eileen (1983c) 'Doing love: tensions in the ideal family', in Gene James (ed.), pp. 35–52.

BARKER, Eileen (1983d) 'With enemies like that. . . : some functions of deprogramming as an aid to sectarian membership', in D. Bromley and J. Richardson (eds.), pp. 329–44.

BARKER, Eileen (1983e) 'New religious movements in Britain: the context and membership', *Social Compass* 30(1): 33–8.

BARKER, Eileen (1983f) 'The ones who got away: people who attend Unification Church workshops and do not become Moonies', in E. Barker (ed.), pp. 309–36.

BARKER, Eileen (1984) *The Making of a Moonie: Choice or Brainwashing?* Oxford: Blackwell.

BARKER, Eileen (1985) 'New religious movements: yet another Great Awakening?', in P. Hammond (ed.) *The Sacred in a Secular Age*, pp. 36–57. Berkeley: University of California.

BARKER, Eileen (1986) 'Religion movements: cult and anti-cult since Jonestown', *Annual Review of Sociology* 12: 329–46.

BARKER, Eileen (1987a) 'New religious movements and cults in Europe', in Mircea Eliade (ed.), *Encyclopedia of Religion*. New York: Macmillan.

BARKER, Eileen (1987b) 'Identity through gender in new religious movements', presented to the Society for the Scientific Study of Religion, Louisville, October.

BARKER, Eileen (1987c) 'The British right to discriminate', pp. 269–80 in T. Robbins and R. Robertson (eds).

BATIUK, Mary Ellen (1987) 'Sociologists and the new religious movements: science, politics and critique', presented to the Association for the Sociology of Religion, Chicago, August.

BECKER, Howard (1960) 'Notes on the concept of commitment', *American Journal of Sociology* 64: 32–40.

BECKFORD, James A. (1975a) *The Trumpet of Prophecy: A Sociological Study of Jehovah's Witnesses*. Oxford: Blackwell.

BECKFORD, James A. (1975b) 'Religious organizations: A trend report and bibliography', *Current Sociology* 21(2): 1–170.

BECKFORD, James A. (1977) 'Explaining religious movements', *International Social Science Journal* 29(2): 235–9.

BECKFORD, James A. (1978a) 'Accounting for conversion', *British Journal of Sociology* 29(2): 249–62.

BECKFORD, James A. (1978b) 'Through the looking-glass and out the other side: withdrawal from Reverend Moon's Unification Church', *Archives de Sciences Sociales des Religions* 45(1): 95–116.

BECKFORD, James A. (1978c) 'Cults and cures', *The Japanese Journal of Religious Studies* 5(4): 225–57.

BECKFORD, James A. (1979) 'Politics and the anti-cult movement', *Annual Review of the Social Sciencs of Religion* 3: 169–90.

BECKFORD, James A. (1981a) 'Functionalism and ethics in sociology', *Annual Review of the Social Sciences of Religion* 5: 106–135.

BECKFORD, James A. (1981b) 'Cults, controversy and control: a comparative analysis of the problems posed by new religious movements in the Federal Republic of Germany and France', *Sociological Analysis* 42(3): 249–64.

BECKFORD, James A. (1982a) 'A typology of family responses to a new religious movement', pp. 41–55 in F. Kaslow and M. Sussman (eds).

BECKFORD, James A. (1982b) 'Beyond the pale: cults, culture and conflict', pp. 284–301 in E. Barker (ed.).

BECKFORD, James A. (1983a) 'The restoration of "power" to the sociology of religion', *Sociological Analysis* 44(1): 11–32 [reprinted in T. Robbins and R. Robertson (eds) (1987), pp. 13–37].

BECKFORD, James A. (1983b) 'Some questions about the relationship between scholars and the new religious movements', *Sociological Analysis* 44(3): 184–95.

BECKFORD, James A. (1983c) 'The "cult problem" in five countries: the social construction of religious controversy', pp. 195–214 in E. Barker (ed.).

BECKFORD, James A. (1983d) '"Brainwashing" and "deprogramming" in Great Britain', pp. 122–38 in D. Bromley and J. Richardson (eds).

BECKFORD, James A. (1983e) 'The state and the control of new religious movements', pp. 115–30 in *Acts of the 17th International Conference of the Sociology of Religion*. Paris: Editions CISR.

BECKFORD, James A. (1984) 'Holistic imagery and ethics in new religious and healing movements', *Social Compass* 31(2–3): 259–72.

BECKFORD, James A. (1985a) *Cult Controversies: The Societal Response to the New Religious Movements*. London: Tavistock.

BECKFORD, James A. (1985b) 'The insulation and the isolation of the sociology of religion', *Sociological Analysis* 46(4): 357–64.

BECKFORD, James A. (1985c) 'Religious organization', pp. 125–38 in P. Hammond (ed.).

BECKFORD, James A. (1985d) 'New religious movements and healing: an overview', pp. 72–93 in R. K. Jones (ed.) *Sickness and Sectarianism*. Aldershot, UK: Gower Press.

BECKFORD, James A. (1986a) 'The role of state and government in the management of contemporary religious movements', presented to the Council on Religion and International Affairs, New York.

BECKFORD, James A. (ed.) (1986b) *New Religious Movements and Rapid Social Change*. London: Sage.

BECKFORD, James A. (1987) 'Cults and new religious movements: an overview', pp. 390–94, Vol. 19 in M. Eliade et al., *The Encyclopedia of Religion*. New York: Macmillan.

BECKFORD, James A. and James RICHARDSON (1983) 'A bibliography of social scientific studies of new religious movements in the U.S. and Europe', *Social Compass* 30(1): 111–35.

BECKFORD, James A. and Melanie COLE (1987) 'British and American responses to new religious movements', presented to the Association for the Sociology of Religion, Chicago, August.

BECKFORD, James A. and Martine LEVASSEUR (1986) 'New religious movements in Western Europe', pp. 29–54 in J. A. Beckford (ed.).

BEHAR, Richard (1986) 'The prophet and profits of Scientology', *Forbes* 138 (9): 314–22.

BELIL, J. M. (1984) 'The religious climate in Spain', *Update* 8(2): 59–61.

BELL, Daniel (1977) 'The return of the sacred?', *British Journal of Sociology* 28(4): 419–44.

BELLAH, Robert (1970) *Beyond Belief*. New York: Harper and Row.

BELLAH, Robert (1975) *The Broken Covenant*. New York: Seabury.

BELLAH, Robert (1976a) 'The new religious consciousness and the crisis of modernity', pp. 335–52 in C. Glock and R. Bellah (eds).

BELLAH, Robert (1976b) 'The new religious consciousness and the Berkeley New Left', pp. 77–92 in C. Glock and R. Bellah (eds).

BELLAH, Robert (1981) 'Religion and the legitimation of the American Republic', in T. Robbins and D. Anthony (eds) pp. 39–50.

BELLAH, Robert, Richard MASDEN, William M. SULLIVAN, Ann SWIDLER and Steven M. TIPTON (1985) *Habits of the Heart: Individualism and Commit-*

ment in American Life. Berkeley: University of California.

BEN-YEHUDA, Nachman (1985) *Deviance and Moral Boundaries: Witchcraft, the Occult, Science Fiction, Deviance Sciences and Scientists*. Chicago: University of Chicago.

BERGER, Bennet M. (1981) *The Survival of a Counterculture*. Los Angeles: University of California Press.

BERGER, Herbert and Peter Hexel (1981) 'Ursachen und Wirkungen gesellschaftlicher Verweigerung junger Menschen unter besonderer Berücksichtigung der "Jugendreligionen"'. Vienna: European Centre for Social Welfare Training and Research, Mimeo.

BERGER, Peter and Thomas LUCKMANN (1963) 'Sociology of religion and the sociology of knowledge', *Sociology and Social Research* 47: 417–27.

BIBBY, Reginald W. (1987) *Fragmented Gods: The Poverty and Potential of Religion in Canada*. Richmond Hill, Canada: Irwin.

BIBBY, Reginald W. and Harold R. WEAVER (1985) 'Cult consumption in Canada', *Sociological Analysis* 46(4): 445–60.

BIEZAIS, H. (ed.) (1975) *New Religions*, vol. VII. Åbo: Scripta Instituti Donneriani Aboensis.

BIRD, Frederick (1977) 'Rituals used by some contemporary movements', pp. 447–61 in P. Salter (ed.) *Religion and Culture in Canada*. Toronto: CCSR.

BIRD, Frederick (1978) 'Charisma and ritual in new religious movements', pp. 173–89 in J. Needleman and G. Baker (eds).

BIRD, Frederick (1979) 'The pursuit of innocence: new religious movements and moral accountability', *Sociological Analysis* 40(4): 335–46.

BIRD, Frederick and William REIMER (1976) 'A sociological analysis of new religious and para-religious movements', in *Canadian Religion*. Toronto: Macmillan.

BIRD, Frederick and William REIMER (1982) 'Participation rates in new religious movements and para-religous movements', *Journal for the Scientific Study of Religion* 21(1): 1–14 [Also (1983) pp. 215–38 in E. Barker (ed.)].

BIRD, Frederick and Francis WESTLEY (1985) 'The economic strategies of new religious movements', *Sociological Analysis* 46(2): 157–70.

BOURG, Carroll J. (1983) 'The politics of religious movements', pp. 45–64 in E. Barker (ed.).

BRADFIELD, Cecil D. (1976) 'Our kind of people: the consequences of Neo-Pentecostalism for social participation', presented to the Association for the Sociology of Religion.

BRECKWOLDT, R. (1973) 'The Hare Krishna movement in Australia', *Australian and New Zealand Journal of Sociology* 9(2): 70–2.

BRINKERHOFF, Merlin B. and Kenneth L. BURKE (1980) 'Disaffiliation: some notes on falling from the faith', *Sociological Analysis* 46(2): 41–5.

BROMLEY, David G. (1983) 'Conservatorships and deprogramming: legal and political prospects', pp. 267–93 in D. Bromley and J. Richardson (eds).

BROMLEY, David G. (1985) 'Financing the millennium: the economic structure of the Unificationist Movement', *Journal for the Scientific Study of Religion* 24(3): 253–75.

BROMLEY, David G. (1987) 'Subversion mythology and the construction of social problems', presented to the Society for the Scientific Study of Religion, October, Louisville.

BROMLEY, David G. (ed.) (1988a) *Falling from the Faith*. Newbury Park: Sage.

BROMLEY, David G. (1988b) 'Hare Krishna and the Anti-Cult movement', in D. Bromley and L. Shinn (eds).

BROMLEY, David G. and Phillip H. HAMMOND (eds) (1987) *The Future of New Religious Movements*. Macon, GA: Mercer University.

BROMLEY, David G. and Katherine PERRY (1987) 'Coercive deprogrammings from the Unification Church: 1972–1986', presented to the Association for the Sociology of Religion, Chicago, August.

BROMLEY, David G. and James T. RICHARDSON (eds) (1983) *The Brainwashing-Deprogramming Controversy: Sociological, Psychological, Legal and Historical Perspectives*. New York: Edwin Mellen.

BROMLEY, David G. and Larry SHINN (eds) (1988) *Krishna Consciousness in the West*. Lewisburg, PA: Bucknell University Press.

BROMLEY, David G. and Anson D. SHUPE (1979a) *The Moonies in America*. Beverly Hills: Sage.

BROMLEY, David G. and Anson D. SHUPE (1979b) 'Just a few years seem like a lifetime: a role theory approach to participation in religious movements', pp. 159–85 in L. Kriesberg (ed.) *Research in Social Movements, Conflicts and Change* 2. Greenwich, CT: JAI Press.

BROMLEY, David G. and Anson D. SHUPE (1979c) 'The TNEVNOC cult', *Sociological Analysis* 40(4): 361–66.

BROMLEY, David G. and Anson D. SHUPE (1980) 'Financing the new religions: a resource mobilization approach', *Journal for the Scientific Study of Religion* 19(3): 227–39.

BROMLEY, David G. and Anson D. SHUPE (1981) *Strange Gods: The Great American Cult Hoax*. Boston: Beacon.

BROMLEY, David G. and Anson D. SHUPE (1986) 'Affiliation and disaffiliation: a role-theory interpretation of joining and leaving new religious movements', *Thought* 61: 192–211.

BROMLEY, David G. and Anson D. SHUPE (1987) 'The future of the Anticult Movement', pp. 221–34 in D. Bromley and P. Hammond (eds).

BROMLEY, David G., Anson D. SHUPE and Joseph C. VENTIMIGLIA (1979) 'Atrocity tales, the Unification Church and the social construction of evil', *Journal of Communication* 29(3): 42–53.

BROMLEY, David G., Anson D. SHUPE and Joseph C. VENTIMIGLIA (1983) 'The role of anecdotal atrocities in the social construction of evil', pp. 139–62 in D. Bromley and J. Richardson (eds).

BROMLEY, David G. Anson D. SHUPE and Donna L. OLIVER (1982) 'Perfect families: visions of the future in a new religious movement', pp. 119–30 in F. Kaslow and M. Sussman (eds).

BROMLEY, David G., Bruce C. BUSCHING and Anson D. SHUPE (1982) 'The Unification Church and the American family: strain, conflict and control', in E. Barker (ed.).

BROMLEY, David G., Jeffrey K. HADDEN and Phillip E. HAMMOND (1987) 'Reflections on the scholarly study of new religious movements', pp. 210–17 in D. Bromley and P. Hammon (eds).

BROOKS, Andre (1986) '"Cults" and the aged: a new family issue', *New York Times* (April 26): 52.

BRUCE, Steve S. (1982) 'Born again: conversion, crusades and brainwashing', *Scottish Journal of Religious Studies* 3: 107–23.

BUNDESMINISTERIUM FÜR JUGEND, FAMILIE UND GESUNDHEIT (1980) *Die Jugendreligionen in der Bundesrepublik Deutschland*. Bonn.

BUSCHING, Bruce and David G. BROMLEY (in press) 'Understanding the structure of covenants: toward a non-heretical sociology of religion', *Sociological Analysis*.

CAMPBELL, Colin (1972) 'The cult, the cultic milieu and secularization', *A Sociological Yearbook of Religion in Britain* 5: 119–36.

CAMPBELL, Colin (1977) 'Clarifying the cult', *British Journal of Sociology* 28(3): 375–88.

CAMPBELL, Colin (1978) 'The secret religion of the educated classes', *Sociological Analysis* 39(2): 146–56.

CAMPBELL, Colin (1982) 'The new religious movements, the new spirituality and post-industrial society', pp. 232–42 in E. Barker (ed.).

CAMPBELL, Colin and Shirley McIVER (1987) 'Cultural sources of support for contemporary occultism', *Social Compass* 34(1): 41–60.

CAMPICHE, Roland J. (1987) 'Sectes et nouveaux mouvements religieux: divergences et convergences', unpublished paper presented to the first Latin American conference on Popular Religion, Identity and Ethnology, Mexico City, 1987.

CARMICHAEL, Carl W., Flo CONWAY, James SIEGELMAN and John COGGINS (1986) 'Information disease: effects of covert induction and deprogramming', *Update* 10(2): 45–57.

CARTER, Lewis F. (1987) 'The "new renunciates" of the Bhagwan Shree Rajneesh: observations and identification of problems of interpreting new religious movements', *Journal for the Scientific Study of Religion* 26(2): 148–72.

CAVANAUGH, Michael (1982) 'Pagan and Christian: sociological euhemerism versus American sociology of religion', *Sociological Analysis* 43(2): 109–30.

CAWLEY, Patrick (1979) 'God's little acres', *Connecticut Magazine* (August).

CHAGNON, Roland (1985) *Trois nouvelles Religions de la Lumière et du Son: la Science de la Spiritualité, Eckankar, La Mission de la Lumière Divine*. Montréal: Les Editions Paulines.

CHIDESTER, David (1983) 'Religious suicide: death and classification at Jonestown', unpublished paper presented to American Academy of Religion, Dallas.

CHIDESTER, David (1988) *Salvation and Suicide: A Religio-Historical Interpretation of The People's Temple*. Bloomington: University of Indiana.

CHOQUETTE, Diane (1985) *New Religious Movements in America: An Annotated Bibliography*. Westport, CT: Greenwood.

CLARK, John G. (1979) 'Cults', *Journal of the American Medical Association* 242: 279–81.

CLARK, John G., Michael D. LANGONE, Robert E. SCHECTER and R. DAILY (1981) *Destructive Cult Conversion: Theory, Research and Treatment*. Weston, MA: American Family Foundation.

COHEN, Albert K. (1955) *Delinquent Boys*. New York: M. Evans.

COLEMAN, James (1970) 'Social inventions', *Social Forces* 49: 163–73.

COLEMAN, John and Gregory BAUM (eds) (1983) *New Religious Movements* (originally *Concilium* 161). New York: Seabury.

COLEMAN, Lee (1985a) 'New religions and "deprogramming": who's brainwashing whom?' pp. 71–80 in T. Robbins, W. Shepherd and J. McBridge (eds).

COLEMAN, Lee (1985b) 'Using psychiatry to fight "cults": three case histories', pp. 40–56 in B. Kilbourne (ed.).

CONWAY, Flo and Jim SIEGELMAN (1978) *Snapping: America's Epidemic of Sudden Personality Change*. Philadelphia: Lippincott.

CONWAY, Flo and Jim SIEGELMAN (1982) 'Information disease: have cults created a new mental illness?' *Science Digest* 90: 88–92.

COOPER, Paulette (1971) *The Scandal of Scientology*. New York: Tower.

COSER, Rose L. and Louis COSER (1979) 'Jonestown as a perverse utopia', *Dissent* 26(2): 158–62.

COX, Harvey (1977) *Turning East*. New York: Simon and Schuster.

COX, Harvey (1978) 'Deep structures in the study of religions', pp. 113–21 in J. Needleman and G. Baker (eds).

CUDDIHY, John (1978) *No Offense: Civil Religion and Protestant Taste*. New York: Seabury.

DAMRELL, Joseph (1978) *Seeking Spiritual Meaning*. Beverly Hills: Sage.

DANER, Francine J. (1976) *The American Children of Krsna*. New York: Holt, Rinehart and Winston.

DAVIDMAN, Lyn (1988) 'Women's search for family, community and roots: a traditional religious solution to a contemporary dilemma', *Jewish Studies* in press.

DAVIS, Rex and James T. RICHARDSON (1975) 'The organization and functioning of the Children of God', *Sociological Analysis* 37(4): 321–40.

D'EAUBONNE, F. (1982) *Dossier S . . . Comme Sectes*. Paris: Alain Moreau.

DELGADO, Richard (1977) 'Religious totalism: gentle and ungentle persuasion under the First Amendment', *Southern California Law Review* 51: 1–99.

DELGADO, Richard (1979–80) 'Religious totalism as slavery', *New York Review of Law and Social Change* 4(1): 51–68.

DELGADO, Richard (1982) 'Cults and conversion: the case for informed consent', *Georgia Law Review* 16(3): 533–74.

DELGADO, Richard (1984) 'When religious exercise is not free', *Vanderbilt Law Review* 37(5).

DERKS, Frans (1983) 'Defections from new religious movements', final unpublished report (summary) of the research project on identity-diffusion in ex-cult members. Nijmegen: Psychologisch Laboratorium.

DOBBELAERE, Karel (1981) 'Secularization: a multi-dimensional concept', *Current Sociology* 29(2): 1–216.

DOBBELAERE, Karel, G. VOET and H. VERBEKE (1987) 'Neue religiöse Bewegungen im Spiegel der belgischen Presse', pp. 230–44 in J. Neumann and M. Fischer (eds).

DOHRMAN, H. T. (1958) *California Cult*. Boston: Beacon.

DORESS, Irving and Jack N. PORTER (1981) 'Kids in cults', pp. 297–302 in T. Robbins and D. Anthony (eds).

DOUGLAS, Mary and Steven TIPTON (eds) (1982) *Religion and America: Spirituality in a Secular Age*, [originally *Daedalus* 111(1)]. Boston: Beacon.

DOWNTON, James V. (1979) *Sacred Journeys: The Conversion of Young Americans to Divine Light Mission*. New York: Columbia University Press.

DOWNTON, James V. (1980) 'An evolutionary theory of spiritual conversion and commitment: the case of the Divine Light Mission', *Journal for the Scientific Study of Religion* 19: 381–96.

DUDDY, Neil T. (1984) 'Editorial', *Update* 8(2): 4–14.

DUPERTIUS, Lucy (1986) 'How people recognize charisma: the case of *Darshan* in Radhasoami and Divine Light Mission', *Sociological Analysis* 47(2): 111–25.

EBAUGH, Helen R. and Sharron Lee VAUGHN (1984) 'Ideology and recruitment in religious groups', *Review of Religious Research* 26(2): 119–30.

EDWARDS, Chris (1979) *Crazy for God: The Nightmare of Cult Life*. Englewood Cliffs, NJ: Prentice-Hall.

EDWARDS, Chris (1982) 'The dynamics of mass conversion', pp. 31–40 in F. Kaslow and M. Sussman (eds).

EICHEL, Steve K., Linda D. EICHEL and Roberta EISENBERG (1984) 'Mental health interventions in cult-related cases: preliminary investigation of outcomes', *Cultic Studies Journal* 1(2): 156–66.

EISTER, Allan W. (1972) 'An outline of a structural theory of cults', *Journal for the Scientific Study of Religion* 11: 319–34.

EISTER, Allan W. (1974) 'Culture crises and new religious movements', pp. 612–27 in I. Zaretsky and M. Leone (eds).

ELLWOOD, Robert S. (1973) *One Way: The Jesus Movement and Its Meaning*. Englewood Cliffs, NJ: Prentice-Hall.

EMORY, Mead and Lawrence ZELENAK (1985) 'The tax exempt status of communitarian religious organizations', pp. 177–205 in T. Robbins, W. Shepherd and J. McBride (eds).

ENROTH, Ronald S. (1977) *Youth, Brainwashing and the Extremist Cults*. Grand Rapids, MI: Zondervan.

ENROTH, Ronald S., Edward ERICSON and C. B. PETERS (1972) *The Jesus People*. Grand Rapids, MI: Erdmans.

ERASMUS, Charles (1977) *In Search of the Common Good: Utopian Experiments Past and Future*. New York: Free Press.

FENN, Richard (1978) *A Theory of Secularization*. Ellington, CT: Society for the Scientific Study of Religion Monograph Series.

FESTINGER, L., H. W. RIECKEN and S. SCHACTER (1956) *When Prophecy Fails*. New York: Harper and Row.

FICHTER, Joseph H. (1979) 'Marriage, family and Sun Myung Moon', *America* (27 October): 226–8.

FICHTER, Joseph H. (1981) 'Youth in the search of the sacred', pp. 21–42 in B. Wilson (ed.).

FICHTER, Joseph H. (ed.) (1983) *Alternatives to American Mainline Churches*. Barrytown, NY: Unification Theological Seminary.

FICHTER, Joseph H. (1985) *The Holy Family of Father Moon*. Kansas City, MO: Leaven.

FILORAMO, G. (1979) 'Nuove religioni: Problemi e prospettive', *Rivista di Storia e Letteratura Religiosa* 15(3): 445–72.

FILORAMO, G. (1986) *I Nuovi Movimenti Religiosi*. Roma: Laterza.

FITZGERALD, Francine (1986) 'Rajneeshpuram', *New Yorker* Part I (11 Sept.): 46–96; Part II (29 Sept.): 83–125.

FLINN, Frank (1983) 'Scientology as technological Buddhism', pp. 89–112 in J. Fichter (ed.).

FOLTZ, Tanice G. (1987) 'The social construction of identity in an alternative healing group', presented to the Society for the Scientific Study of Religion, Louisville, October.

FOSS, Daniel and Ralph W. LARKIN (1976) 'Roar of the lemming: Youth, post-movement groups and the life construction crisis', in H. Johnson (ed.) *Religious Change and Continuity*, pp. 264–85. San Francisco: Jossey-Bass.

FOSS, Daniel and Ralph LARKIN (1978) 'Worshipping the absurd: the negation of social causality among the followers of the Guru Maharaji', *Sociological Analysis* 39(2): 157–64.

FOSS, Daniel and Ralph LARKIN (1986) *Beyond Revolution: A Theory of Social Movements*. Massachusetts: Bergin and Garvey.

FOUCART, Eric (1982) 'Répertoire bibliographique: sectes et mouvements religieux marginaux de l'Occident contemporain', *Etudes et Documents en Sciences de la Religion*. Québec.

FRIEDRICHS, Robert W. (1974) 'Social research and theology: the end of detente?' *Review of Religious Research* 15: 113–27.

GALANTER, Marc (1978) 'The "relief effect": a sociobiological model for neurotic distress and large-group therapy', *American Journal of Psychiatry* 135: 588–91.

GALANTER, Marc (1980) 'Psychological induction into the large group: findings from a modern religious sect', *American Journal of Psychiatry* 137: 1574–9.

GALANTER, Marc (1982) 'Charismatic religious sects and psychiatry: an overview', *American Journal of Psychiatry* 139: 1539–98.

GALANTER, Marc (1983a) 'Engaged "Moonies": the impact of a charismatic group on adaptation and behavior', *Archives of General Psychiatry* 40: 1197–201.

GALANTER, Marc (1983b) 'Unification ("Moonie") Church drop-outs: psychological readjustment after membership in a charismatic sect', *American Journal of Psychiatry* 140: 994–9.

GALANTER, Marc (1985) 'New religious groups and large-group psychology', pp. 64–80 in B. Kilbourne (ed.).

GALANTER, Marc (1986) ' "Moonies" get married: a psychiatric follow-up study of a charismatic religious sect', *American Journal of Psychiatry* 143: 1245–9.

GALANTER, Marc and P. BUCKLEY (1978) 'Evangelical religion and meditation: psychological effects', *Journal of Nervous and Mental Disease* 166: 685–91.

GALANTER, Marc and C. DIAMOND (1981) ' "Relief" of psychiatric symptoms in evangelical religious sects', *British Journal of Hospital Medicine* 26(5): 495–8.

GALANTER, Marc, Richard RABKIN, I. RABKIN and A. DEUTSCH (1979) 'The "Moonies": a psychological study of conversion and membership in a contemporary religious sect', *American Journal of Psychiatry* 136: 165–70.

GALANTI, Geri-Ann (1984) 'Brainwashing and the Moonies', *Cultic Studies Journal* 1(1): 27–36.

GALPER, Marvin (1982) 'The cult phenomenon: behavioral science perspectives applied to therapy', pp. 141–50 in F. Kaslow and M. Sussman (eds).

GARCÍA, A. (1986) *Guia del Orientalismo en España*. Barcelona: Martinez Roca.

GARTRELL, C. David and Zane K. SHANNON (1985) 'Contacts, cognitions and conversion: a rational choice approach', *Review of Religious Research* 27(1): 32–48.

GARVEY, Kevin (1985) 'Warlocks among the warriors: Delta Force and the myth of Superman', presented to the conference on 'Other Realities, New Religions and Revitalization Movements', Omaha, April.

GERLACH, Luther and Virginia HINE (1970) *People, Power and Change*. Indianapolis: Bobbs-Merrill.

GELDBACH, E. (1987) 'Religiöse Polemik gegen "neue Religionen" im Deutschland des 19 Jahrhunderts', pp. 170–97 in J. Neumann and M. Fischer (eds).

GIBBON, Edward (1932) *Decline and Fall of the Roman Empire*, Vol. II. New York: Modern Library.

GLOCK, Charles (1976) 'Consciousness among contemporary youth: an interpretation', pp. 353–66 in C. Glock and R. Bellah (eds.).

GLOCK, Charles and Robert BELLAH (eds) (1976) *The New Religious Consciousness*. Berkeley: University of California.

GLOCK, Charles and Thomas PIAZZA (1981) 'Exploring reality structures', pp. 67–83 in T. Robbins and D. Anthony (eds).

GLOCK, Charles and Rodney STARK (1965) 'On the origin and evolution of religious groups', in C. Glock and R. Stark (eds) *Religion and Society in Tension*, p. 245. New York: Rand McNally.

GORDON, David F. (1974) 'The Jesus People: an identity synthesis interpretation', *Urban Life and Culture* 3(2): 159–79.

GORDON, David F. (1984a) 'The role of the local social context in social movements: a case study of two Jesus People groups', *Journal for the Scientific Study of Religion* 23(4): 381–95.

GORDON, David F. (1984b) 'Dying to self: self-control through self-abandonment', *Sociological Analysis* 45(1): 41–55.

GORDON, David F. (1987) 'Getting close by staying distant: field work with proselytizing groups', *Qualitative Sociology* 10(3): Fall.

GORDON, David F. (1988) 'Psychiatry and Krishna consciousness', in D. Bromley and L. Shinn (eds).

GORDON, Suzanne (1980) 'You can't go home again', *Working Papers for a New Society* 7(4): 10–12.

GORDON-McCUTCHAN, Robert (1977) 'The social and the celestial: Mary Douglas and Transcendental Meditation', *Princeton Journal of the Arts and Sciences* 1(2): 130–63.

GRACE, James H. (1985) *Sex and Marriage in the Unification Movement*. New York: Edwin Mellen.

GRAFSTEIN, Laurence (1984) 'Messianic capitalism', *New Republic* 190(7): 14–16.

GREELEY, Andrew M. (1972) *Unsecular Man*. New York: Schocken.

GREELEY, Andrew M. (1973) 'Implications for the sociology of religion of occult behavior in the youth culture', pp. 295–302 in E. Tiryakian (ed.) *On the Margin of the Visible*. New York: Wiley.

GREELEY, Andrew M. (1975) *Sociology of the Paranormal: A Reconnaissance*. Beverly Hills: Sage.

GREELEY, Andrew M. (1979) 'Superstition, ecstasy, and tribal consciousness', *Social Research* 37: 202–11.

GREGG, Roy G. (1973) 'Getting it on with Jesus: a study of adult socialization', PhD dissertation, University of Southern California.

GREIL, Arthur L. (1977) 'Previous dispositions and conversion to perspectives of social and religious movements', *Sociological Analysis* 38(3): 115–25.

GREIL, Arthur L. and David R. RUDY (1984a) 'What have we learned from process models of conversion? An examination of ten studies', *Sociological Focus* 17(4): 306–23.

GREIL, Arthur L. and David R. RUDY (1984b) 'Social cocoons: encapsulation and identity transformation organizations', *Sociological Inquiry* 54(3): 260–78.

GROVES, Mary Ann (1986) 'Marginal religious movements as precursors of a sociocultural revolution', *Thought* 61: 267–76.

GUIZZARDI, Gustavo (1974) 'New religious phenomena in Italy: towards a post-Catholic era', presented to the Eighth World Congress of Sociology, Toronto.

HACKETT, David G. (1981) *The New Religions: An Annotated Introductory Bibliography*. Berkeley, CA: Center for the Study of New Religions.

HADDEN, Jeffrey K. (1980) 'Religion and the construction of social problems', *Sociological Analysis* 41(2): 99–108.

HADDEN, Jeffrey K. (1987a) 'Toward desacralizing secularization theory', *Social Froces* 65(3): 587–611.

HADDEN, Jeffrey K. (1987b) 'Religious broadcasting and the New Christian Right', *Journal for the Scientific Study of Religion* 26(1): 1–24.

HADDEN, Jeffrey K. and Theodore LONG (eds) (1983) *Religion and Religiosity in America*. New York: Crossroads.

HADDEN, Jeffrey K. and Anson D. SHUPE (1987) Televangelism in America', *Social Compass* 34(1): 61–70.

HALL, John H. (1981) 'The apocalypse at Jonestown', pp. 171–90 in T. Robbins and D. Anthony (eds). [See also Levi (ed.) (1982).]

HALL, John H. (1987) *Gone from the Promised Land: Jonestown in American Cultural History*. New Brunswick, NJ: Transaction.

HALLOMAN, Regina E. (1974) 'Ritual opening and individual transformation', *American Anthropologist* 76: 265–80.

HALPERIN, John (ed.) (1983) *Psychodynamic Perspectives on Religion, Sect and Cult*. Boston: PSG.

HAMMOND, Phillip E. (1987) 'Cultural consequence of cults', pp. 261–73 in D. Bromley and P. Hammond (eds).

HAMMOND, Phillip and Robert GORDON-McCUTCHAN (1981) 'Cults and civil religion', *Revue française d'études américaines* 12: 173–83.

HAMPSHIRE, Annette P. and James A. BECKFORD (1983) 'Religious sects and the concept of deviance: the Moonies and the Mormons', *British Journal of Sociology* 34(2): 208–29.

HANNIGAN, John A. (1987) 'Apples and oranges: new religious movements and the new social movements compared', presented to the Association for the Sociology of Religion, Chicago.

HARDER, Mary W. (1974) 'Sex roles in the Jesus Movement', *Social Compass* 21: 345–53.

HARDER, Mary W., J. T. RICHARDSON and R. B. SIMMONDS (1976) 'Lifestyle, marriage and the family in a Jesus Movement communal organization', *International Review of Modern Sociology* 6(1): 155–72.

HARDIN, Berg (1983) 'Quelques aspects du phénomène des nouveaux mouvements religieux en République Fédérale de l'Allemagne', *Social Compass* 30(1): 13–32.

HARDIN, Bert and Günter KEHRER (1982) 'Some social factors affecting the rejection of new belief systems', pp. 267–83 in E. V. Barker (ed.).

HARGROVE, Barbara (1982) 'On studying the "Moonies" as a political act', *Religious Studies Review* 8(3): 1–4.

HARGROVE, Barbara (1983) 'Social sources and consequences of the brain-washing controversy', pp. 299–308 in D. Bromley and J. Richardson (eds).

HARPER, Charles L. (1982) 'Cults and communities: the community interfaces of three marginal religious communities', *Journal for the Scientific Study of Religion* 21(1): 26–36.

HARPER, Charles L. (1986) 'The social construction of malevolence: rethinking theories of the new religions', presented to the Midwest Sociological Society, Chicago.

HARRIS, Marvin (1981) *America Now: The Anthropology of a Changing Culture.* New York: Simon and Schuster.

HARRISON, Michael I. (1974) 'Sources of recruitment to Catholic Pente-costalism', *Journal for the Scientific Study of Religion* 13:19–64.

HARRISON, Michael I. (1975) 'The maintenance of enthusiasm in a new religious movement', *Sociological Analysis* 36(2): 150–60.

HARRINGTON, Michael (1983) *The Politics at God's Funeral.* New York: Penguin.

HASHIMOTO, Hideo and William McPHERSON (1976) 'Rise and decline of Sokagakkai in Japan and the United States', *Review of Religious Research* 17(2): 83–92.

HAYWOOD, Carol L. (1983) 'The authority and empowerment of women among spiritualist groups', *Journal for the Scientific Study of Religion* 22(2): 156–66.

HEENAN, Edward F. (1973) *Mystery, Magic and Miracle.* Englewood Cliffs, NJ: Prentice-Hall.

HEINO, Harri (1984) 'New religious communities in Finland', *Update* 8(2): 27–31.

HEINS, Marjorie (1981) 'Other peoples' faiths: the Scientology litigation and the justiciability of religious fraud', *Hastings Constitutional Law Quarterly* 9: 153–97.

HEINZ, Donald (1976) 'The Christian World Liberation Front', pp. 143–61 in C. Glock and R. Bellah (eds).

HEIRICH, Max (1977) 'Change of heart: a test of some widely held theories about religious conversion', *American Journal of Sociology* 85(3): 653–80.

HERBERG, Will (1960) *Protestant, Catholic, Jew.* Garden City, NJ: Doubleday.

HERSHELL, Marie and Ben HERSHELL (1982) 'Our involvement with a cult', pp. 131–40 in F. Kaslow and M. Sussman (eds).

HERVIEU-LÉGER, Danièle (1986) *Vers un nouveau Christianisme?* Paris: Cerf.

HERVIEU-LÉGER, Danièle (1987) 'Le travail de la religion dans les mouvements sociaux: un problème de production de significations collectives', pp. 117–26 in *Acts of the 19th International Conference for the Sociology of Religion.* Lausanne: CISR.

HEXHAM, Irving and Karla POEWE (1986) *Understanding Cults and New Religions.* Grand Rapids: Erdmans.

HILLER, Harry (1975) 'A reconceptualization of the dynamics of social move-ment development', *Pacific Sociological Review* 17(3): 342–59.

HOFFMAN, Eva (1977) 'Est: the magic of brutality', *Dissent* 24(2): 209–12.

HOLM, Nils G. (ed.) (1981) *Aktuella religösa rörelser i Finland: ajankohtaisin uskonnollisin liikketä Suomessa*. (summaries in English). Åbo.

HOROWITZ, Irving (ed.) (1978) *Science, Sin and Scholarship: The Politics of Reverend Moon and the Unification Church*. Cambridge, MA: MIT Press.

HOROWITZ, Irving (1981) 'The politics of new cults', pp. 161–70 in T. Robbins and D. Anthony (eds).

HOROWITZ, Irving (1983a) 'Universal standards, not uniform beliefs: further reflections on scientific method and religious sponsors', *Sociological Analysis* 44(3): 179–82.

HOROWITZ, Irving (1983b) 'A reply to critics and crusaders', *Sociological Analysis* 44(3): 221–6.

HUBER, John and Lindsay GRUSON (1987) 'Dial OM for murder, *Rolling Stone* 497: 53–9.

HUMMEL, Robert and Bert HARDIN (1983) 'Asiatic religions in Europe', *Concilium* 161: 23–8 [see also J. Coleman and G. Baum (eds)].

HUNTER, James (1981) 'The new religions: demodernization and the protest against modernity', pp. 1–20 in B. Wilson (ed.).

HUNTER, James (1983) *American Evangelicalism*. New Brunswick, NJ: Rutgers.

HUNTER, James (1987) *Evangelicalism: The Coming Generation*. Chicago: University of Chicago.

JACKSON, John and Ray JOBLING (1968) 'Towards an analysis of contemporary cults', pp. 94–105 in D. Martin (ed.) *Yearbook of Religion in Britain*, 1. London: SCM Press.

JACOBS, Janet L. (1984) 'The economy of love in religious commitment: the deconversion of women from non-traditional religious movements', *Journal for the Scientific Study of Religion* 23(2): 155–71.

JACOBS, Janet L. (1986) 'The effects of ritual healing on female victims of abuse: a study of empowerment and transformation', paper presented to the Society for the Scientific Study of Religion, Washington. [Submitted for publication.]

JACOBS, Janet L. (1987) 'Deconversion from religious movements: an analysis of charismatic bonding and spiritual commitment', *Journal for the Scientific Study of Religion* 26(3): 294–308.

JACOBSEN, Cardell K. and Thomas PILARZYCK (1974) 'Croissance, développement et fin d'une secte conversionniste: les Jesus People de Milwaukee', *Social Compass* 21(3): 255–68.

JAMES, Gene G. (ed.) (1983) *The Family and the Unification Church*. Barrytown, NY: Unification Seminary.

JAMES, Gene G. (1986) 'Brainwashing: the myth and the actuality', *Thought* 61: 241–58.

JOHNSON, Benton (1961) 'Do Holiness sects socialize in dominant values?' *Social Forces* 39: 309–16.

JOHNSON, Benton (1963) 'On church and sect', *American Sociological Review* 28: 589–99.

JOHNSON, Benton (1971) 'Church and sect revisited', *Journal for the Scientific Study of Religion* 10: 124–37.

JOHNSON, Benton (1977) 'Sociological theory and religious truth', *Sociological Analysis* 38: 368–88.

JOHNSON, Benton (1981) 'A sociological perspective on new religions', pp. 51–66 in T. Robbins and D. Anthony (eds).

JOHNSON, Benton (1987a) 'A sociologist of religion looks at the future of new religious movements', pp. 251–64 in D. Bromley and P. Hammond (eds).

JOHNSON, Benton (1987b) 'On founders and followers: some obstacles to the stabilization of charismatic movements', presidential address [forthcoming, *Sociological Analysis*] to the Association for the Sociology of Religion, Chicago.

JOHNSON, Doyle P. (1980) 'Dilemmas of charismatic leadership: the case of the People's Temple', *Sociological Analysis* 40(4): 315–23.

JOHNSON, Gregory (1976) 'The Hare Krishna in San Francisco', pp. 31–51 in C. Glock and R. Bellah (eds).

JOHNSTON, H. (1980) 'The marketed social movement: a case study of the rapid growth of TM', *Pacific Sociological Review* 23: 333–54.

JORGENSEN, Danny L. (1980) 'The social construction and interpretation of deviance — Jonestown and the mass media', *Deviant Behavior* 1(3–4): 309–32.

JORGENSEN, Danny L. (1982) 'The esoteric community: an ethnographic investigation of the cultic milieu', *Urban Life* 10(4): 383–408.

JUDAH, J. Stillson (1974) *Hare Krishna and the Counterculture*. New York: Wiley.

JULES-ROSETTE, Bennetta (1981) 'Disavowal and disengagement: a new look at the conversion process in religious sects', paper presented to the Conference on Conversion, Coercion and Commitment in New Religious Movements, Berkeley, CA.

KANTER, Rosabeth M. (1972) *Commitment and Community: Communes and Utopias in Sociological Perspective*. Cambridge, MA; Harvard University Press.

KASLOW, Florence W. and Marvin K. SUSSMAN (eds) (1982) *Cults and the Family* [originally in *Marriage and Family Review* 4((3–4)]. New York: Haworth.

KEISER, Thomas W. and Jacqueline L. KEISER (1987) *The Anatomy of an Illusion: Religious Cults and Destruction Persuasion*. Springfield: Charles Thomas.

KELLEY, Dean (1972) *Why the Conservative Churches are Growing*. New York: Harper and Row.

KENISTON, Kenneth (1977) *All Our Children: The American Family Under Siege*. New York: Norton.

KENT, Stephen (1987) 'Puritan radicalism and the "new" religious organizations', *Comparative Social Research* 10.

KENT, Stephen (1988) 'Slogan chanters to mantra chanters: a Mertonian deviance analysis of conversion to the new religious movements', *Sociological Analysis* 49(2), in press.

KHALSA, Kirpal S. (1986) 'New religious movements turn to worldly success', *Journal for the Scientific Study of Religion* 25(2): 233–47.

KHERRINE, Theodore and Richard NEUHAUS (1979) 'Mediating structures: a paradigm for democratic pluralism', *Annals of the American Association for Political and Social Science* 446: 10–18.

KILBOURNE, Brock K. (1983) 'The Conway and Siegelman claims against religious cults: an assessment of their data', *Journal for the Scientific Study of Religion* 22(4): 380–5.

KILBOURNE, Brock K. (ed.) (1985) *Scientific Research of New Religions: Divergent Perspectives*. Proceedings of the annual meeting of the Pacific Division of the American Association for the Advancement of Science, and the 59th Meeting of the Rocky Mountain Division. San Francisco: AAAS.

KILBOURNE, Brock K. (1986a) 'A reply to Maher and Langone's statistical critique of Kilbourne', *Journal for the Scientific Study of Religion* 25(1): 110–23.

KILBOURNE, Brock K. (1986b) 'Equity or exploitation: the case of the Unification Church', *Review of Religious Research* 28(2): 145–50.

KILBOURNE, Brock K. and James T. RICHARDSON (1982) 'Cults vs. families: a case of a misattribution of cause', pp. 81–100 in F. Kaslow and M. Sussman (eds).

KILBOURNE, Brock K. and James T. RICHARDSON (1984a) 'Psychotherapy and new religions in a pluralistic society', *American Psychologist* 39(3): 237–51.

KILBOURNE, Brock K. and James T. RICHARDSON (1984b) 'The DSM-III and new religions: a critique', paper presented to the Society for the Scientific Study of Religion, Chicago.

KILBOURNE, Brock K. and James T. RICHARDSON (1986) 'Cultphobia', *Thought* 61: 258–61.

KILBOURNE, Brock K. and James T. RICHARDSON (1988) 'A social psychological analysis of healing', *Journal of Integrative and Eclective Psychotherapy*, forthcoming.

KIM, Byong-Suh (1979) 'Religious deprogramming and subjective reality', *Sociological Analysis* 40(3): 197–207.

KÖLLEN, K. (1980) *Jeugdsekten en Nederland*. Amsterdam: Allert de Lange.

KRAMER, Fred (1983) 'Cult members as victims and victimizers', *Annual Review of Studies of Deviance* 7: 163–82.

KUNER, Wolfgang (1983) 'New religious movements and mental health', pp. 255–64 in E. Barker (ed.).

LANGONE, Michael (1984) 'Deprogramming: an analysis of parental question- naires', *Cultic Studies Journal* 1(1): 63–78.

LANGONE, Michael (1985) 'Cults, evangelicals and the ethics of social influence persuasion', *Cultic Studies Journal* (2): 371–88.

LANGONE, Michael and John G. CLARK (1985) 'New religions and public policy', pp. 90–113 in B. Kilbourne (ed.).

LASCH, Christopher (1979) *The Culture of Narcissism*. New York: Warner.
LATKIN, Richard Hagan, Richard LITTMAN and Norman D. SUNDBERG (1987) 'Who lives in Utopia? A brief report on the Rajneeshpuram research project', *Sociological Analysis* 48(1): 73–81.
LECERF, Yves (ed.) (1975) *Les Marchands de Dieu: Analyses socio-politiques de l'Affaire Melchior*. Bruxelles: Complexe.
LECHNER, Frank (1985) 'Fundamentalism and sociocultural revitalization in America', *Sociological Analysis* 46(3): 243–60.
LEVI, Kenneth (ed.) (1982) *Violence and Religious Commitment: Implications of Jim Jones' People's Temple Movement*. University Park, PA: Penn State.
LEVIN, Jack and James ALAN (1984) 'Cults: a response to alienation', *USA Today* (May 16): 8A.
LEVINE, Edwin M. (1980a) 'Deprogramming without tears', *Society* 17(3): 34–8.
LEVINE, Edwin M. (1980b) 'Rural communes and religious cults: refuges for middle-class youth', *Adolescent Psychiatry* 8: 138–53.
LEVINE, Edwin M. (1985) 'Religious cults: a social-psychiatric analysis', pp. 114–23 in B. Kilbourne (ed.).
LEVINE, Edwin M. and Charles SHAIOVA (1987) 'Religious cult leaders as authoritarian personalities', *Areopagus* 11(1–2): 19–28.
LEVINE, Saul V. (1978) 'Youth and religious cults: a societal and clinical dilemma', *Adolescent Psychiatry* 8: 138–53.
LEVINE, Saul V. (1984) 'Radical departures', *Psychology Today* 18(8): 20–9.
LEWIS, James (1987) 'The sociology of cults and the cult of sociology', *Dharma* 12(2): 96–107.
LEWIS, James (1986) 'Reconstructing the "cult" experience', *Sociological Analysis* 47(2): 151–9.
LEWIS, James (1987) 'Religious insanity past and present', paper presented to the Association for the Sociology of Religion.
LEWIS, James and David G. BROMLEY (1988) 'Cult "information disease": a misattribution of cause?', *Journal for the Scientific Study of Religion* 26(1): 508–22.
LIEBMAN, Robert C. and Robert WUTHNOW (eds) (1983) *The New Christian Right*. New York: Aldine.
LIFTON, Robert J. (1961) *Thought Reform and the Psychology of Totalism*. New York: Norton.
LIFTON, Robert J. (1979) 'The appeal of the death trip', *New York Times Magazine* (7 Jan.).
LIFTON, Robert J. (1985) 'Cult processes, religious totalism and civil liberties', pp. 59–70 in T. Robbins, W. Shepherd and J. McBride (eds).
LINCOLN, C. Eric and L. MAMIYA (1980) 'Daddy Jones and Father Divine: the cult as political religion', *Religious Life* 49(Spring): 6–23.
LINDSEY, Robert (1986) 'Isolated strongly led sects growing in U.S.', *New York Times* (22 June): 1, 12.
LINDT, Gillian (1981–82) 'Journeys to Jonestown: accounts and interpretations

of the rise and demise of the People's Temple', *Union Seminary Quarterly Review* 37: 159–74.

LOFLAND, John (1977) *Doomsday Cult: A Study of Conversion, Proselytization, and Maintenance of Faith*, enlarged ed. New York: Irvington [original ed., 1966].

LOFLAND, John (1978) 'Becoming a world-saver revisited', pp. 805–18 in J. Richardson (ed.).

LOFLAND, John (1979) 'White-hot mobilization: strategies of a millenarian movement', pp. 157–66 in M. Zald and J. McCarthy (eds) *The Dynamics of Social Movements*. Cambridge, MA: Winthrop.

LOFLAND, John (1985) *Protest: Studies of Collective Behavior and Social Movements*. New Brunswick, NJ: Transaction.

LOFLAND, John (1987) 'Social movement culture and the Unification Church', pp. 91–108 in D. Bromley and P. Hammond (eds).

LOFLAND, John and Michael JAMISON (1984) 'Social movement locals: modal member structures', *Sociological Analysis* 45(2): 115–29.

LOFLAND, John and James T. RICHARDSON (1984) 'Religious movement organizations: elemental forms and dynamics', in L. Kriesberg (ed.) *Research in Social Movements, Conflicts and Change*. Greenwich, CT: JAI.

LOFLAND, John and L. N. SKONOVD (1981) 'Conversion motifs', *Journal for the Scientific Study of Religion* 20(4): 373–85.

LOFLAND, John and L. N. SKONOVD (1983) 'Patterns of conversion', pp. 1–24 in E. Barker (ed.).

LOFLAND, John and Rodney STARK (1965) 'Becoming a world-saver: a theory of conversion to a deviant perspective', *American Sociological Review* 30: 862–75.

LONG, Theodore F. (1979) 'Cult, culture and conversion: three different tillings of a common plot', *Journal for the Scientific Study of Religion* 18: 419–23.

LONG, Theodore and Jeffrey K. HADDEN (1980) 'Sects, cults and religious movements', *Sociological Analysis* 40(2): 280–2.

LONG, Theodore E. and Jeffrey K. Hadden (1983) 'Religious conversion and the concept of socialization: integrating the brainwashing and drift models', *Journal for the Scientific Study of Religion* 22(1): 1–14.

LYNCH, Frederick R. (1977) 'Field research and future history: problems posed for ethnographic sociologists by the "Doomsday Cult" making good', *American Sociologist* 12: 80–8.

LYNCH, Frederick R. (1978) 'Toward a theory of conversion and commitment to the occult', pp. 91–112 in J. Richardson (ed.).

MACHALEK, Richard and David A. SNOW (1985) 'Neglected issues in the study of conversions', pp. 123–30 in B. Kilbourne (ed.) *Scientific Research on New Religious Movements*. San Francisco: Pacific Division AAAS.

MACIOTI, Maria Immacolata (1987) 'Nouveaux mouvements religieux dans un pays de tradition Catholique: continuité et innovation dans les croyances et dans les devoirs des fidèles', pp. 111–16 in *Acts of the 19th International Conference for the Sociology of Religion*. Lausanne: CISR.

MAHER, Brendan A. and Michael D. LANGONE (1985) 'Kilbourne on Conway and Siegelman: a statistical critique', *Journal for the Scientific Study of Religion* 24(3): 325–6.

MALESON, F. G. (1981) 'Dilemma in evaluation and management of religious cultists', *American Journal of Psychiatry* 138: 925–9.

MARCIANO, Teresa D. (1982) 'Families and cults', pp. 101–18 in F. Kaslow and M. Sussman (eds).

MARIN, Peter (1973) 'The new narcissism: the trouble with the Human Potential Movement', *Harpers* 251: 45–56.

MARKOWITZ, Arnold and David A. HALPERIN (1984) 'Cults and children: the abuse of the young', *Cultic Studies Journal* (1(2): 143–55.

MARSHALL, Gordon (1987) 'Which way for the sociology of religion?', *Comparative Studies in Society and History* 29(2): 375–80.

MARTIN, David (1982) 'Revived dogma and new cult', pp. 111–29 in S. Tipton and M. Douglas (eds).

MARTIN, David (1983) 'A definition of cult: terms and approaches', pp. 27–42 in J. Fichter (ed.).

MARTIN, Walter (1968) *The Kingdom of the Cults*. Minneapolis: Bethany Fellowship.

MARTY, Martin (1985) 'Transpositions: American religion in the 1980s', *Annals of the Academy of Political and Social Sciences* 480 (July): 11–23.

MARX, John D. and David L. ELLISON (1975) 'Sensitivity training and communes: contemporary quests for community', *Pacific Sociological Review* 18(4): 441–60.

MARX, John H. and Burhardt HOLZNER (1975) 'Ideological primary groups in contemporary cultural movements', *Sociological Focus* 8(4): 312–29.

MARX, John H. and Joseph SELDIN (1975) 'At the crossroads of crisis: therapeutic sources and quasi-therapeutic functions of post-industrial communes', *Journal of Health and Social Behavior* 14: 39–52.

MAT-HASQUIN, Michèle (1982) *Les Sectes contemporaines*. Bruxelles: Editions de l' Université de Bruxelles.

MAUSS, Armand L. and Donald PETERSEN (1974) 'Les "Jesus Freaks" et retour à la respectabilité, ou la prédiction des fils prodigues', *Social Compass* 21(3): 283–304.

MAYER, Jean-François (1985a) *Une honteuse Exploitation des Esprits et des Porte-Monnaie?* Fribourg: Les Trois Nornes.

MAYER, Jean-François (1985b) *Les nouvelles Sectes*. Paris: Cerf.

McGEE, Michael (1974) 'Meher Baba: the sociology of religious conversion', *Graduate Student Journal* 9(1–2): 43–71.

McGUIRE, Meredith B. (1974) 'An interpretive comparison of elements of the Pentecostal and the Underground Church movements in American Catholicism', *Sociological Analysis* 35: 51–65.

McGUIRE, Meredith B. (1975) 'Toward a sociological interpretation of the "Catholic Pentecostal" movement', *Review of Religious Research* 16(2): 94–104.

McGUIRE, Meredith B. (1977) 'Testimony as a commitment mechanism in Catholic Pentecostal prayer groups', *Journal for the Scientific Study of Religion* 16(2): 165–8.

McGUIRE, Meredith B. (1982) *Pentecostal Catholics: Power, Charisma and Order in a Religious Movement*. Philadelphia: Temple University.

McGUIRE, Meredith B. (1983a) 'Discovering religious power', *Sociological Analysis* 44(1): 1–10.

McGUIRE, Meredith B. (1983b) 'Words of power: personal empowerment and healing', *Culture, Medicine, and Psychiatry* 7: 1–20.

McGUIRE, Meredith B. (1985) 'Religion and healing', pp. 268–84 in P. Hammond (ed.).

McGUIRE, Meredith B. (1986) *Religion: The Social Context*, 2nd ed. Belmont, MA: Wadsworth.

McLOUGHLIN, William G. (1978) *Revivals, Awakenings and Reform*. Chicago: University of Chicago Press.

MELTON, J. Gordon (1978) *Encyclopedia of American Religions*, 2 vols [2nd edition in preparation]. Wilmington, NC: McGrath (A Consortium Book).

MELTON, J. Gordon (1982) *Magic, Witchcraft, and Paganism in America: A Bibliography*. New York: Garland.

MELTON, J. Gordon (1984) *Biographical Dictionary of American Cult and Sect Leaders*. New York: Garland.

MELTON, J. Gordon (1985) 'Violence and the cults', *Nebraska Humanist* 8(2): 51–60.

MELTON, J. Gordon (1986) *The Encyclopedic Handbook of Cults in America*. New York: Garland.

MELTON, J. Gordon (1987) 'How new is new? The flowering of the "new" religious consciousness since 1965', pp. 46–56 in D. Bromley and P. Hammond (eds).

MELTON, J. Gordon and Robert L. MOORE (1982) *The Cult Experience: Responding to the New Religions*. New York: Pilgrim.

MICHAEL, R. Blake (1988) 'Heaven, West Virginia: legitimation techniques in ISKONs New Vrindaban', in D. Bromley and L. Shinn (eds).

MICKLER, Michael L. (1987) 'Future prospects for the Unification Church', pp. 175–86 in D. Bromley and P. Hammond (eds).

MILLER, Donald E. (1983) 'Deprogramming in historical perspective', pp. 15–28 in D. Bromley and J. Richardson (eds).

MILLS, Edward W. (1982) 'Cult extremism: the reduction of normative dissonance', pp. 75–87 in K. Levi (ed.).

MOL, Hans (1985) 'Review of Roy Wallis's *The Elementary Forms of the New Religious Consciousness*', *Review of Religious Research* 27(1): 94–5.

MOORE, Joey P. (1980) 'Piercing the religious veil of the so-called cults', *Pepperdine Law Review* 7: 655–710.

MOORE, R. Laurence (1985) *Religious Outsiders and the Making of Americans*. New York: Oxford University Press.

MORELLI, Anne (1981) 'Les sectes religieuses sont-elles en Belgique un danger montant?' *Cahiers Marxistes* 91: 7–18.

MORELLI, Anne (1983) 'A propos des sectes religieuses en Belgique: les recherches à l'Université de Bruxelles', *Social Compass* 30(1): 137–41.

MORTH, Ingo (1987) 'Elements of religious meanings in science-fiction literature', *Social Compass* 34(1): 87–108.

NAIPAUL, Shiva (1981) *Journey to Nowhere: A New World Tragedy*. New York: Simon and Schuster.

NEEDLEMAN, Jacob L. and George BAKER (eds) (1978) *Understanding the New Religions*. New York: Seabury.

NEITZ, Mary-Jo (1987) *Charisma and Community: A Study of Religion and Commitment Among the Catholic Charismatic Renewal*. New Brunswick, NJ: Transaction.

NEITZ, Mary-Jo (1988) 'Sacramental sex in modern witchcraft groups', paper presented to the Midwest Sociological Society, Minneapolis.

NELSON, Geoffrey K. (1968a) 'The concept of cult', *Sociological Review* 16(3): 351–62.

NELSON, Geoffrey K. (1968b) 'The analysis of a cult: spiritualism', *Social Compass* 15(6): 649–81.

NELSON, Geoffrey K. (1969a) *Spiritualism and Society*. London: Routledge and Kegan Paul.

NELSON, Geoffrery K. (1969b) 'The spiritualist movement and the need for a redefinition of cult', *Journal for the Scientific Study of Religion* 8(1): 152–60.

NESTI, Arnaldo (1973) 'Groupes, idéologie religieuse, société', pp. 165–78 in *Acts of the 12th International Conference for the Sociology of Religion*. Lille: CISR.

NEUHAUS, Richard (1984) 'The naked public square', *Christianity Today* 28 (5 Oct.): 26–32.

NEUMANN, Johannes and Michael FISCHER (eds) (1987) *Toleranz und Repression: zur Lage religiöser Minderheiten in modernen Gesellschaften*. Frankfurt am Main: Campus Verlag.

NIEBUHR, H. Richard (1929) *The Social Sources of Denominationalism*. New York: Holt, Rinehart and Winston.

NIEBUHR, H. Richard (1950) *Christ and Culture*. New York: Harper and Row.

NIELSON, Donald A. (1984) 'Charles Manson's family of love: a case of anonism, puerilism and transmoral consciousness in civilizational perspective', *Sociological Analysis* 45(4): 315–17.

NOCK, A. D. (1933) *Conversion*. New York: Oxford University Press.

NORDQUIST, Ted (1978) *Ananda Cooperative Village*. Uppsala: Religionhistoriska Institute, Uppsala University.

NORDQUIST, Ted (1982) 'New religious movements in Sweden', pp. 173–88 in E. Barker (ed.).

ODEN, Thomas (1972) *The Intensive Group Experience: The New Pietism*. New York: Westminster.

ODEN, Thomas (1982) 'The intensive group experience: the new pietism', pp. 86–106 in E. Barker (ed.).

OFSHE, Richard (1976) 'Synanon: the people's business', pp. 116–38 in C. Glock and R. Bellah (eds).

OFSHE, Richard (1980a) 'Shifts in opportunities and accountability and the regulation of religious organizations', presented to the Association for the Sociology of Religion, August, New York.

OFSHE, Richard (1980b) 'The social development of the Synanon Cult', *Sociological Analysis* 41(2): 109–27.

OFSHE, Richard (1982) 'Regulating diversified social movements', presentation to the Seminar on The Law and the New Religions, Berkeley.

OFSHE, Richard (1986) 'The role of tax law in the promotion of cult deviance', paper presented to the American Sociological Association, New York.

OFSHE, Richard and Margaret SINGER (1986) 'Attacks on peripheral versus central elements of self and the impact of thought reforming techniques', *Cultic Studies Journal* 3(1): 2–24.

OTTINGER, Congressman Richard (1980) 'Cults and their slaves', *Congressional Record* (24 July): E3578–9.

PACE, Enzo (1980) 'Dal' ascesi alla mistica: nuovi movimenti religiosi', *Schema* 5.

PACE, Enzo (1983) *Asceti e Mistici in una Società Secolarizzata*. Venezia: Marsilio Editori.

PAGELS, Elaine (1981) *The Gnostic Gospels*. New York: Vintage.

PALMER, Susan (1986a) 'Purity and danger in the Rajneesh Foundation', *Update* 10(3): 18–30.

PALMER, Susan (1986b) 'Community and commitment in the Rajneesh Foundation', *Update* 10(4): 3–15.

PALMER, Susan (1987a) 'Therapy, charisma, and social control in the Rajneesh Foundation International', paper presented to the Association for the Sociology of Religion, Chicago.

PALMER, Susan (1987b) 'Women in new spiritual communes: Rajneesh lovers, Moon sisters, Krishna mothers', paper presented to the Society for the Scientific Study of Religion, Louisville.

PALMER, Susan (1988) 'Charisma and abdications: the leadership of Shree Rajneesh', *Sociological Analysis* in press.

PALMER, Susan (forthcoming) 'Virus as metaphor: religious responses to AIDS', prepared for T. Robbins and D. Anthony (eds), 2nd ed. (1981).

PARRUCI, D. J. (1968) 'Religious conversion: a theory of deviant behavior', *Sociological Analysis* 29: 144–54.

PARSONS, Arthur (1974) 'Yoga in a Western setting: youth in search of religious prophecy', *Soundings* 57: 222–35.

PARSONS, Arthur (1985) 'Redemptory intimacy: the family culture of the Unification Church', *Communal Societies: Journal of the National Historic Communal Societies Association* 5: 137–75.

PARSONS, Arthur (1986) 'Messianic personalism: a role analysis of the Unification

Church', *Journal for the Scientific Study of Religion* 25(2): 141–161.

PARSONS, Arthur (1987a) 'The culture of narcissism: is it a threat to religion?', presented to the Society for the Scientific Study of Religion, Louisville.

PARSONS, Arthur (1987b) 'The social origins of religious innovation: the Unification Church and contemporary society', unpublished paper.

PARSONS, Arthur (forthcoming) 'The social origins of cultic innovation: the secular contribution to religious revival', *Sociological Analysis*.

PELLETIER, Pierre (1986) '*est*, une nouvelle religion?', *Studies in Religion* 15(1): 3–15.

PESHKIN, Alan (1984) 'Odd man out: the participant observer in an absolutist setting', *Sociology of Education* 57: 254–64.

PESHKIN, Alan (1986) *God's Choice: The Total World of a Fundamentalist Christian School*. Chicago: University of Chicago.

PETERSEN, Donald W. and Armand L. MAUSS (1973) 'The cross and the commune: an interpretation of the Jesus Movement', pp. 261–79 in C. Glock (ed.) *Religion in Sociological Perspective*. Belmont, CA: Wadsworth.

PILARZYK, Thomas (1978a) 'Conversion and alternation processes in the youth culture', *Pacific Sociological Review* 21(4): 379–405 [reprinted in Bromley and Shupe (eds), 1983: 51–72].

PILARZYK, Thomas (1978b) 'The origin, development, and decline of a youth culture religion: an application of sectarianization theory', *Review of Religious Research* 20(1): 33–43.

PILARZYK, Thomas and L. BHARADNAJ (1979) 'What is real? Problems with the phenomenological approach in a field study of Divine Light Mission', *Humanity and Society* 3: 14–34.

PILARZYK, Thomas and Cardell JACOBSEN (1977) 'Christians and the youth culture: a life history of an urban commune', *Wisconsin Sociologist* 14: 136–51.

POLOMA, Margaret M. (1982) 'Toward a Christian sociological perspective', *Sociological Analysis* 43(2): 95–108.

POLOMA, Margaret M. (1987) 'Faith healing and well-being: beyond the belief dimension', presented to the Society for the Scientific Study of Religion, Louisville.

PRESTON, David L. (1981) 'Becoming a Zen practitioner', *Sociological Analysis* 42(1): 47–55.

PRICE, Maeve (1979) 'The Divine Light Mission as a social organization', *Sociological Review* 27(2): 279–96.

PRITCHARD, Linda K. (1976) 'Religious change in nineteenth-century America', pp. 297–330 in C. Glock and R. Bellah (eds).

PROUDFOOT, Wayne and Phillip SHAVER (1975) 'Attribution theory and the psychology of religion', *Journal for the Scientific Study of Religion* 14(4): 317–30.

QUARANTELLI, E. L. and Dennis WENGER (1973) 'Characteristics and conditions for the emergence of a Ouija Board cult', *Urban Life and Culture* 1(4): 379–400.

QUEBEDEAUX, Richard (1976) *The New Charismatics*. Garden City, NJ: Doubleday.

RAMBO, Lewis R. (1982) 'Bibliography: current research on religious conversion', *Religious Studies Review* 8: 146–59.

REGAN, Richard (1986) 'Regulating cult activities: the limits', *Thought* 61(241): 185–96.

RICHARDSON, Herbert (ed.) (1980) *New Religions and Mental Health: Understanding the Issues*. New York: Edwin Mellen.

RICHARDSON, James T. (ed.) (1978a) *Conversion Careers: In and Out of the New Religions*. Beverly Hills, CA: Sage [originally in *American Behavioral Scientist* 20(6), 1977].

RICHARDSON, James T. (1978b) 'An oppositional and general conceptualization of cult', *Annual Review of the Social Sciences of Religion* 2: 29–52.

RICHARDSON, James T. (1979) 'From cult to sect: creative eclecticism in new religious movements', *Pacific Sociological Review* 22(2): 139–66.

RICHARDSON, James T. (1980) 'People's Temple and Jonestown: a corrective comparison and critique', *Journal for the Scientific Study of Religion* 19(3): 239–55.

RICHARDSON, James T. (1982a) 'Financing the new religions: comparative and theoretical considerations', *Journal for the Scientific Study of Religion* 21(3): 255–68.

RICHARDSON, James T. (1982b) 'A comparison between Jonestown and other cults', pp. 21–34 in K. Levi (ed.).

RICHARDSON, James T. (1983) 'Financing the new religions: a broader view', pp. 65–88 in E. Barker (ed.).

RICHARDSON, James T. (1985a) 'The active vs. passive convert: paradigm conflict in conversion/recruitment research' *Journal for the Scientific Study of Religion* 24(2): 163–79.

RICHARDSON, James T. (1985b) 'The "deformation" of new religions: impacts of societal and organizational factors', pp. 163–75 in T. Robbins, W. Shepherd and J. McBride (eds).

RICHARDSON, James T. (1985c) 'Studies of conversion: secularization or re-enchantment', pp. 104–21 in P. Hammond (ed.).

RICHARDSON, James T. (1985d) 'Methodological considerations in the study of new religions', pp. 130–9 in B. Kilbourne (ed.).

RICHARDSON, James T. (1986) 'Consumer protection and deviant religion', *Review of Religious Research* 28(2): 168–79.

RICHARDSON, James T. (1987) 'Battle for legitimacy: psychiatry and the new religions in America', paper presented to the International Conference for the Sociology of Religion, Tübingen.

RICHARDSON, James T. (1988a) 'Proselytizing process in the new religions', forthcoming in F. Greenspan (ed.) *Proselytization and Jews*. Crossroads Press.

RICHARDSON, James T. (1988b) 'Jewish participation in new religions', forthcoming.

RICHARDSON, James T. (1988c) 'Religion, economics and the law', *Socio-logical Analysis* [originally, presidential address to the Association for the Sociology of Religion, 1986, Chicago].

RICHARDSON, James T. (ed.) (1988d) *Money and Power in New Religious Movements*. New York: Edwin Mellen.

RICHARDSON, James T. and Rex DAVIS (1983) 'Experiential fundamentalism: revisions of orthodoxy in the Jesus Movement', *Journal of the American Academy of Religion* 51(3): 398–425.

RICHARDSON, James T. and Brock K. KILBOURNE (1983a) 'Classified and contemporary applications of brainwashing models: a comparison and critique', pp. 29–45 in D. Bromley and J. Richardson (eds).

RICHARDSON, James T. and Brock K. KILBOURNE (1983b) 'Violence and the new religions: an interactional perspective', unpublished paper.

RICHARDSON, James T. and M. T. V. REIDY (1980) 'Form and fluidity in two contemporary glossolalic movements', *Annual Review of the Social Sciences of Religion* 4: 183–220.

RICHARDSON, James T. and Mary H. STEWART (1978) 'Conversion process models and the Jesus Movement', pp. 24–42 in J. Richardson (ed.).

RICHARDSON, James T. and Barendt VAN DRIEL (1984) 'Public support for anti-cult legislation', *Journal for the Scientific Study of Religion* 23(4): 412–8.

RICHARDSON, James T., Robert B. SIMMONDS and Mary W. HARDER (1972) 'Thought reform and the Jesus Movement', *Youth and Society* 4: 185–200.

RICHARDSON, James T., Mary H. STEWART and Robert B. SIMMONDS (1978) 'Researching a fundamentalist commune', pp. 235–51 in J. Needleman and G. Baker (eds).

RICHARDSON, James T., Mary W. STEWART and Robert B. SIMMONDS (1979) *Organized Miracles: A Study of a Contemporary Youth, Communal, Fundamentalist Organization*. New Brunswick, NJ: Transaction.

RICHARDSON, James T., Jan van der LANS and Franz DERKS (1986) 'Leaving and labeling: voluntary and coerced disaffiliation from religious social movements', *Research in Social Movements* 9: 97–126.

RIDDLE, Donald W. (1931) *The Martyrs: A Study in Social Control*. Chicago: University of Chicago Press.

ROBBINS, Thomas (1969) 'Eastern mysticism and the resocialization of drug users', *Journal for the Scientific Study of Religion* 8(2): 308–17.

ROBBINS, Thomas (1979) 'Cults and the therapeutic state', *Social Policy* (May/June): 42–6.

ROBBINS, Thomas (1979–80) 'Religious movements, the state and the law: reconceptualizing "the cult problem"', *New York University Review of Law and Social Change* 9(11): 33–49.

ROBBINS, Thomas (1980) 'Brainwashing and the persecution of "cults"', *Journal of Religion and Health* 19(1): 66–9.

ROBBINS, Thomas (1981) *Civil Liberties, 'Brainwashing' and 'Cults': A Select*

Annotated Bibliography. Berkeley, CA: Center for the Study of New Religious Movements.

ROBBINS, Thomas (1983a) 'The beach is washing away: controversial religion and the sociology of religion', *Sociological Analysis* 44(3): 207–14.

ROBBINS, Thomas (1983b) 'Sociological studies of new religious movements: a selective review', *Religious Studies Review* 9(3): 233–8.

ROBBINS, Thomas (1984) 'Constructing cultist "mind control"', *Sociological Analysis* 45(3): 241–56.

ROBBINS, Thomas (1985a) 'Government regulatory powers over religious movements: deviant groups as test cases', *Journal for the Scientific Study of Religion* 24(32): 237–51.

ROBBINS, Thomas (1985b) 'Are conflicting images of "cults" susceptible to empirical resolution?', pp. 139–49 in B. Kilbourne (ed.).

ROBBINS, Thomas (1985c) 'Nuts, sluts and converts: studying religious groups as social problems', *Sociological Analysis* 46(2): 171–8.

ROBBINS, Thomas (1985d) 'New religious movements on the frontier of Church and State', pp. 7–30 in T. Robbins, W. Shepherd and J. McBride (eds).

ROBBINS, Thomas (1985e) 'Religious movements and church autonomy conflicts', *Nebraska Humanist* 8(2): 40–51.

ROBBINS, Thomas (1985f) 'New religious movements, brainwashing, and deprogramming: the view from the law journals', *Religious Studies Review* 11(4): 361–70.

ROBBINS, Thomas (1986a) 'Religious mass suicide before Jonestown: the Russian Old Believers', *Sociological Analysis* 41(1): 1–20.

ROBBINS, Thomas (1986b) 'Objectionable aspects of cults: rhetoric and reality', *Cultic Studies Journal* 2(2): 58–71.

ROBBINS, Thomas (1986c) '"Uncivil religions" and religious deprogramming', *Thought* 62(241): 277–90.

ROBBINS, Thomas (1986d) 'Goodbye to Little Red Ridinghood', *Update* 10(2): 1–8.

ROBBINS, Thomas (1987) 'Church–State tensions and marginal movements', pp. 135–49 in T. Robbins and R. Robertson (eds).

ROBBINS, Thomas (1988a) 'The transformative impact of the study of new religious movements on the sociology of religion', *Journal for the Scientific Study of Religion* 27(1) (in press).

ROBBINS, Thomas (1988b) 'Profits for prophets: legitimate and illegitimate economic practices in new religious movements', forthcoming in J. Richardson (ed.) *Money and Power in New Religious Movements*. New York: Edwin Mellen.

ROBBINS, Thomas and Dick ANTHONY (1972) 'Getting straight with Meher Baba: a study of drug rehabilitation, mysticism and post-adolescent role-conflict', *Journal for the Scientific Study of Religion* 11(2): 122–40.

ROBBINS, Thomas and Dick ANTHONY (1978) 'New religious movements and the social system: integration, disintegration or transformation', *Annual Review of the Social Sciences of Religion* 21: 1–28.

ROBBINS, Thomas and Dick ANTHONY (1979a) 'Cults, brainwashing and counter-subversion', *Annals of the American Academy of Political and Social Science* 446: 78–90.

ROBBINS, Thomas and Dick ANTHONY (1979b) 'The sociology of contemporary religious movements', *Annual Review of Sociology* 4:75–89.

ROBBINS, Thomas and Dick ANTHONY (1980) 'The limits of "coercive persuasion" as an explanation for conversion to authoritarian sects', *Political Psychology* 2(2). 22–37.

ROBBINS, Thomas and Dick ANTHONY (eds) (1981) *In Gods We Trust: New Patterns of Religious Pluralism in America*. New Brunswick, NJ: Transaction [2nd edition in preparation].

ROBBINS, Thomas and Dick ANTHONY (1982a) 'Deprogramming, brainwashing and the medicalization of new religious movements', *Social Problems* 29(3): 283–97.

ROBBINS, Thomas and Dick ANTHONY (1982b) 'Cults, culture and community', pp. 57–9 in F. Kaslow and M. Sussman (eds).

ROBBINS, Thomas and Dick ANTHONY (1984) 'The Unification Church', *The Ecumenicist* Sept.–Oct.

ROBBINS, Thomas and Dick ANTHONY (1987) ' "Cults" in the later twentieth century", in C. Lippy and P. Williams (eds) *Encyclopedia of Religion in America*. New York: Scribners.

ROBBINS, Thomas and Roland ROBERTSON (eds) (1987) *Church–State Relations: Tensions and Transitions*. New Brunswick, NJ: Transaction.

ROBBINS, Thomas, Dick ANTHONY and Thomas CURTIS (1973) 'The limits of symbolic realism: problems of empathetic field observation in a sectarian context', *Journal for the Scientific Study of Religion* 12: 259–72.

ROBBINS, Thomas, Dick ANTHONY and Thomas CURTIS (1975) 'Youth culture religious movements: evaluating the integrative hypothesis', *Sociological Quarterly* 16(1): 48–64.

ROBBINS, Thomas, Dick ANTHONY, Thomas CURTIS and Madaline DOUCAS (1976) 'The last civil religion: the Unification Church of Reverend Sun Myung Moon', *Sociological Analysis* 37(2): 111–25. [See also Horowitz (ed.)].

ROBBINS, Thomas, Dick ANTHONY and James T. RICHARDSON (1978) 'Theory and research on today's "new religions" ', *Sociological Analysis* 39(2): 95–122.

ROBBINS, Thomas, William SHEPHERD and James McBRIDE (eds) (1985) *Cults, Culture and the Law*. Chico, CA: Scholars Press.

ROBERTSON, Roland (1979) 'Religious movements and modern societies: toward a progressive problemshift', *Sociological Analysis* 40(4): 297–314.

ROBERTSON, Roland (1981) 'Considerations from within the American context on the significance of church–state tension', *Sociological Analysis* 42(3): 193–208.

ROBERTSON, Roland (1985a) 'The cultural context of contemporary religious movements', pp. 43–58 in T. Robbins, W. Shepherd and J. McBride (eds).

ROBERTSON, Roland (1985b) 'Scholarship, sponsorship and "the Moonie

Problem"'', *Sociological Analysis* 49(2): 179–84.

ROBERTSON, Roland (1985c) 'Beyond the sociology of religion', *Sociological Analysis* 46(4): 355–60.

ROBERTSON, Roland and Joann Chirico (1985) 'Humanity, globalization, and worldwide religious resurgence', *Sociological Analysis* 46(3): 219–42.

ROCHFORD, E. Burke (1982) 'Recruitment strategies, ideology and organization in the Hare Krishna movement', *Social Problems* 29(4): 339–410. [Reprinted, pp. 283–299 in E. Barker (ed.).]

ROCHFORD, E. Burke (1985) *Hare Krishna in America*. New Brunswick, NJ: Rutgers University.

ROCHFORD, E. Burke (1987) 'Ideology and structure in the career of a Krishna Consciousness Church', presented to the British Sociological Association, Sociology of Religion Conference, Preston, England.

ROCHFORD, E. Burke, Sheryl PURVIS and NeMar EASTMAN (1988) 'New religions, mental health and social controls', forthcoming in M. Lynn and D. Moberg (eds) *Research in the Social Scientific Study of Religion*. Greenwich, CT: JAI Press.

RODRIGUEZ, P. (1985) *Les sectas hoy y aqui*. Barcelona. Tibidabo Ediciones.

ROMARHEIM, Arild (1977) *Moderne religiositet: en oversikt over ca. 30 nyere bevegelser og retninger som arbeider aktivt i dagens Skandinavia*. Oslo: H. Aschehong.

ROMARHEIM, Arild (1979) 'Litteratur om nyreligiose bevegelser', *Tidskrift for Teologi og Kirke*, 50.

ROSE, Susan (1987) 'Women warriors: the negotiation of gender in a charismatic community', *Sociological Analysis* 48(3): 245–58.

ROSE, Susan (forthcoming) 'Gender, education and the New Christian Right' in T. Robbins and D. Anthony (eds) 2nd ed.

ROSZAK, Betty (1979) *A Select Filmography on New Religious Movements*. Berkeley, CA: Center for the Study of New Religious Movements.

ROULEAU, Jean-Paul and Jacques ZYLBERBERG (1984) *Les Mouvements religieux aujourd'hui: Théories et Pratiques*. Montréal: Bellarmin [*Cahiers de Recherches en Sciences de la Religion* vol. 4].

RUDIN, James and Marcia RUDIN (1980) *Prison or Paradise: The New Religious Cults*. Philadelphia: Fortress.

RUDIN, Marcia (1984) 'Women, elderly and children in religious cults', *Cultic Studies Journal* 1(1): 8–26.

SAGE, Wayne (1976) 'The war on cults', *Human Behavior* 5(10): 40–9.

SALVATORI, Diane (1987) 'Cults and the aged: a new family issue', *Ladies' Home Journal* July: 46, 48, 148.

SCHEIN, Edwin, I. SCHNEIER and C. H. BARKER (1961) *Coercive Persuasion*. New York: Norton.

SCHULER, Jeanne (1983–4) 'Review of S. Tipton, *Getting Saved from the Sixties*', *Telos* 58: 231–5.

SCHUR, Edwin (1976) *The Awareness Trap: Self-Absorption Instead of Social Change*. New York: McGraw-Hill.

SCHWARTZ, Lita L. (1979) 'Psychohistorical perceptions of involuntary conversion', *Adolescence* (Summer): 351–60.

SCHWARTZ, Lita L. (1985) 'Viewing the cults: differences of opinion', pp. 150–61 in B. Kilbourne (ed.).

SCHWARTZ, Lita L. and Florence W. KASLOW (1979) 'Religious cults, the individual and the family', *Journal of Marriage and Family Therapy* 5: 15–26.

SCHWARTZ, Lita L. and Florence W. KASLOW (1982) 'The cult phenomenon: historical sociological and familial factors contributing to their development and appeal', pp. 3–31 in F. Kaslow and M. Sussman (eds).

SCHWARTZ, Lita L. and Jacqueline L. ZEMEL (1980) 'Religious cults: family concerns and the law', *Journal of Marriage and Family Therapy* 6: 301–8.

SCOTT, Gini G. (1980) *Cult and Countercult: A Study of a Spiritual Growth Group and a Witchcraft Order*. Westport, CT: Greenwood.

SEGGAR, John and Phillip KUNZ (1972) 'Conversion: evaluation of a step-like process for problem-solving', *Review of Religious Research* 13: 178–84.

SHAPIRO, E. (1977) 'Destructive cultism', *American Family Physician* 15(2): 80–3.

SHARMA, Arvind (1985) 'The Rajneesh Movement', pp. 115–29 in R. Stark (ed.).

SHEPHERD, William C. (1979) 'Conversion and adhesion', pp. 251–64 in H. Johnson (ed.) *Religious Change and Continuity*. San Francisco: Jossey-Bass.

SHEPHERD, William C. (1982) 'The prosecutor's reach: legal issues stemming from the new religious movements', *Journal of the American Academy of Religion* 50(2): 187–214.

SHEPHERD, William C. (1985) *To Secure the Blessings of Liberty: American Constitutional Law and the New Religious Movements*. Baltimore: Scholars Press [also distributed by Crossroads Publishing].

SHINN, Larry D. (1985a) 'Conflicting networks: guru and friend in ISKON', pp. 95–115 in R. Stark (ed.).

SHINN, Larry D. (1985b) 'Review of R. Wallis's *The Elementary Forms of the New Religious Consciousness*', *Journal for the Scientific Study of Religion* 24(3): 329–30.

SHINN, Larry D. (1987) *The Dark Lord: Cult Images and the Hare Krishnas in America*. Philadelphia: Westminster.

SHUPE, Anson D. (1976) 'Disembodied access and technological constraints on organizational development: a study of mail-order religions', *Journal for the Scientific Study of Religion* 15: 177–85.

SHUPE, Anson D. (1981) *Six Perspectives on New Religions: A Case Study Approach*. New York: Edwin Mellen.

SHUPE, Anson D. (1982) 'The Guardians: anti-organizational fetishism in a mail-order cult', pp. 189–99 in R. Browne (ed.) *Fetishes and Fetishism in American Society*. Bowling Green, OH: Popular Press.

SHUPE, Anson D. (1985) 'The routinization of conflict in modern cult/anticult controversy', *Nebraska Humanist* 8(2): 26–40.

SHUPE, Anson D. (1987) 'Problems of constructing histories for liminal social movements', paper presented to the Society for the Scientific Study of Religion, Louisville, KY.

SHUPE, Anson D. and David G. BROMLEY (1979) 'The Moonies and the anti-cultists: movement and countermovement in conflict', *Sociological Analysis* 40(4): 325–34.

SHUPE, Anson D. and David G. BROMLEY (1980a) *The New Vigilantes: Deprogrammers, Anti-Cultists and the New Religions.* Beverly Hills, CA: Sage.

SHUPE, Anson D. and David G. BROMLEY (1980b) 'Walking a tightrope: dilemmas of participant observation of groups in conflict', *Qualitative Sociology* 2: 3–21.

SHUPE, Anson D. and David G. BROMLEY (1981a) 'Witches, Moonies and evil', pp. 247–62 in T. Robbins and D. Anthony (eds).

SHUPE, Anson D. and David G. BROMLEY (1981b) 'Apostates and atrocity stories: some parameters in the dynamics of deprogramming', pp. 179–215 in B. Wilson (ed.).

SHUPE, Anson and David G. BROMLEY (1984) *New Christian Politics.* Mercer: Mercer University Press.

SHUPE, Anson D. and David G. BROMLEY (1985a) 'Social responses to cults', pp. 58–72 in P. Hammond (ed.).

SHUPE, Anson D. and David G. BROMLEY (1985b) *A Documentary History of the Anti-Cult Movement.* New York: Edwin Mellen.

SHUPE, Anson D., Roger SPIELMANN and Sam STIGALL (1978) 'Deprogramming: the new exorcism', pp. 145–60 in J. Richardson (ed.).

SHUPE, Anson D., Roger SPIELMANN and Sam STIGALL (1980) 'Cults of anti-cultism', *Society* March/April: 43–6.

SHUPE, Anson D., Bert HARDIN and David G. BROMLEY (1983) 'A comparison of anti-cult groups in the United States and West Germany', pp. 177–93 in E. Barker (ed.).

SHUPE, Anson D., David G. BROMLEY and Donna L. OLIVER (1984) *The Anti-Cult Movement in America: A Bibliography and Historical Survey.* New York: Garland.

SIHVO, Juoko (1973) 'Expanding revival movements and their circumstances in Finland', pp. 251–69 in *Acts of the 12th International Conference for the Sociology of Religion.* Lille: CISR.

SIMMONDS, Robert B. (1978) 'Conversion or addition: consequences of joining a Jesus Movement group', pp. 113–28 in J. Richardson (ed.).

SIMMONDS, Robert B., James T. RICHARDSON and Mary W. HARDER (1974) 'Organizational aspects of a Jesus Movement community', *Social Compass* 21(3): 269–81.

SIMON, T. (1978) 'Observations on 67 patients who took Erhard Seminars training', *American Journal of Psychiatry* 135: 636–91.

SINGER, Margaret T. (1979) 'Coming out of the cults', *Psychology Today* 12: 72–82.

SINGER, Margaret T. and Louis J. WEST (1980) 'Cults, quacks and non-professional psychotherapies', pp. 3295–358 in H. Kaplan, A. Freedman and B. Sadock (eds) *Comprehensive Textbook of Psychiatry* 3. Baltimore: Williams and Wilkins.

SKERRY, Peter (1970) 'Christian schools vs. the IRS', *The Public Interest* 61: 18–41.

SKONOVD, L. Norman (1981) 'Apostasy: the process of defection from religious totalism', unpublished PhD dissertation, University of California, Davis.

SKONOVD, L. Norman (1983) 'Leaving the cultic religious milieu', pp. 91–106 in D. Bromley and J. Richardson (eds).

SNELLING, Clarence H. and Oliver R. WHITELEY (1974) 'Problem-solving behavior in religious and para-religious groups: an initial report', pp. 315–34 in A. Eister (ed.) *Changing Perspectives in the Scientific Study of Religion*. New York: Wiley.

SNOW, David A. (1976) 'The Nicheren Shoshu Buddhist movement in America: a sociological examination of its value orientations, recruitment effort, and spread', unpublished PhD dissertation, UCLA.

SNOW, David A. (1979) 'A dramaturgical analysis of movement accommodation: building idiosyncrasy credit as a movement mobilization strategy', *Symbolic Interaction* 2: 23–44.

SNOW, David A. (1980) 'The disengagement process: a neglected problem in participant observation research', *Qualitative Sociology* 3(2): 100–22.

SNOW, David A. and Richard MACHALEK (1982) 'On the presumed fragility of unconventional beliefs', *Journal for the Scientific Study of Religion* 21(1): 15–26.

SNOW, David A. and Richard MACHALEK (1983) 'The convert as social type', pp. 259–89 in R. Collins (ed.) *Sociological Theory 1983*. San Francisco: Jossey-Bass.

SNOW, David and Richard MACHALEK (1984) 'The sociology of conversion', *Annual Review of Sociology* 10: 167–90.

SNOW, David A. and Cynthia PHILLIPS (1980) 'The Lofland–Stark conversion model: a critical reassessment', *Social Problems* 27: 430–47.

SNOW, David A. and E. Burke ROCHFORD (1983) 'Structural availability: the alignment process and movement recruitment', paper presented to the Society for the Scientific Study of Religion, Detroit.

SNOW, David A., Louis A. ZURCHER and Sheldon EKLAND-OLSON (1980) 'Social networks and social movements: a microstructural approach to differential recruitment', *American Sociological Review* 45: 787–801.

SNOW, David A., E. Burke ROCHFORD, Steven K. WORDEN and Robert D. BENFORD (1986) 'Frame alignment processes, micromobilization, and movement participation', *American Sociological Review* 51(4): 464–82.

SOLOMON, Trudy (1981) 'Integrating the 'Moonie' experience: a survey of ex-members of the Unification Church', pp. 275–95 in T. Robbins and D. Anthony (eds).

SOMIT, Albert (1968) 'Brainwashing', in David Sills (ed.) *International Encyclopedia of the Social Sciences*, Vol. 2, pp. 138–43.

SPENCER, Jim (1987) 'Worshipping the goddesses', *Chicago Tribune* (25 October) Section 6: 1, 7.

SPERO, Moshe (1982) 'Psychotherapeutic procedure with religious cult devotees', *Journal of Nervous and Mental Diseases* 170(6): 332–44.

STAPLES, Clifford L. and Armand L. MAUSS (1987) 'Conversion or commitment? A reassessment of the Snow and Machalek approach to the study of conversion', *Journal for the Scientific Study of Religion* 26(2): 133–47.

STARK, Rodney (1981) 'Must all religions be supernatural?', pp. 159–78 in B. Wilson (ed.).

STARK, Rodney (1984) 'The rise of a new world faith', *Review of Religious Research* 26(1): 18–27.

STARK, Rodney (ed.) (1985a) *Religious Movements: Genesis, Exodus and Numbers*. New York: Paragon.

STARK, Rodney (1985b) 'Europe's receptivity to religious movements', pp. 301–44 in R. Stark (ed.).

STARK, Rodney (1987a) 'How new religions succeed: a theoretical model', pp. 11–29 in D. Bromley and P. Hammond (eds).

STARK, Rodney (1987b) 'Quantitative approaches to the rise of Christianity', presented to the Society for the Scientific Study of Religion, Lousiville.

STARK, Rodney and William S. BAINBRIDGE (1979) 'Of churches, sects and cults: preliminary concepts for a theory of religious movements', *Journal for the Scientific Study of Religion* 18(2): 117–33.

STARK, Rodney and William S. BAINBRIDGE (1980a) 'Networks of faith: interpersonal bonds and recruitment to cults and sects', *American Journal of Sociology* 85(6): 1376–95.

STARK, Rodney and William S. BAINBRIDGE (1980b) 'Towards a theory of religion: religious commitment', *Journal for the Scientific Study of Religion* 19(2): 114–28.

STARK, Rodney and William S. BAINBRIDGE (1980c) 'Secularization, revival and cult formation', Annual Review of the Social Sciences of Religion 4: 85–119.

STARK, Rodney and William S. BAINBRIDGE (1981) 'Secularization and cult formation in the Jazz Age', *Journal for the Scientific Study of Religion* 20: 360–73.

STARK, Rodney and William S. BAINBRIDGE (1983) 'Concepts for a theory of religious movements', pp. 3–26 in J. Fichter (ed.).

STARK, Rodney and William S. BAINBRIDGE (1986) *The Future of Religion: Secularization, Revival and Cult Formation*. Berkeley: University of California.

STARK, Rodney, William S. BAINBRIDGE and D. P. DOYLE (1979) 'Cults in America: a reconnaissance in time and space', *Sociological Analysis* 40(4): 347–59.

STARK, Rodney, William S. BAINBRIDGE and Lori KENT (1981) 'Cult membership in the roaring twenties: assessing local receptivity', *Sociological Analysis* 42(2): 137–62.

STARK, Rodney and Lynn ROBERTS (1982) 'The arithmetic of social movements', *Sociological Analysis* 43(1): 53–68.

STOFFELS, H. (1982) 'Tien jaar na de Jesus revolutie: evangelische jeugdbewegingen in Nederland', *Jeugd en Samenleving* 12(3): 147–61.

STONE, Donald (1976) 'The Human Potential Movement', pp. 93–115 in C. Glock and R. Bellah (eds).

STONE, Donald (1978a) 'On knowing what we know about new religions', pp. 141–52 in J. Needleman and George Baker (eds).

STONE, Donald (1978b) 'The new religious consciousness and personal religious experience', *Sociological Analysis* 39(2): 123–34.

STONE, Donald (1981) 'Social consciousness in the Human Potential Movement', pp. 215–27 in T. Robbins and D. Anthony (eds).

STONE, Donald (1982) 'The charismatic authority of Werner Erhard', pp. 141–77 in R. Wallis (ed.).

STRAUS, Roger B. (1976) 'Changing oneself: seekers and the creative transformation of life experience', pp. 252–72 in J. Lofland (ed.) *Doing Social Life*. New York: Wiley.

STRAUS, Roger B. (1979a) 'Inside Scientology', paper presented to the annual meeting of the Pacific Sociological Association.

STRAUS, Roger B. (1979b) 'Religious conversion as a personal and collective accomplishment', *Sociological Analysis* 40(2): 158–65.

STRAUS, Roger B. (1986) 'Scientology "ethics": deviance, identity and social control in a cult-like social world', *Symbolic Interaction* 9(1): 67–82.

STRAUS, Roger B. (forthcoming) 'But we *are* a religion: "religion" and "technology" in Scientology's struggle for legitimacy', *Sociological Analysis*.

SULLIVAN, Lawrence, B. (1984a) 'Family perspectives on involvements in new religious groups', *Cultic Studies Journal* 1(1): 79–102.

SULLIVAN, Lawrence B. (1984b) 'Counseling and involvements in new religious groups', *Cultic Studies Journal* 1(2): 178–195.

SUNDBACQ, S. (1980) 'New religious movements in Finland', *Temeros* 16: 132–9.

SWATOS, William H. (1975) 'Monopolism, pluralism, acceptance and rejection', *Review of Religious Research* 40: 297–314.

SWATOS, William H. (1981) 'Church–sect and cult: bringing mysticism back in', *Sociological Analysis* 42(1): 17–26.

Symposium (1983) 'On scholarship and sponsorship', *Sociological Analysis* 44(3).

TAYLOR, David (1976) 'Conversion and cognition: an area for empirical study in the microsociology of religious knowledge', *Social Compass* 21(3): 325–44.

TAYLOR, David (1978) 'The social organization of recruitment in the Unification Church', unpublished masters thesis, University of Montana.

TAYLOR, David (1982a) 'Thought reform and the Unification Church', pp. 73–90 in D. Bromley and J. Richardson (eds).

TAYLOR, David (1982b) 'Becoming new people: the recruitment of young Americans into the Unification Church', pp. 177–230 in R. Wallis (ed.).

Thought: A Review of Culture and Idea (1986) Special issue, *New Religions* 61(241) June.

TIPTON, Steven M. (1979) 'New religious movements and the problem of modern ethic', pp. 286–312 in H. Johnson (ed.) *Religious Change and Continuity*. San Francisco: Jossey-Bass.

TIPTON, Steven M. (1982a) *Getting Saved from the Sixties: Moral Meaning in Conversion and Cultural Change*. Berkeley: University of California.

TIPTON, Steven M. (1982b) 'The moral logic of alternative religions', pp. 79–107 in M. Douglas and S. Tipton (eds).

TIPTON, Steven M. (1983) 'Making the world work: ideas of social responsibility in the Human Potential Movements', pp. 265–82 in E. Barker (ed.).

TIPTON, Steven M. (1985) 'Therapy as a way of life', in R. Bellah et al. (eds).

TIPTON, Steven M. (1986) 'Zen practice and moral meaning', pp. 211–34 in D. Anthony, K. Wilber and T. Ecker (eds).

TIRYAKIAN, Edward (1967) 'A model of social change and its lead indicators', in S. Klausner (ed.) *The Study of Total Societies*, pp. 59–67. Garden City, NJ: Anchor.

TIRYAKIAN, Edward (1973) 'Toward a sociology of esoteric culture', *American Journal of Sociology* 78: 491–512.

TIRYAKIAN, Edward (1974) *On the Margin of the Visible*. New York: Wiley.

TOBEY, Alan (1976) 'The summer solstice of the Happy–Healthy–Holy organization', pp. 5–30 in C. Glock and R. Bellah (eds).

TOURAINE, Alain (1977) *The Self-Production of Society*. Chicago: University of Chicago Press.

TOURAINE, Alain (1981) *The Voice and the Eye: An Analysis of Social Movements*. Cambridge: Cambridge University Press.

TRAVISANO, Richard V. (1970) 'Alternation and conversion as qualitatively different transformations', pp. 594–606 in G. Stone and H. Faberman (eds) *Social Psychology Through Symbolic Interaction*. Waltham, MA: Ginn-Blaisdell.

TRUZZI, Marcello P. (1971) 'The occult revival as popular culture', *Sociological Quarterly* 13: 16–36.

TRUZZI, Marcello P. (1974) 'Toward a sociology of the occult', pp. 628–45 in I. Zaretsky and M. P. Leone (eds).

TRUZZI, Marcello P. (1975) 'Astrology as popular culture', *Journal of Popular Culture* 8: 906–11.

TURNER, Bryan (1983) *Religion and Social Theory*. London: Heinemann.

TURNER, Ralph (1976) 'The real self: from institution to impulse', *American Journal of Sociology* 81: 989–1016.

UNGERLEIDER, Thomas J. and D. K. WELLISCH (1979) 'Coercive persuasion (brainwashing), religious cults and deprogramming', *American Journal of Psychiatry* 136(3): 279–82.

VALENTIN, F. (1984) 'New religions in Austria', *Update* 8(2): 60–4.

VAN DER LANS, J. and F. DERKS (1982) 'Reakties in Nederland: media overheid en kerken in Nederland over jeugdreligies', *Jeugd en Samenleving* 12(3): 213–23.

VAN DER LANS, J. and F. DERKS (1983) 'Les nouvelles religions aux Pays-Bas: contexte, appartenance, réactions', *Social Compass* 30(1): 63–83.

VAN DRIEL, Barendt and James T. RICHARDSON (1988) 'Print media and new religious movements: a longitidunal study', *Journal of Communication* (forthcoming).

VAN DRIEL, B. and J. VAN BELSEN (1987) 'The print media and the downfall of Rajneeshpuram: A cross-national study', presented to the 19th International Conference for the Sociology of Religion, Tübingen.

VERDIER, Paul A. (1980) *Brainwashing and the Cults: An Exposé in Capturing the Human Mind*. North Hollywood, CA: Wilshire.

VIVIEN, Alain (1985) *Les Sectes en France: Expression de la Liberté morale ou Facteurs de Manipulations?* Paris: Documentation Française.

VOLINN, Ernest (1985) 'Eastern meditation groups: why join?' *Sociological Analysis* 46(2): 147–56.

WAGNER, Melinda B. (1983) 'Spiritual Frontiers Fellowship', pp. 45–66 in J. Fichter (ed.).

WAGNER, Melinda B. (1984) *Metaphysics in Midwestern America*. Columbus, OH: Ohio State University.

WALKER, Andrew (1983) 'Pentecostal power: the charismatic renewal movement and the politics of Pentecostal experience', pp. 89–108 in E. Barker (ed.).

WALLIS, Roy (1974) 'Ideology, authority and the development of cultic movements', *Social Research* 41(2): 299–327.

WALLIS, Roy (ed.) (1975a) *Sectarianism*. New York: Halstead.

WALLIS, Roy (1975b) 'Societal reaction to Scientology', pp. 86–116 in R. Wallis (ed.).

WALLIS, Roy (1975c) 'The cult and its transformation', pp. 35–49 in R. Wallis (ed.).

WALLIS, Roy (1975d) 'Scientology: therapeutic cult to religious sect', *Sociology* 9(1): 89–99.

WALLIS, Roy (1976) 'Observations of the Children of God', *Sociological Review* 24(4): 807–27.

WALLIS, Roy (1977) *The Road to Total Freedom: A Sociological Analysis of Scientology*. New York: Columbia.

WALLIS, Roy (1978a) 'Recruiting Christian manpower', *Society* 14(4): 72–4.

WALLIS, Roy (1978b) 'Fishing for men', *The Humanist* 38(1): 14–15.

WALLIS, Roy (1978c) 'The rebirth of the Gods', *New Lecture Series* 18. Belfast: The Queen's University.

WALLIS, Roy (1979) *Salvation and Protest*. London: Francis Pinter.

WALLIS, Roy (1981) Yesterday's children: cultural and structural change in a new religious movement', pp. 97–132 in B. Wilson (ed.).

WALLIS, Roy (ed.) (1982a) *Millennialism and Charisma*. Belfast: The Queen's University.

WALLIS, Roy (1982b) 'Charisma, commitment and control in a new religious movement', pp. 73–140 in R. Wallis (ed.).

WALLIS, Roy (1982c) 'The social construction of charisma', *Social Compass* 29(1): 25–39.

WALLIS, Roy (1982d) 'The new religions as social indicators', pp. 218–31 in E. Barker (ed.).

WALLIS, Roy (1983) 'Religion, reason and responsibility', *Sociological Analysis* 44(3): 215–20.

WALLIS, Roy (1984) *Elementary Forms of the New Religious Life*. London: Routledge and Kegan Paul.

WALLIS, Roy (1985) 'The dynamics of change in the Human Potential movement', pp. 129–56 in R. Stark (ed.).

WALLIS, Roy (1986a) 'Figuring out cult receptivity', *Journal for the Scientific Study of Religion* 25(4): 494–503.

WALLIS, Roy (1986b) 'How and why does the treatment of new religions differ in Britain and America?', *Update* 10(1): 3–9.

WALLIS, Roy (1987a) 'Hostages to fortune: thoughts on the future of Scientology and the Children of God', pp. 80–90 in D. Bromley and P. Hammond (eds).

WALLIS, Roy (1987b) 'New religions and the potential for world re-enchantment: religion as way of life, preference and commodity', pp. 87–98 in *Acts of the 19th International Conference for the Sociology of Religion*. Lausanne: CISR.

WALLIS, Roy (1987c) 'Zum problem religiöser minoritäten in Grossbritannien und den USA', pp. 287–312 in J. Neumann and M. Fischer (eds).

WALLIS, Roy (1988) 'Paradoxes of freedom and regulation: the case of new religious movements in Britain and America', *Sociological Analysis* 48(4): 355–71.

WALLIS, Roy and Steven BRUCE (1982) 'Network and clockwork', *Sociology* 16(1): 102–7.

WALLIS, Roy and Steve BRUCE (1984) 'The Stark–Bainbridge theory of religion', *Sociological Analysis* 45(1): 29–40.

WALLIS, Roy and Steven BRUCE (1986) *Sociological Theory, Religion and Collective Action*. Belfast: The Queen's University.

WALLIS, Roy and Peter MORELY (eds) (1976) *Marginal Medicine*. New York: Free Press.

WEBER, Max (1947) *The Theory of Social and Economic Organization*. New York: Free Press.

WEBER, Max (1948) 'The sociology of charismatic authority', in H. Gerth and C. Mills (eds) *From Max Weber*. New York: Free Press.

WEIGHTMAN, Judith (1983) *Making Sense of the Jonestown Suicides*. New York: Edwin Mellen.

WEISSMAN, Gerald (1985) *The Woods Hole Cantata: Essays on Science and Society*. New York: Dodd, Mead.

WERBLOWSKY, R. Zwi (1982) 'Religions new and not so new', pp. 32–96 in E. Barker (ed.).

WEST, Loûis J. (1982) 'Contemporary cults: utopian image and infernal reality', *The Center Magazine* 13(2): 10–13.

WESTLEY, Francis (1978a) 'The "cult of man": Durkheim's predictions and the new religious movements', *Sociological Analysis* 39(2): 135–45.

WESTLEY, Francis (1987b) 'Searching for surrender: a Catholic charismatic renewal group's attempt to become glossolalic', pp. 129–44 in J. Richardson (ed.).

WESTLEY, Francis (1983) *The Complex Forms of the New Religious Life: A Durkheimian View of New Religious Movements*. Chico, CA: Scholars Press.

WHITE, James (1970) *The Sokagakkai and Mass Society*. Palo Alto, CA: Stanford University Press.

WIKSTROM, Lester (1984) 'Strategies in the 80s of new religions in Sweden', *Update* 8(2): 31–6.

WILBER, Ken (1980) 'The pre/trans fallacy', *Re-vision* 3(2): 1980.

WILBER, Ken (1983) *A Sociable God*. New York: McGraw-Hill.

WILBER, Ken (1987) 'The spectrum model', pp. 237–60 in D. Anthony, K. Wilber and B. Ecker (eds).

WILSON, Bryan (1973) *Magic and Millennium*. London: Heinemann.

WILSON, Bryan (1975) *The Noble Savage: The Primitive Origins of Charisma*. Berkeley: University of California.

WILSON, Bryan (1976) *Contemporary Transformation of Religion*. New York: Harper and Row.

WILSON, Bryan (1978) *Sects and Society*. London: Greenwood.

WILSON, Bryan (ed.) (1981) *The Social Impact of New Religious Movements*. New York: Edwin Mellen.

WILSON, Bryan (1982) *Religion in Sociological Perspective*. Oxford: Oxford University Press.

WILSON, Bryan (1983) 'Sympathetic detachment and disinterested involvement', *Sociological Analysis* 44(3): 183–8.

WILSON, Bryan (1985) 'Secularization: the inherited model', pp. 9–20 in P. Hammond (ed.).

WILSON, Bryan (1987) 'Factors in the failure of the new religious movements', pp. 30–45 in D. Bromley and P. Hammond (eds).

WILSON, Bryan and Karel DOBBELAERE (1987) 'Unificationism – a study of the Moonies in Belgium', *British Journal of Sociology* 38: 184–98.

WILSON, John and Harvey K. CLOW (1981) 'Themes of power and control in a pentecostal assembly', *Journal for the Scientific Study of Religion* 20(3): 241–50.

WILSON, Stephen R. (1984) 'Becoming a yogi', *Sociological Analysis* 45(3).

WIMBERLEY, Ronald C., Thomas HOOD, C. LIPSEY and M. HAY (1980) 'Conversion in a Billy Graham crusade', pp. 278–85 in M. Pugh (ed.) *Collective Behavior: A Source Book*. St Paul, MN: West.

WITTEVEEN, Tweede Kamer der Staten-Generaal (1984) 'Onderzoek be treffende sekten', *Overheid en Nieuwe Religieuze Bewegingen*. The Hague (16,635 No. 4).

WOLF-PETRUSKY, Julie C. (1979) 'The social construction of the cult problem', paper presented to the annual meetings of the Association for the Sociology of Religion, Boston.

WOODEN, Kenneth (1981) *The Children of Jonestown*. New York: McGraw-Hill.

WOODROW, A. (1977) *Les nouvelles sectes*. Paris: Le Seuil.

WOODRUM, Eric (1977) 'The development of the Transcendental Meditation movement', *The Zetetic Scholar* 1(2): 38–48.

WOODRUM, Eric (1982) 'Religious organization change: an analysis based on the TM Movement', *Review of Religious Research* 24: 98–103.

WRIGHT, Stuart A. (1983) 'Defection from new religious movements: a test of some theoretical propositions', pp. 106–21 in D. Bromley and J. Richardson (eds).

WRIGHT, Stuart A. (1984) 'Post-involvement attitudes of voluntary defectors from new religious movements', *Journal for the Scientific Study of Religion* 23(2): 172–82.

WRIGHT, Stuart A. (1985) 'The dynamics of cult disengagement: an analysis of exiting modes', unpublished paper presented to the Society for the Scientific Study of Religion, Savannah, GA.

WRIGHT, Stuart A. (1986) 'Dyadic intimacy and social control in three cult movements', *Sociological Analysis* 47(2): 151–9.

WRIGHT, Stuart A. (1987) *Leaving Cults: The Dynamics of Defection*. Washington DC: Society for the Scientific Study of Religion.

WRIGHT, Stuart A. and Elizabeth S. PIPER (1986) 'Families and cults: familial factors related to youth leaving or remaining in deviant religious groups', *Journal of Marriage and the Family* 48: 15–25.

WUTHNOW, Robert (1976a) 'The new religions in social context', pp. 267–93 in C. Glock and R. Bellah (eds).

WUTHNOW, Robert (1976b) *The Consciousness Reformation*. Berkeley, CA: University of California.

WUTHNOW, Robert (1978) *Experimentation in American Religion: The New Mysticisms and Their Implications for the Churches*. Berkeley, CA: University of California.

WUTHNOW, Robert (1981a) 'Two traditions in the study of religion', *Journal for the Scientific Study of Religion* 20(1): 16–32.

WUTHNOW, Robert (1981b) 'Political aspects of the quietistic revival', pp. 229–93 in T. Robbins and D. Anthony (eds).

WUTHNOW, Robert (1982) 'World order and religious movements', pp. 47–65 in E. Barker (ed.).

WUTHNOW, Robert (1983) 'The political rebirth of American evangelicals', in R. Leibman and R. Wuthnow (eds).

WUTHNOW, Robert (1985) 'The cultural context of contemporary religious movements', pp. 43–56 in T. Robbins, W. Shepherd and J. McBride (eds).

WUTHNOW, Robert (1986) 'Religious movements and counter-movements in North America', pp. 1–28 in J. Beckford (ed.).

WUTHNOW, Robert (1987) *Meaning and Moral Order: Explorations in Cultural Analysis*. Berkeley: University of California.

YANOFF, Morris (1984) 'Some Lessons from Jonestown', *Chicago Tribune* Op. Ed. (18 Nov.).

YINGER, J. Milton (1946) *Religion and the Struggle for Power*. Durham, NC: Duke University.

ZARETSKY, Irving and Marc P. LEONE (eds) (1974a) *Religious Movements in Contemporary America*. Princeton, NJ: Princeton University.

ZARETSKY, Irving and Marc P. LEONE (eds) (1974b) 'The common foundation of religious diversity', pp. xvii–xxxvi in I. Zaretsky and M. Leone (eds).

ZERIN, Marjorie F. (1985) 'The pied piper phenomenon: family systems and vulnerability to cults', pp. 161–74 in B. Kilbourne (ed.).

ZYGMUNT, J. F. (1972) 'When prophecies fail', *American Behavioral Scientist* 16: 245–68.

Index

CURRENT SOCIOLOGY
La sociologie contemporaine

A Journal of the International Sociological
Association

Edited by **William Outhwaite** *University of Sussex*

Each issue of this unique journal is devoted to a comprehensive Trend Report on a topic of interest to the international community of sociologists. Authors review current trends and tendencies in all areas of sociological work — theories, methods, concepts, substantive research and national or regional developments. The aim is to review new developments, to discuss controversies, and to provide extensive bibliographies. From time to time, Commentaries on Trend Reports are published in subsequent issues of the journal.

Recent reports have focused on the multinational version of social science, different traditions of sociology and the human body, the sociology of law, migration in Europe, the sociology of industrial and post-industrial societies, and the sociology of humour and laughter.

Issues are published in French or English, but a text in one language is always accompanied by an extensive resume in the other. **Current Sociology** is an official journal of the International Sociological Association. Its main aim is to review international developments in the discipline and to provide a forum from which professional sociologists from all countries can communicate with the widest group of colleagues.

Current Sociology is published three times a year in Spring, Summer and
Winter
ISSN: 0011-3921

Subscription Rates, 1988

	Institutional	Individual
one year	£50.00($75.00)	£22.00($33.00)
two years	£99.00($148.50)	£44.00($66.00)
single copies	£17.00($25.50)	£8.00($12.00)

 SAGE Publications Ltd, 28 Banner Street, London EC1Y 8QE
SAGE Publications Ltd, PO Box 5096, Newbury Park, CA 91359